SO-BNR-028

FLORIDA STATE
UNIVERSITY LIBRARIES

APR 21 1999

TALLAHASSEE, FLORIDA

BLACKS AND JEWS
ON THE COUCH

BLACKS AND JEWS ON THE COUCH

Psychoanalytic Reflections on
Black-Jewish Conflict

Edited by
Alan Helmreich and Paul Marcus

PRAEGER

Westport, Connecticut
London

E
185.615
.B5533
1998

Library of Congress Cataloging-in-Publication Data

Blacks and Jews on the couch : psychoanalytic reflections on Black-
  Jewish conflict / edited by Alan Helmreich and Paul Marcus.
    p. cm.
  Includes bibliographical references and index.
  ISBN 0–275–95666–0 (alk. paper)
    1. Afro-Americans—Relations with Jews—Psychological aspects.
  2. Psychoanalysis—Social aspects—United States. I. Helmreich,
  Alan, 1974– . II. Marcus, Paul, 1953– .
  E185.615.B5533 1998
  305.896'073—dc21   98–15620

British Library Cataloguing in Publication Data is available.

Copyright © 1998 by Alan Helmreich and Paul Marcus

All rights reserved. No portion of this book may be
reproduced, by any process or technique, without the
express written consent of the publisher.

Library of Congress Catalog Card Number: 98–15620
ISBN: 0–275–95666–0

First published in 1998

Praeger Publishers, 88 Post Road West, Westport, CT 06881
An imprint of Greenwood Publishing Group, Inc.

Printed in the United States of America

The paper used in this book complies with the
Permanent Paper Standard issued by the National
Information Standards Organization (Z39.48–1984).

10 9 8 7 6 5 4 3 2 1

Copyright Acknowledgments

The editors and publisher gratefully acknowledge permission to reprint the following
material:

Excerpts from Lerner and West, *Jews and Blacks: A Dialogue on Race, Religion, and
Culture in America* (New York: Penguin Books, 1996). Reprinted by permission of The
Putnam Publishing Group from *Jews and Blacks* by Michael Lerner and Cornel West.
Copyright © 1995 by Michael Lerner and Cornel West. Reprinted by permission of
Michael Lerner and Cornel West and the Watkins/Loomis Agency.

Excerpts from G. Hartman, "Public Memory and Its Discontents," *Raritan Review*
(Summer 1994): 24–40. Used by permission of *Raritan Review*.

Poem from Rabindranath Tagore, *A Tagore Reader*, edited by Amiya Chakravarty (New
York: Macmillan Co., 1961), p. 257. Reprinted by permission of HarperCollins Publishers.

To my father who showed me that boundaries only
exist if you place them there.

—AH

To my late father who worked forty years in Harlem as
a dentist devoted to his patients.

—PM

The tie with the Other is knotted only as responsibility ... whether accepted or refused, whether knowing or not knowing how to assume it, whether able or unable to do something concrete for the Other. To say: here I am. To do something for the Other. To give. To be human spirit, that's it.

—Emmanuel Levinas

Contents

Preface

PAUL MARCUS

The idea for this anthology grew out of my eye-opening experience amidst a conference I organized and chaired entitled "Racial and Ethnic Conflict in America: Black/Jewish Tensions in New York." The interdisciplinary conference was sponsored by the National Psychological Association for Psychoanalysis (The Center for the Psychoanalytic Study of Social Trauma) and took place on May 7, 1995.[1]

The purpose of the conference I had thought, was to examine black-Jewish conflict in New York City from a scholarly psychoanalytic perspective with the hope of improving things. I had envisioned a rather dreary academic conference, but this meeting quickly became a forum for the expression of a wide range of intense feelings, in particular palpable black anger directed at the other mostly white Jewish panelists and the one black "integrationalist," anti-Farrakhan speaker. While I came into this conference with what I thought were the best of intentions—to facilitate critical psychoanalytic inquiry into a complex interethnic problem, one in which as a Jew I had a personal stake—I was frankly taken aback at the avalanche of unjustified (in my view) anger and hostility directed toward the panelists. I was also dumbfounded at what I viewed as the bizarre and unreasonable ways of construing black-Jewish conflict that emanated mostly from the black audience participants and some of the Jewish ones and the strange group dynamics that were enacted during the conference. The fact that most of the other panelists concurred with my view of what had transpired did not tone down my internal response.

It was only after about six months of "self-analysis," in which I mulled things over and took a critical look at my own feelings toward blacks, race, and Jewish and group identity, that I came to recognize that I had underestimated the depth, magnitude, and complexity of the feelings that underlie black-Jewish conflict (and probably all interethnic conflict), a range of ambivalent, confusing, and powerful emotions that I myself was feeling. It was mainly this "learning" experience—the conference and its troubling psychological aftermath and my self-analysis, as well as my attending more empathically to racial and black-Jewish themes in my psychoanalytic work with black and Jewish patients, that brought about my idea to assemble a diversified group of psychoanalytically informed thinkers to tackle the problem of black-Jewish conflict. If I, a white, liberal-minded, Orthodox Jewish, Freudian analyst had felt such strong, confusing, and at times "irrational" emotions toward blacks—but also toward Jews following the conference, my hunch was that perhaps many others, Jews and blacks, were probably also vulnerable to such reactions, at least to some extent some of the time. Perhaps a psychoanalytic volume on the subject could make a worthwhile contribution to "working through" the many affect driven problems between blacks and Jews and possibly improve things a bit. This was my abiding hope and main motivation for co-editing this anthology.

ACKNOWLEDGMENTS

The editors would like to thank Professors William B. Helmreich and Irving Louis Horowitz for their gracious efforts in reading parts of the manuscript and offering their very helpful suggestions on how to improve it.

Paul Marcus would like to thank the members of the Center for the Psychoanalytic Study of Social Trauma of the National Psychological Association for Psychoanalysis for their support and encouragement throughout this project. My wife Irene, a child and adult psychoanalyst, also helped evaluate critically each essay encouraging me to sharpen my editorial focus, and I hope together with my co-editor, bring out the best in each author. To my children Raphael and Gabriela, I thank them for allowing their father to quietly work on the manuscript without making him feel too guilty for not being outside playing with them.

NOTE

1. The participants were C. Fred Alford, William B. Helmreich, Edith Kurzweil, Michael Meyers, Paul H. Ornstein, and Paul L. Wachtel.

Introduction:
Black-Jewish Conflict

ALAN HELMREICH AND PAUL MARCUS

Recently there has been a steady stream of publications lamenting the state of black-Jewish relations. Paul Berman's anthology, *Blacks and Jews: Alliances and Arguments* (1994); Murray Friedman's *What Went Wrong? The Creation and Collapse of the Black-Jewish Alliance* (1995); Michael Lerner and Cornel West's *Jews and Blacks: Let the Healing Begin* (1995); Jack Salzman and Cornel West's anthology, *Struggles in the Promised Land: Toward a History of Black-Jewish Relations in the United States* (1997); and most recently, Seth Forman's *Blacks in the Jewish Mind: A Crisis in Liberalism* (1998)—all testify to the fact that members of each community are deeply troubled by the deterioration in black-Jewish relations. Moreover, in a certain sense, the black-Jewish conflict is a subspecies of the larger racial problem in this country between people of color and whites. Our hope is that this volume will not only provide some new insights into black-Jewish conflict and its amelioration, but it will also serve as a useful point of entry into gaining greater understanding of the larger racial conflict in which it resides.

As Freud noted, most intimate and meaningful relationships between individuals have their fair share of ambivalence. The same can be said about intergroup relations between minorities with a long-standing history of involvement with each other. The black-Jewish relationship, as we have noted, is certainly no exception. Friedman for example, documents the mistaken but widely held notion that blacks and Jews throughout American history came together in a common fight against prejudice and racism until the alliance began to fall apart in the mid-1960s. Rather, says Friedman,

from the beginning there were differences, disputes, and bad feelings between both groups: "mutual distrust was always present alongside the sense
of common experience and a willingness to cooperate in overcoming prejudice and discrimination" (1995, 89).

By the 1970s according to Friedman, there was a major breach between
both communities over such issues as community control over the Ocean
Hill–Brownsville public schools, affirmative action, and the increasingly
pro-Palestinian position of many black leaders. These developments were
accompanied by the emergence of a new generation of black leaders whose
rhetoric and gestures were frequently antisemitic—Sonny Carson, Gus Savage, Louis Farrakhan and others. As many have noted, in the last few years
black-Jewish relations have fallen to an all time low. Says Cornel West,
"Black-Jewish relations—at the symbolic level—are in shambles" (1997,
415). Blacks and Jews, as communities, have lived through some terrible
episodes together. One has only to recall the 1991 Crown Heights tragedy
and its aftermath to recognize to what extent black-Jewish relations have
deteriorated. Such moments not only reflect badly on both communities,
but also raise tough questions about race relations, our democracy, and the
social fabric of our nation.

Almost all the analyses of the deteriorated state of black-Jewish relations
have been written from a largely sociocultural, historical, and literary point
of view. While these publications have contributed much to our understanding, we think that a crucial piece of the story is missing, especially
when it comes to actually improving black-Jewish relations. By this we
mean the potentially illuminating and socially beneficial application of psychoanalysis to intergroup, interethnic conflict. As Mark Bracher has
pointed out, while cultural values, social structures, and material conditions—the main focus of the aforementioned books—clearly influence individual and group behavior, these forces are always mediated by the
subjectivity of the behaving subject, that is by psychological motives,
wishes, beliefs, and desires. It is precisely in this psychological realm that
psychoanalysis as an interpretive tool has historically been most robust.
Bracher continues,

> An analysis of socially significant behavior [e.g., black-Jewish conflict] that
> aspires to adequacy . . . must focus on motives—psychological causes—and
> to achieve an adequate grasp of the pertinent motives, it must employ a model
> of subjectivity that accounts for all the various complex and often mutually
> contradictory psychological forces that produce human behavior. That is,
> taking account of subjects' subjectivity means more than simply identifying
> their subject positions or locations in culture—i.e., their memberships in var-
> ious kinds of identity groups (nationality race, ethnicity, class, gender, sexual
> preference, and so on). Taking account of subjectivity means identifying and
> addressing not only the complex of identities constituting one's location in

culture but also multiple and often conflicting values, drives, desires, enjoyments, anxieties, and defenses that both derive from and help produce this location and that constitute the psychological roots of social and cultural formations. (Bracher 1996, 2)

In short, says Bracher, it is necessary to investigate how psychological processes function as both cause and effect in relation to material, social, and cultural variables. By investigating the material, social, and cultural context of subjectivity, on the one hand, and the behavior that emanates from this subjectivity, on the other, we can draw some inferences concerning the structure and dynamics of that subjectivity. With this knowledge in hand, we can thus develop possible interventions in that subjectivity, both direct and indirect, to modify the target behavior (ibid., 2–3). In our view, psychoanalysis, viewed as a comprehensive theory of human experience, offers a powerful conceptual tool and set of strategies for understanding and intervening in those psychological processes that along with material, social, and cultural conditions, foster interethnic conflict such as the type we see between blacks and Jews in the United States.

Clearly, indisputably, no one can fail to recognize that all intergroup, especially interethnic conflict involves conscious and unconscious passions— usually a mixture of variations of hate and love—that together with situational determinants frequently produce explosive, violent, and other destructive behavior. The Crown Heights episode mentioned above for example, involved some of the most "regressive" passions and "core" aspects of subjectivity—rivalry, territoriality, hate, narcissistic rage, beliefs and ideology, meaning, identity, and fantasy. Let's briefly remind ourselves what happened during that terrible episode so that perhaps we can have a more experience-near and visceral appreciation of the emotionally incendiary terrain through which this volume treads—Crown Heights being an extreme example of black-Jewish conflict in America at its all time worst:

1. A black child named Gavin Cato was accidentally and tragically killed by a Hassidic driver who was part of the Lubavitcher Hassidic procession transporting their community leader and chief rabbi, Menachem Schneerson.

2. There was no immediate public apology on the part of the Hassidic community for the child's death; no organized public communal prayer at the place where the child died—a symbolic act that might have greatly diffused the situation and prevented the violence that followed. For a community that greatly cherishes its children and the family unit, for a community that can bring together thousands of Hassidim for a demonstration in support of some issue of concern to the safety and continuity of their way of life, for a community that prides itself on its commitment to the "ethical life"—one wonders what muted the moral, psychological, and political response of the Hassidic leadership. The fact that, as some have intimated, the Hassidic leadership was advised by legal counsel to

say and do nothing at the time of the incident, in our view, is not an acceptable excuse for their inaction.

3. And then the most shocking and morally grotesque scene: a murderous black mob charging through the streets shouting anti-Jewish slogans such as "kill the Jews," beating men, women, and children, destroying their property, and worst of all, murdering one yeshiva student, Yankel Rosenbaum. The ineffectiveness of the police in maintaining law and order, raises troubling questions about the effectiveness of local government.

4. Sometime later, another shocking scene: a mob of Hassidic Jews marching around the neighborhood chanting (peacefully thankfully) that blacks should go back to Africa.

5. While a few black leaders, especially the clergy, vigorously spoke out against the black violence against Jews, by and large, there was either silence or feeble apologetics. And almost no one in the Jewish community criticized the Hassidim for their lack of an immediate morally responsible reaction to the death of the black child and for their racist demonstration against blacks.

6. Then a trial in which Lemrick Nelson, the alleged murderer of the yeshiva student was incredibly, found innocent, after which the black jurors shamelessly celebrated Nelson's acquittal together with him at a local restaurant.

Black-Jewish relations cannot, should not, be reduced to this one horrible episode, and keeping in mind that this specific episode has its own complex social dynamics and history, it does nevertheless put into sharp focus the fact that intense conscious and unconscious passions in both communities makes it at times difficult for blacks and Jews to live together in a civil manner. Blacks and Jews do not have to agree on everything. Reasonable and decent people can disagree for example about quotas, racial preference and affirmative action. Nor do blacks and Jews have to love each other, although that surely would be the ideal. However, on the individual and communal level, they do need to respect each other within the realms of law and politics. This is certainly one of the main goals of all black-Jewish dialogue and efforts at reconciliation, and it is one of the ends that this volume hopes to contribute to.

As we have said, in our view, psychoanalysis offers a unique and compelling way of conceptualizing and intervening in the motivations that we think are at the root of much of black-Jewish conflict. There is a long-standing tradition regarding the use of psychoanalytic theory to study culture and society, going back to Freud and his early followers. Most of this work, however, has been on the application of psychoanalysis to understanding works of art, music, literature, religion and other such "applied" subjects. To date, however, this appropriation has generally been limited in its potential for bringing about real-life social benefits although there have been some exceptions such as Bruno Bettelheim's work on education (Luel 1994) and Vamik D. Volkan's work on interventions in international conflict (Volkan 1988). Like Bettelheim, Volkan, and others, this volume is dedicated to the application of psychoanalytic theory to real-life problems, in our case, to those problems effecting the black and Jewish communities as they try and live and flourish together in this country.

Practically speaking, psychoanalysis can be helpful as a psychologically nuanced "mode of thinking" about intergroup conflict. As we have intimated, psychoanalysis emphasizes the fact that almost always, certainly in the case of blacks and Jews, we are confronted with very complex, ambivalent, and "messy" emotions: strongly felt fears, anxieties, envy, anger—but also uncomfortable and usually disavowed kinship and "merging" wishes. These interfere in the development of effective communication and a reasonable relationship between the two groups. Public policy makers, communal leaders, and those who are charged with negotiating the problems between blacks and Jews must recognize that we are not, strictly speaking, dealing with participants who are governed by rationality and logic. Rather, these people have deeply felt, conscious, and unconscious passions that need to be ventilated and empathically addressed before we can expect a reasonable discussion and resolution of conflicts to take place.

For example, Heinz Kohut's notion of chronic narcissistic rage—rage that follows repeated assaults on self-esteem—has a heuristic value in understanding the often intense antisemitic, antiwhite attitudes among certain segments of the black community. Beginning with slavery, through institutional and other forms of racism, right up to the recent contentious claims by the authors of *The Bell Curve*, Charles Murray and Richard J. Herrnstein, alleging the intellectual inferiority of blacks, the African American community has experienced, and continues to experience, profound narcissistic injuries to their sense of competency, dignity, and humanity. Such assaults on what Kohut calls the "group-self," can create a feeling of shame and inferiority that frequently is defended by the destructive expression of narcissistic rage. Without oversimplifying extremely complex dynamics, suffice it to say, that according to this view, only with an empathic understanding of the narcissistic matrix and thus the role of group humiliation versus group pride, can black rage be adequately comprehended and transformed into constructive self-assertion. Programs that fully acknowledge and address the narcissistic injuries committed against blacks by whites, including some Jews, are more likely to promote the transformation of black rage into constructive self-assertion and a desire to coalesce with Jews and other potential allies against common enemies such as racism and bigotry.

A second example follows. Educational programs against white racism, including Jewish racism, have usually been based on the assumption among pedagogues and social engineers that the most effective way to combat racism and prejudice is to expose students to information and values that contradict their racist attitudes. So, for instance, students are encouraged to learn more about other marginalized and negatively stereotyped groups and the importance of respecting others who are different from themselves. While these programs have been successful to some degree, from a psychoanalytic viewpoint they don't go "deep" enough into the motives that usually sustain racist attitudes and drive individuals to racist behavior. As Bracher further points out, "the more profound and intractable causes of intolerance includes the presence of a rigid but threatened sense of identity and the use of primitive defense mechanisms, such as projection, to maintain this sense of identity by refusing to recognize elements of one's own being that contradict this idealized self-image" (Bracher 1996, 9). From a psychoanalytic point of view then, an effective intervention emanating from this way of conceptualizing racism would focus on increasing the student's self-acceptance of his unacceptable tendencies, in contrast to the received view, that aims to increase the student's self-esteem by stressing attributes and achievements that they take pride in. That is, to reduce racist and bigoted attitudes and behavior, it is precisely those unacceptable feelings, attitudes, and attributes that students are ashamed of and have disavowed, repressed, and projected that need to be "worked through" (ibid.).

While we think that psychoanalysis can be a most illuminating tool for understanding and intervening in interethnic and racial conflict, we recognize that it is not a metaphysical master key. To be most effective, psychoanalysis must integrate itself with other disciplines, in particular social theory. It must concern itself with understanding how the socioeconomic and political institutions of our society and the power relations of ethnicity, race, class, and gender shape our personal worlds and vice versa. Moreover, without social theory, psychoanalysis will never be able to make the leap adequately from individual psychology to group behavior, an issue of great importance in this volume as we try and understand and intervene in the behavior of communities and not simply the behavior of discrete individuals.

OUTLINE OF THE BOOK

In light of the above, this anthology addresses, among other problems, how two profoundly different groups with at times divergent interests, can respectfully and peacefully live together and possibly work together, on mutually enhancing, common goals that also strengthen our democracy. Specifically, contributors were asked to answer from their particular psychoanalytic perspective the following three straightforward although deceptively complex and demanding questions: (1) What is the problem? (2) How did it get there? (3) How can we "fix" it?

It should be emphasized that the authors were instructed to give special attention to the interweaving of psychoanalytic and social theory in their chapters and, most important, to generate some theoretically sophisticated, pragmatic suggestions on how to improve black-Jewish relations. This volume thus aims to contribute to understanding and ameliorating a specific case of interethnic, interracial conflict that we think is in some ways emblematic for other intergroup conflicts including the very troubling racial problem in this country. Moreover, by encouraging the merging of psychoanalysis with social theory we hope to further the development of a theoretically coherent psychoanalytic social psychology, one that does not, as has too often been the case, reduce phenomenological and political multiplicities into causal singularities.

Every anthology, to some extent, reflects the convictions, biases, and prejudices of its editors. While this introduction is not the place to situate this book in its personal, historical, and ideological context we do think that it is necessary to at least say something about the editors' perspective as it relates to the aims of this book. The editors are of course radically different people with very different ways of looking at things, in part because they are very unlike in age and circumstance. The first editor (Alan Helmreich), an unmarried journalist with a degree in philosophy from Columbia University is more than twenty years younger than the second editor (Paul Marcus), a practicing psychoanalyst who is married with children. Thus, merging our particular life perspectives into one coherent editorial strategy was not always so easy. However, there was at least always one important common point of orientation between the editors and this should be acknowledged in this introduction. Both editors consider themselves Orthodox Jews who are strongly influenced in their world-views, sensibilities, and concerns by their commitment to Jewish ethics, learning, continuity, and survival. Moreover, it is the philosophical anthropology of the renowned French Jewish philosopher Emmanuel Levinas that serves as the "common ground" between the editors. While Levinas is not actually overtly "used" by us in this book, his "presence," especially his notion that responsibility for and obligation to the Other are absolute, both helped to inspire and editorially inform this anthology as a whole.

Thus, saying all of this, it needs to be emphasized that while this volume strives to be psychoanalytic, that is, in a certain sense "impartial" in orientation, neither the editors nor any of the contributors are "neutral" observers looking at black-Jewish conflict from a scientifically privileged, "God's-eye" view, that somehow reveals the "truth" about blacks and Jews or about black-Jewish conflict. Psychoanalysts, like everyone else, are subject to the range of political, social, historical, economic, and personal forces that shape a person's views. We have assembled psychoanalytic thinkers from a variety of backgrounds and convictions: blacks, Jews, non-Jews, a Pakistani—and each of these contributors comes to our evocative subject with their own biases, political sensibilities, and concerns, and perhaps most important, "unfinished business" and baggage. To make matters even more complicated, no single psychoanalytic theory will likely be able to embrace adequately the wide-ranging contemporary, multidimensional identities of blacks and Jews, again emphasizing the magnitude of the conceptual-practical complexity embedded in grappling with black-Jewish conflict.

The book begins with a "Time Line of Black-Jewish Relations" that summarizes what we think are the most important moments in black-Jewish relations: beginning in 1619 when the first shipload of African slaves arrived in Virginia, right up to the 1997 civil rights conviction and imprisonment of Lemrick Nelson, the alleged murderer of Yankel Rosenbaum during the Crown Heights riots, and the tragic death of the heroic Betty Shabbaz, the widow of Malcolm X, who was murdered by her grandson, and whose death brought together important black and Jewish luminaries from the civil rights era. Our hope is that this time line will help contextualize current black-Jewish relations and problems by providing an easily accessible historical perspective. We have generously drawn from Murray Friedman's (1995) thoughtful and we think balanced history of black-Jewish relations in constructing the time line.

Chapter 2, "Black-Jewish Conflict and the Regions of the Mind," accounts for black-Jewish conflict in terms of the discomforting realities that the Jewish group narrative represents for African Americans. As issues of identity and self-constitution have become increasingly important for African Americans, the authors argue these unsettling realities related to the Jewish experience and their troubling symbolic ramifications, have become increasingly threatening. These developments can be seen in the context of a fundamental shift in the orientation to blacks of the African American community from a preoccupation with practical, legislative concerns toward a focus on the more intangible and emotional realms. The result of the overall shift in emphasis, which seems to have started on the heels of the civil rights revolution, has resulted in an escalation in black antisemitism, since it is primarily in the symbolic and emotional sphere where Jews pose the greatest threat.

In chapter 3 by C. Fred Alford, "If I Am You, Then You Are . . . Fake" we learn that psychoanalysts of social conflict generally hold that feuding groups, such as blacks and Jews, desperately need each other in order to define themselves by contrast. We need our enemies as much, or more, than we need our friends. Our friends tell us who we are, our enemies tell us who we are not. Enemies, in other words, provide an important identity-enhancing function. In the case of blacks and Jews, however, this conflict has additional complications. A few blacks, such as Khalid Abdul Muhammad, representative of Minister Louis Farrakhan, hold not that the Jew is the enemy, but that the Jew is not truly Jewish. Blacks are the real Jews. Here we see, says Alford, a phenomenon that is usually more obscure, a profound identification with the enemy that in this case, is rooted in the historical relations of blacks and Jews. In an Afrocentric refashioning of history, the black is now the Jew, the one who deserves historical recognition and respect. Such an identification, argues Alford, indicates such an extreme degree of enmeshment and confused and confusing boundaries that the first step must be not reconciliation but separation. Psychoanalysis can help untangle this complex relationship by taking seriously the concept of unconscious identification and its consequences.

In "Black Liberation and the Jewish Question," E. Victor Wolfenstein, a Marxist-psychoanalytic scholar, asks the question: How might we understand the relationship of blacks and Jews if we view it from the perspective of identity politics and multiculturalism, specifically the struggle against white racism? The answer, he suggests, is that the focus of the relationship—whether originating with Jews or blacks—is for the most part a displacement from the primary focus of conflict. It is, in this quite psychoanalytic sense, symptomatic. From this perspective, according to Wolfenstein, the main reason for analyzing black-Jewish relationships is to dissolve the symptom and undo the displacement so that the central conflict can be forthrightly confronted. Wolfenstein claims that for many Jews, the remembered trauma of the European Jewish religious-*racial* past (e.g., the Holocaust) distorts perception of the American Jewish religious-*ethnic* present. The consequence is a certain blindness to the continuing traumatic impact of white racism on black people and a corresponding tendency to misinterpret black attitudes toward white people, Jews included. In his view, a psychoanalytic perspective can help Jews and blacks recognize that a renewed black-Jewish alliance is unrealistic in that it is no longer maintained by a situational play of power and interests. The focus rather should be on inclusive interracial discourse.

While Wolfenstein's essay suggests that black-Jewish conflict is largely a function of how Jewish attitudes toward blacks are determined by the persecution of their European past and not owning up to their present power, Mortimer Ostow views black-Jewish conflict as mainly an issue of black antisemitism. In his "Black Myths and Black Madness: Is Black Antisemitism Different?," Ostow provides a psychoanalytic narrative on Louis Farrakhan's fantasies about Jews. In Ostow's view, Farrakhan's fantasies about Jews display the paradoxicality, the ambivalence, the creation of and reliance upon myth, and the fluctuating quality that characterized antisemitism since the early years of the Christian era. The basic psychodynamic that determines Farrakhan's antisemitism is the designation of the Jew as the cosmic principle of evil alongside Satan. When this psychodynamic is embedded in a fundamentalist group that relies on apocalyptic thinking, such as in the case of The Nation of Islam, it is most dangerous. Ostow sees very little evidence of a Jewish animus, symmetrical and reciprocal to black antisemitism. A prophylactic psychoanalytically informed educational strategy that focuses on exposing antisemitic myths in individuals before others are coopted by fundamentalist groups, is perhaps the best form of defense against Black antisemitism.

Maurice Apprey and Howard F. Stein's "Ruptures in Time: The Branch That Holds the Fork in African American and Jewish American History" situates black-Jewish conflict in terms of their common group's history in which enslavements, expulsions, exclusions, lynchings, and exterminations have been historically "normal." In the authors' view, both groups have a profound experience of historical traumatic rupture, a feeling of brokenness that is both embedded in, and further shaped by our larger national history. Focusing on these gaps in black and Jewish group memory and how these gaps are manifested in the extremely ambivalent, symbiotic relationship between blacks and Jews, Apprey and Stein suggest that it is a cycle of group woundedness and the narcissistic infliction of woundedness that is at the root of black-Jewish conflict. That is, each group enacts its own disavowed, repressed traumatic past through the dehumanized other, frequently in terms of black antisemitism and Jewish racism. Psychoanalysis can help resolve black-Jewish conflict by helping these two transgressed groups fill in gaps in their collective memory by creating new narratives to preserve their traumatic memories and new stories to define the identity of their culture. By "working through" their internal griefs, blacks and Jews can build on their common human interests in their relations with each other.

Cynthia Burack and Bonnie J. Morris's chapter " 'Unlearning Racism' at Women's Music Festivals," describes black-Jewish conflict within the context of politically progressive, largely lesbian-feminist music festivals. In their view, festivals are opportunities for developing a vehicle for antiracist political discourse; however, they are also places where racial and ethnic conflict erupt as sites of radicalized struggles for territory and visibility, frequently involving stereotyping. In this sense what occurs at music festivals are to some extent emblematic for black-Jewish and black-white conflict in other social contexts. The "unlearning racism" workshop model assumes that racism is learned and can therefore be unlearned, and in this sense it is cognitive-behavioral in psychological orientation. However, as Burack and Morris demonstrate, when a psychoanalytically oriented piece is added to the workshop, for example the exploration of the personal roots of one's experience of race and racism, inequality and privilege, as well as the associated "primitive" feelings of fear, contempt, anxiety, and envy— these unlearning workshops as pedagogical strategies are enormously useful to reduce black antisemitism and Jewish racism.

Aisha Abbasi (originally from Pakistan), in her chapter "Speaking the Unspeakable," approaches the problem of black-Jewish conflict from the point of view of what is left unsaid and unshared between Jews and blacks with regard to the conflicts between them. Such feelings as hate, envy, blame, disappointment, and betrayal felt toward the other group are "unspeakable" because they are viewed as psychologically dangerous, politically incorrect and/or inappropriate for civilized discussion. At times these disavowed, suppressed, and repressed feelings—part projections of unacceptable parts of one's group self onto members of the other group and partly a response to real-life suffering—become the emotional basis for conflict between blacks and Jews. Abbasi suggests among other things, that psychologically sophisticated facilitators in a variety of educational contexts be used to help conflicting parties "process" that which is unspeakable and often unheard. "Working through" feelings about race, white privilege, prejudice, and bigotry will increase empathy between blacks and Jews. Moreover, as individuals "reality test" their own projections, they will strengthen their ego-functioning and thus their ability as groups to both live more harmoniously with each other and work together in mutually enhancing ways.

In chapter 9, A. Michele Morgan begins "Sharing the Mark of Cain: The Jewish and African American Communities in America" by pointing out that, by and large, the so-called black-Jewish conflict is not one between average blacks and Jews living their everyday lives, but rather, it has been African American and Jewish scholars who have been duking it out. This suggests that what goes for black-Jewish conflict, at least on the symbolic level, may to some extent be a function of unresolved power and other issues between black and Jewish intellectuals on campus who attract a lot of media attention. Morgan accounts for black-Jewish conflict in terms of three interrelated themes: reciprocally unrealistic expectations of each other, making use of the other community as Other to diminish the Other in themselves, and insensitivity to the experience of the other group. She makes the important point that the reduction of conflict between blacks and Jews can only take place if there is first an internal shift in each community. For Jews it means owning up to their white-skin privilege in this country and racism in their community, and for blacks it means strengthening their ability to be self-critical such as facing up to their antisemitism.

Mark Bracher's "The Conflict between Blacks and Jews: A Lacanian Analysis," situates black-Jewish conflict in terms of four basic psychological needs. Individuals and groups have a need for identity, meaning, a shared object of positive or negative fantasy, and an opportunity, a space upon which to confront their self-division. Bracher claims that each of these needs can contribute to intergroup conflict. For example: (1) the quest to fill each need can lead to competition, rivalry, and hatred with another group that threatens to deprive one of the means to satisfy a particular need; (2) an enemy can help fulfill a particular need by serving as a foil or defining antithesis for the fulfilling object; (3) or an enemy can relieve one of a particular need, and of the intraspsychic conflict it involves, by functioning as a receptacle into which one can deposit that need. Each of these needs functions as a causal factor in the conflict between blacks and Jews. Bracher suggests that only after blacks and Jews "work through" the various repressed drives, desires, fantasies, enjoyments, anxieties, and defenses that are associated with these above-mentioned needs, especially about each other, can the roots of the conflict be adequately addressed and sublimated. He describes some promising psychoanalytically informed problem-solving workshops that may be helpful in facilitating this process of conflict resolution and reconciliation.

Lee Jenkins in "Black-Jewish Relations: A Social and Mythic Alliance" suggests that the historical experience of the intolerance and bigotry expressed toward Jews and blacks has enmeshed the two in a mythic kinship, while at the same time the emphasis upon the similarity of historical and social experience has served as a source of ambivalence and conflict. Says Jenkins, Jews and blacks are mythic doubles, each seeing both an unwanted reflections of themselves in the other and a mutual recognition of similarity, yet driven by the self-evident experience of the uniqueness of a separate identity and a necessary emphasis upon such difference. Jenkins argues that one of the main dynamics that ought to be addressed between blacks and Jews is their need to emphasize their respective distinctiveness, to the denigration of the other. While Jenkins recognizes that blacks and Jews are different as groups in many important ways, he nevertheless believes that it is only a commitment to the notion of the sanctity of a common humanity—emanating from blacks and Jews reclaiming their hostile projectiles and integrating their ambivalences toward each other—that an improved relationship can be brought about.

This book closes with some additional observations pertaining to the most pressing question underlying this volume: How can psychoanalysis be applied effectively to improve real-life relations between blacks and Jews? Realizing that much of what has been written in this book has been strong on explaining "why" there is black-Jewish conflict, that is, elucidating the possible psychodynamics and psychological realities at work, it has been less successful at generating "solutions." This is not surprising in light of the fact that psychoanalysis has historically been most powerful as a way of understanding the origins and significance of psychological and social realities and less effective at intervention on both the individual and group level. In this sense, practice has not kept up with theory. Thus, chapter 12, "Some Practical Psychoanalytically Informed Suggestions for Communal Leaders for Improving Black-Jewish Relations," tries to delineate some pragmatic recommendations directed toward those individuals who are actually involved on the "front line" of black-Jewish conflict and its resolution.

REFERENCES

Berman, Paul, ed. 1994. *Blacks and Jews: Alliances and Arguments*. New York: Delacorte Press.

Bracher, Mark. 1996. "Editor's Introduction." *Journal for the Psychoanalysis of Culture and Society* 1, no. 1 (spring):1–13.

Forman, Seth. 1998. *Blacks in the Jewish Mind: A Crisis of Liberalism.* New York: New York University Press.

Friedman, Murray. 1995. *What Went Wrong? The Creation and Collapse of the Black-Jewish Alliance.* New York: Free Press.

Lerner, Michael, and Cornel West. 1995. *Jews and Blacks: Let the Healing Begin.* New York: G. P. Putnam's Sons.

Luel, Steven. 1994. "Bettelheim on Education." Bruno Bettelheim's Contribution to Psychoanalysis. A Special Issue of *The Psychoanalytic Review* 81, no. 3 (fall):565–80.

Salzman, Jack, and Cornel West, eds. 1997. *Struggles in the Promised Land: Toward a History of Black-Jewish Relations in the United States.* New York: Oxford University Press.

Volkan, Vamik D. 1988. *The Need to Have Enemies and Allies: From Clinical Practice to International Relationships.* Northvale, N.J.: Jason Aronson.

West, Cornel. 1997. "Walking the Tightrope: Some Personal Reflections on Blacks and Jews." In *Struggles in the Promised Land: Toward a History of Black-Jewish Relations in the United States,* edited by Jack Salzman and Cornel West, 411–16. New York: Oxford University Press.

1

Time Line of Black-Jewish Relations

ALAN HELMREICH AND PAUL MARCUS

1619: First shipload of African slaves arrives in Virginia.

1777: Northern states begin to abolish slavery. By 1804 states north of Maryland have outlawed the institution.

1787: Constitutional Convention puts into place twenty-year timetable to establish prohibition on slave trading. By 1807 new slaves are no longer allowed into the United States.

1800s: Abolitionism movement gains momentum in the North. However, in contrast to their later role in the civil rights struggle, Jews play negligible part in the cause.

1860: Abraham Lincoln elected president on emancipation platform. Southern states secede, and Civil War breaks out.

JEWS AND SLAVERY: The question of Jews and slavery, long virtually ignored, has been reexamined of late as the topic has become an academic sore-point of black-Jewish relations. It appears that Jews played a limited though not inconsequential role in the slave trade. Certain Dutch Sephardic (of Spanish origin) Jewish clans were known to be "slave trading families"; however, the percentage of Jewish slave traders is believed never to have exceeded about 10 percent. As small a role as Jews played in slave trading, they were even more marginal as slave owners. Jews, who up through the mid-1800s were just barely gaining a foothold in this country, were mostly too poor to afford slaves. However, there were exceptions: Judah P. Benjamin, the most important Southern Jew of the antebellum era, was reported to have owned 140 slaves. Despite the zeal American Jews would later display for social justice and civil rights, Jews played a rather small role in the abolitionist movement, and the opinions of Jewish leadership on the issue of slavery were typically ambivalent.

1861–65: Civil War—Jews, essentially, do not make waves and line up to fight in accordance with geographic locale. Six thousand Jews serve on the Union side while fifteen hundred join the Confederate ranks. 210,000 blacks fight in the Union Army and Navy.

1862: Benjamin Emancipation Plan—Proposal presented by Jewish Confederate Secretary of State Judah P. Benjamin offers emancipation to Southern slaves who volunteer to fight in the Confederate Army. Though perhaps seemingly perverse, the plan was in fact too progressive for the Confederate congress, which voted it down. (Ultimately, a pared-down version of the plan was passed that allowed slaves to fight without the promise of freedom.)

1865: Thirteenth Amendment Passed—With the emancipation of blacks following the South's defeat in the Civil War, the stage is set for the first chapter of the black-Jewish relationship. Almost immediately, one of the most important patterns that would come to characterize that relationship in later years takes hold—the merchant-customer relationship—as Jews are among the only Southern shopkeepers willing to do business with blacks.

1860s: Formation of the Ku Klux Klan.

Judah P. Benjamin: Secretary of war and later secretary of state to Confederate President Jefferson Davis. Next to Davis, Benjamin was the most important figure in the rebel government and probably the most important American Jew of that era. In the words of one scholar, he "achieved greater political power than any other Jew in the nineteenth century, perhaps in all of American history." Though he was a staunch supporter of slavery, some of his most public gestures were on the antislavery front. In defending a group of insurance companies against a slaveholders' suit, he offered a stirring indictment of slavery, denouncing it as a "contravention of the laws of nature." Along these lines, Benjamin was probably best known for his ill-fated emancipation plan (see above, 1862).

1868: Immigrant Jewish merchant is lynched by the Ku Klux Klan in Franklin, Tennessee; was an employer of blacks and was believed to harbor "radical" views.

1881: Tuskegee Institute founded by Booker T. Washington—Washington would go on to establish ties with upper-crust German Jews through his fundraising efforts for Tuskegee, pioneering a type of dependency that would become emblematic of the black-Jewish relationship of subsequent years.

Booker T. Washington: Much of the complexity of the black-Jewish relationship was embodied in the thought and action of this seminal African American figure. On the one hand, Washington often professed admiration for Jewish industriousness and group solidarity and urged blacks to follow the Jews' lead. However, such sentiments can at times also be just a short stride away from antisemitism, and Washington was known to have his share of mildly antisemitic impulses. It is likely that the degree of Washington's antisemitism was typical for Americans of that day—black or white. Regardless of the nuances of Washington's feelings toward Jews, he did not hesitate in soliciting their financial backing, and New York's wealthy German Jews became the backbone of Washington's fundraising efforts for endeavors such as the Tuskegee Institute.

1882: Schiff Proposal—As a member of the New York Board of Education, German Jewish financier Jacob Schiff proposes to end the city's segregated school system and close its "colored schools." His proposal is passed by the board, though "de facto" school segregation continues well into the twentieth century.

1895: Dreyfus Affair—Sentencing of accused French Jewish spy becomes one of the early litmus tests for the fledgling black-Jewish relationship: The black press harshly criticizes what it sees as unfair persecution.

1903: Kishinev Massacre—Forty-nine Jews are killed and hundreds more injured in bloody Russian *pogrom*. Tensions begin to surface as American blacks use this incident to contrast attention and sympathy garnered by Jews, with public indifference to the plight of blacks.

1909: National Association for the Advancement of Colored People (NAACP) Formed—Over the next several decades this organization would become perhaps the most important embodiment of the emerging black-Jewish alliance. Some of the early participants in the NAACP were wealthy German Jews, and Jews would continue to play key roles in the organization right up through the zenith of the civil rights movement in the 1960s. Though the NAACP was certainly a critical factor in solidifying the black-Jewish alliance, at least on the organizational level, it also embodied some of the more questionable components of the black-Jewish relationship such as Jewish paternalism and black dependence on outside expertise.

OUR CROWD: The New York–based German Jewish aristocracy played a crucial role in the early black-Jewish alliance. Names such as Jacob Schiff, Felix Warburg, Isaac Seligman, and James Loeb were often the financial might behind many of the seminal endeavors to address the plight of blacks in this country, including the Urban League and the NAACP. Philanthropist Julius Rosenwald would make a huge individual contribution toward educating Southern black children (see below, 1914) and other German Jews, such as Louis Marshall, Jacob Schiff, and Joel Spingarn also made important contributions on the legislative and legal fronts. In the next generation or two, Jews with immigrant Eastern European, and often labor-left backgrounds, would take these German Jews' place at the forefront of the black-Jewish partnership.

1913: Leo Frank Affair—Jewish Atlanta factory manager Leo Frank is convicted and hanged for the alleged murder of a thirteen-year-old white Christian female employee. Defense efforts on behalf of Frank, both legal and public relations, focus on the guilt of a black janitor, one of only two other people present in the factory on the day of the alleged killing. Blacks join ranks with Southern whites in insisting on Frank's guilt while incendiary antiblack rhetoric is employed by Frank's defenders. Frank's name would eventually be cleared many years later, but the event marked a low point in the burgeoning black-Jewish relationship.

1914: Rosenwald Fund Established—Jewish philanthropist Julius Rosenwald sets up fund to educate Southern black children. Until its expiration in 1932, fund contributes over $4 million and educates over one-fourth of Southern black children.

Marcus Garvey: One of the foremost figures in black history, Garvey was to the twenties and thirties, what figures such as Malcolm X, Amiri Baraka, and Stokely Carmichael would be to the sixties and seventies: the vanguard voice of black nationalism and separatism. Garvey was, in many respects, a forerunner to the developments that would, arguably, play a large role in bringing down the black-Jewish alliance several decades later. Garvey's preaching of black pride and "back to Africa" was coupled with a robust antisemitism. In his publication, *The Blackman*, Garvey wrote: "Hitler's ways could make the Negroes the man he ought to be" (*sic*). Garvey scapegoated Jews for many of the woes of urban blacks, as well as for some of his own personal problems. Though his message was no doubt inspiring to many blacks who were living in the throes of a racist and oppressive society, the emergence of Marcus Garvey was a decidedly ominous development for black-Jewish relations.

1920s: West Side Improvement Association Formed—Group run mainly by Jews on Manhattan's upper West side seeks to limit the presence of blacks in the area to "protect property values."

1922: Marcus Garvey prosecuted in mail fraud case in which both prosecutor and judge are Jews. Fact does not go unnoted by Garvey.

THE TWO GREAT MIGRATIONS: In the early decades of the twentieth century, Southern blacks began in large numbers to migrate north in search of jobs and greater opportunities. This migration coincided with the era of large-scale Jewish immigration to this country. Often, Jews and blacks met each other in the teeming urban neighborhoods of such cities as New York, Philadelphia, Detroit, Boston, and Chicago. Not infrequently, as blacks were on the way in, Jews were on the way out. However, a strong Jewish presence remained in these neighborhoods right up through the 1960s and 1970s as many Jews stayed on as storeowners and landlords. Whether justly or not, these Jewish merchants and building owners were often perceived to be exploitative and were accused of unsavory practices such as profiteering and price gouging. The unequal and, in many ways, problematic economic relationship established between blacks and Jews under these circumstances may have contributed to the later poisoning of the black-Jewish relationship.

1925: A. Philip Randolph Forms the Brotherhood of Sleeping Car Porters—Much of Randolph's union activity was conducted in concert with Jewish labor figures such as Morris Hillquit and Jewish politicians such as Emmanuel Celler. Such activity would form the foundation of the black-Jewish labor alliance, which would play a central role in the civil rights movement in later decades.

1929: Stock Market Crashes—Blacks, already on the bottom rungs of the economic ladder, are hit especially hard by the ensuing Great Depression. Crushing poverty in the ghettoes exacerbates economic tensions with Jewish merchants and landlords.

1931: Nathan Margold, a Jewish Harvard-trained lawyer hired by the NAACP, drafts a report urging the NAACP to direct its legal efforts toward attacking segregation as a principle, as opposed to fighting discrimination on a case by case basis. The new strategy would revolutionize the way civil rights campaigns are waged.

1931: Scottsboro Case—Eight black youths are sentenced to death and one to life imprisonment on scant evidence for the rape of two white women aboard an Alabama train. The Yiddish press is at the forefront of the national furor over the miscarriage of justice, and the boys are defended by Jewish attorneys Joseph Brodsky and Samuel Liebowitz, who ultimately win their acquittal on appeal.

March 25, 1935: Harlem Riots—Harlem erupts after a false rumor spreads that a Puerto Rican youth, arrested for shoplifting, was beaten to death by police. Jewish stores are targeted in the looting and mayhem.

1936: Adolph Hitler Takes Power in Germany—Blacks have recurring flirtations with support for the Nazi leader, indicative of growing currents of antisemitism in the urban ghettoes.

1941: Japanese Forces Bomb Pearl Harbor—Sense of national unity brought on by the war seems to offer a respite in mounting black-Jewish tension.

THE HOLOCAUST: Perenially a flashpoint of black-Jewish tension, ostensibly, the Holocaust might be a unifying factor in the black-Jewish relationship: It serves as a powerful testimony for blacks that Jews have suffered profoundly as well. For Jews, the Holocaust may heighten awareness of the dangers of discrimination of any kind. However, by and large, the Holocaust has been a divisive force between the two groups. Blacks have often appeared to resent the attention given to the Holocaust at the expense of their own causes. And the apparent postwar economic success of Holocaust survivors seems to be a sort of "in your face" for blacks, many of whom are still languishing in poverty more than one hundred years after the end of slavery. Some reactionary Jews have used the Holocaust as a justification for taking an insular, defensive posture, shutting out the needs of other groups and causes, including African Americans. The contentiousness of the Holocaust was graphically captured in Jesse Jackson's alleged remark while on a trip to Israel that he is "sick and tired of hearing about the Holocaust."

1943: Detroit and Harlem Riots—Street fighting breaks out between whites and blacks in Detroit, resulting in the deaths of twenty-five blacks and nine whites. Blacks in another area of the city respond to white violence by looting Jewish stores, leading to the exodus of Jews from inner-city Detroit. A similar episode in Harlem is sparked by the shooting of a black soldier by a white policeman. Hundreds of businesses along 125th Street are destroyed.

1948: State of Israel Established—Israel would become a particularly sore point for black-Jewish relations, particularly after Israel's victory in the Six Day War. Not only did blacks choose to identify with Third World anti-Israel elements, but the Zionist enterprise may have also siphoned off Jewish energy and romance from the civil rights struggle.

1950: Leadership Conference on Civil Rights Formed—Spawned as an outgrowth of the drive to establish a permanent Fair Employment Protection Committee, the organization would play a major role in some of the important civil rights endeavors of subsequent years. It would also usher in a new era of black-Jewish civil rights collaboration with the NAACP's Roy Wilkins and the National Jewish Community Relations Council's Arnold Aronson at the center of its formation.

May 17, 1954: _Brown_ v. _Board of Education_ Topeka, Kansas—Supreme Court issues landmark ruling deeming public school segregation unconstitutional. Jewish attorney Jack Greenberg and Supreme Court Justice Felix Frankfurter play key roles in the initiative.

December 1955: Rosa Parks refuses to move to the back of a Montgomery, Alabama, bus. The Montgomery bus boycott, organized by Martin Luther King and other Southern black leaders follows.

May 17, 1957: Prayer Pilgrimage for Freedom—Gathering in Washington, D.C., on the third anniversary of the _Brown_ decision unites NAACP with "In Friendship," a newly formed civil rights body, and with members of the black-Jewish labor alliance. This event solidifies a blossoming black-Jewish civil rights partnership.

GLORY DAYS: The years 1954 through approximately 1965 marked the most fruitful period for the civil rights movement. It was during these years that the bulk of the most important civil rights legislation was passed. These years, perhaps not coincidentally, also marked the best times for the black-Jewish alliance. Not only did high-profile Jews such as Stanley Levison, Jack Greenberg, and Allard Lowenstein play significant roles in the civil rights organizational apparatus, but young Jews, especially students, provided much of the grass-roots support and manpower for the sit-ins and mass demonstrations. More than any other period, it is this era that people envision when they speak of the fabled black-Jewish partnership. As the

1960s wore on, it appears that black activists began to "outgrow" their former Jewish partners, as the movement started to chart a more militant as well as separatist course. The assassination of Martin Luther King Jr. in 1968 may have killed the last hope that the growing fissure could ever be fully repaired.

1957: Southern Christian Leadership Conference (SCLC) Founded—The organization headed by Martin Luther King Jr., would become perhaps the preeminent force in the civil rights struggle. It would also be a major organ for the advancement of the black-Jewish alliance, with Jewish left-wing lawyer Stanley Levison playing a critical behind-the-scenes role. Another civil rights organization that similarly united blacks and Jews was the Congress on Racial Equality (CORE).

February 1960: Sit-ins—"Sit-in Movement" spearheaded when four black students demand service at a whites only lunch counter at a Woolworth's in Greensboro, North Carolina. Success of the move leads CORE to organize sit-ins on segregated interstate buses in the South.

April 1960: Student Non-Violent Coordinating Committee (SNCC) Formed—Movement is formed as a sort of breakaway from SCLC. Offered as a more radical and student-oriented alternative. The black leadership of SNCC does not become as heavily intertwined with Jewish figures as their SCLC counterparts, and the movement eventually becomes highly militant and separatist, alienating many of its former Jewish sympathizers.

Martin Luther King Jr.: The great civil rights leader was perhaps the most important figure in perpetuating and nurturing the black-Jewish alliance. Throughout his life, King worked closely with Jews such as Stanley Levison, Harry Wachtel, and Jack Greenberg and forged spiritual alliances with Jewish religious leaders Rabbi Joachim Prinz and Rabbi Abraham Joshua Heschel. In the latter years of the movement, King was increasingly caught between separatist as well as antisemitic elements of the civil rights movement and the more liberal Jewish forces that had been with him from the beginning. However, King never severed, or even loosened, his Jewish ties and continued to speak out against antisemitism and anti-Zionism even when it was becoming less and less fashionable to do so. King was, in many ways, the thread that held the black-Jewish alliance together, and after his assassination in 1968, things would never quite be the same between the two groups.

Summer 1961: The Freedom Riders—Interracial bands of young activists set out on interstate buses to provoke hostile Southerners into displays of racism and brutality. This move is also engineered to expose the lack of enforcement of integration laws. Much of the manpower is supplied by white Northern students, two-thirds of whom are Jews.

1963: Norman Podhoretz, one of the "founders" of "neoconservativism," publishes an essay "My Negro Problem and Ours" in which he writes of being victimized, both physically and psychologically, by his contact with blacks during his Brooklyn childhood. A landmark piece in the dialogue on black-Jewish relations, the essay deals with the often neglected terrain of Jewish attitudes toward black physicality and sexuality, in contrast to Jewish physical ineptitude and bookishness.

August 28, 1963: March on Washington—Civil rights movement (as well as the black-Jewish alliance) reaches its high-water mark with the march. Nearly 200,000 people turn out as Martin Luther King Jr. delivers his rousing, "I Have a Dream" speech. The march is a milestone for black-Jewish relations, as Jews provide much of the behind-the-scenes work and Rabbi Joachim Prinz, then president of the American Jewish Congress, addresses the crowd.

1964: Freedom Summer—Up to a thousand mostly white college students from the North descend upon Mississippi to volunteer in registering blacks to vote and other civil rights efforts. Approximately half of the volunteers are Jewish.

Summer 1964: Three young civil rights activists, working on a voter registration drive in Mississippi during the Freedom Summer, are murdered by the Ku Klux Klan under the cover of night. Two of the victims, Michael Schwerner, a twenty-three-year-old teacher from New York City and Andrew Goodman, a student at Queens College, are Jews. The third, twenty-one-year-old James Chaney is a black man from Meridian, Mississippi, who had met Schwerner through voter registration work.

1964: Omnibus Civil Rights Act—In one of the greatest moments of the civil rights struggle, this measure is passed that grants power to attorney generals to file discrimination suits against state and city officials and attempts to insure fairness in hiring with the establishment of the Equal Employment Opportunity Commission. Along with the Voting Rights Act that would soon follow, the measure represents the most tangible achievement of the movement. Jewish lawyers, lobbyists, and legislators play important roles in gaining the bill's passage.

1964–68: Race riots break out in urban black ghettoes across the country. Jewish businesses in areas such as Newark, Watts, and Detroit are targeted.

1965: Voting Rights Act—Another huge civil rights milestone, this event arguably represented the zenith of the civil rights era. This provision offers blacks broad protection in exercising their constitutional right to vote. Again, Jews play an important role in its enactment.

Stanley Levison: In a way, Levison was the very personification of the black-Jewish alliance. Trained as a lawyer, Levison, who had close ties to the Communist party, may well have been Martin Luther King Jr.'s closest friend and confidant. Levison greatly influenced some of King's most important decisions, while making a prolific contribution as a speechwriter. It can be argued that no figure, other than King himself, played a more important role in the civil rights struggle. And yet, Levison received little public note, serving more as a behind-the-scenes planner. Ironically, in the later years of the movement, despite his communist background, Levison urged moderation as King was sometimes tempted to follow the rest of the movement down an increasingly radical and leftist path. On the flip side, Levison may also have represented some of the more problematic elements of the black-Jewish relationship: Levison provided the strategic savvy and connections, upon which King and other black activists were so dependent.

1965: SNCC Openly Breaks with SCLC—From then on, SNCC would chart its own course and eschew many of the white and Jewish figures who had played a central role in the civil rights struggle.

1966: Stokely Carmichael Takes Over as Head of SNCC—Carmichael steers movement in increasingly radical, and then internationalist Third World direction, alienating many Jews.

1967: Harold Cruse's *The Crisis of the Negro Intellectual* Is Released—A literary voice to the growing sentiment among blacks that the time had come to unleash themselves from their white, liberal, and Jewish "patrons."

June 1967: Six Day War—Israel's victory thrusts the Jewish nation into the perceived role of oppressor of dark-skinned people. This event also reinvigorates Zionism, shifting somewhat the focus of American Jews.

Malcolm X: A link in the chain from Marcus Garvey to Louis Farrakhan, the charismatic Black Muslim leader was a sort of anti-King. While King was known for his concilliatory nonviolent approach, Malcolm X was associated with the phrase "By any means necessary." His strident separatist approach precluded any real alliance with Jews, and his now heralded autobiography reveals elements of antisemitism. Though in many ways Malcolm X differed from the more leftist oriented black separatists such as the Black Panther party, as well as some of the later incarnations of SNCC, he is widely seen as the symbol of the Black Nationalist approach that began to gain strength after his death. Incidentally, it has been alleged that Louis Farrakhan played a role in Malcolm X's assassination. Malcolm was a compelling as well as complex figure, and shortly before his death he embarked on a trip to Mecca that caused him to reassess his antiwhite views, as well as his antisemitism. But despite this, even as he continues to be lionized in films such as Spike Lee's *X*, his legacy will forever be as one of the more divisive racial forces in U.S. history.

1967: SNCC Folds—By this point SNCC is unrecognizable from its coalition building beginning.

Labor Day Weekend, 1967: Palmer House Conference for a New Politics—One of the last gasps of the black-Jewish alliance, this event attempts to unite various strands of the progressive left, including the remnants of the black-Jewish civil rights coalition. The conference turns into a travesty as Martin Luther King Jr. is jeered and attendees pass a number of anti-Zionist resolutions.

April 4, 1968: King Assassination—Devastating event for the nation as well as the black-Jewish alliance. Subsequent black leaders are much less willing and able to maintain black-Jewish cooperation.

JEWZ N' THE HOOD: In a development that began to take hold after World War II and continued on through the 1970s, many of the nation's former Jewish working-and middle-class urban areas were transformed into black ghettoes. The trend occurred in areas such as Brownsville–East New York, North Philadelphia, and large swaths of Detroit and Newark. The development can be attributed to a number of factors, including the historical coinciding of black migration from the South with Jewish migration from urban areas to the suburbs. However, not infrequently, Jewish reaction to the newcomers accelerated the process. Many of the Jews, who often considered themselves middle class, were fearful and suspicious of the new arrivals who usually were further down the socioeconomic scale. Unscrupulous real estate agents and mortgage interests fanned and capitalized on these fears with the infamous practice of blockbusting. As a result, sometimes entire neighborhoods were racially transformed in just a few short years. White flight, often perpetrated by Jews, both uncovered and exacerbated black-Jewish tension as the wholesale fleeing of Jews appeared to betray racism, while Jews lamented that their neighborhoods were being "ruined" by blacks.

1968: Democratic National Convention—Civil rights movement splits over demands by Mississippi Freedom Democrats, a radical spinoff of SNCC, to replace Mississippi party regulars in the state's delegation. Liberal "Jewish" branch of the movement favors compromise position that allows party regulars to remain, while radical black nationalist elements are staunchly opposed to any concessions. Discord in the movement is considered a turning point for the civil rights movement as well as for black-Jewish relations.

1968: Ocean Hill–Brownsville—Newly elected black superintendent of heavily black Brooklyn school district, in an act allegedly motivated by antisemitism though, seemingly, as much by personal vindictiveness, abruptly fires nineteen district teachers, most of whom are Jewish. Three hundred and fifty teachers strike in protest. Antisemitic fliers are distributed in the schools, and the episode heightens mounting animus between blacks and Jews.

RACE MATTERS: In a development that may have had its roots with the founding of SNCC in 1963, but which became much more visible as the 1960s came to a close, blacks in the civil rights movement begin to take a more nationalist as well as militant, separatist stance. It becomes increasingly passe to work with whites, and when the opportunity arises, whites, many of whom had devoted their entire life to civil rights, are snubbed at civil rights gatherings. The civil rights movement shifts its focus from achieving rights to the rhetoric of "liberation" and "black power." Coupled with this trend is the increasing tendency for the movement to identify with Arab causes and express antisemitic and anti-Zionist sentiments. Needless to say, these developments did not bode well for the black-Jewish alliance, and some feel they are practically synonymous with its demise.

1969: Jewish Defense League (JDL) Formed—Organization is started by New York City rabbi and Jewish activist Meir Kahane, ostensibly to protect Jews living on the figurative "front lines" in racially transitional neighborhoods. This militaristic

Brooklyn-based organization also serves as an outlet for increasing resentment toward blacks by lower middle-class and working-class Jews.

WITH FRIENDS LIKE THESE ... With the civil rights struggle fading into the past, a new, bleaker era of black-Jewish relations emerges. For the first time, Jews and blacks find themselves on opposing sides of a political issue, affirmative action. The affirmative action issue brings into full relief the fact that Jews and blacks are no longer natural coalition partners with common interests. The question becomes, What can sustain the alliance now?

1970: Federal judge Charles Weiner hands down decision in favor of establishing racial preference in hiring as the era of affirmative action begins. In subsequent years, Jews—who feel that they will bear the greatest brunt of affirmative action policies—become a visible force in opposing racial quotas.

NEOCONSERVATISM: Intellectual movement dominated by Jews, many of whom were formerly active in the civil rights movement. The tenets of traditional liberalism come to be questioned in the pages of journals such as *Commentary* and *The New Republic* by "neocons" Irving and William Kristol, Norman Podhoretz (see above, 1963), Nathan Glazer, and Midge Decter. The movement flourishes in the new era of black-Jewish mistrust and remains a potent intellectual force today.

1974: *Bakke* Case—Alan Bakke, a white medical school applicant denied admission by the University of California, files suit against the school charging that racial quotas are unconstitutional. Jewish groups back Bakke. Bakke wins his case in state court in 1976 and is again vindicated by the U.S. Supreme Court two years later in the case's appeal. (The Court does rule that race may be considered in school admissions, but numerical and statistical quotas may not be applied.)

June 1975: Civil rights veteran Bayard Rustin forms Black Americans in Support of Israel (BASIC) in an effort to curb growing black hostility toward Israel.

November 1977: Edward I. Koch Elected Mayor of New York City.

Edward I. Koch: Though not necessarily a major figure in the black-Jewish alliance, the talkative ex–New York City Mayor—perhaps the very personification of that city—merits mention since he seems to embody individually much of the complexity and ambivalence of the black-Jewish relationship. During the early 1960s, Koch went South to show support for blacks and, as an attorney, wound up defending a group of civil rights protesters. For his efforts, Koch narrowly escaped being attacked by white hoodlums. Koch's own stance toward blacks seems to have reflected the changing nature of the black-Jewish relationship. Though in the past he had been an outspoken advocate for civil rights, in later years he became (and remains) a vocal opponent of racial preferences, and his strongest voting base had always been among outer borough Jews who were often becoming increasingly wary of blacks. Caustic, yet compassionate, and never easy to pin down ideologically, Koch is once again in the courtroom presiding on NBC's *The People's Court*.

1979: U.S. ambassador to the UN Andrew Young, a former point man in the civil rights struggle as well as the black-Jewish alliance, is forced to step down after revelations that he secretly met with Zehdi Labib Terzi of the PLO. The meeting is considered to be in violation of a Carter administration policy that bans contact with terrorists. Resignation leads to African Americans' resentment of Jews, whom blacks perceive to be the driving force behind the ouster.

1979: In the wake of the Young flap, NAACP officials convene in New York and issue a much publicized statement, construed by many Jews to be antisemitic. The episode is, in many ways, a harbinger of things to come.

1979: Jesse Jackson travels to Israel and refers to a Jewish "persecution complex" after visiting Yad Vashem. During the same trip he is pictured in the *New York Times* embracing Yassir Arafat (well before the days of the Israeli-Palestinian peace process). The photo is in many ways an epitaph to the now disintegrated black-Jewish alliance.

1984: Jesse Jackson utters the infamous "hymietown" remark, quoted in the *Washington Post*. In response, a "Jews Against Jesse" ad appears in the *New York Times*.

1984: "Hymies for Jesse" bumper stickers and pins briefly appear. Some feel that by this point, the notion of a black-Jewish alliance is something of a joke.

Jesse Jackson: Arguably the foremost black leader of the post–civil rights era, Jackson symbolized the black-Jewish rift when he became associated with a series of seemingly antisemitic utterances, including the infamous "hymietown" remark. Jackson had also become known—and not so loved—in Jewish quarters, for his controversial embrace of Yassir Arafat during a 1979 trip to the Middle East. As Jackson's hopes for national political office have grown, and perhaps as he has matured as a leader, he has taken steps to distance himself from his antisemitic past. He has offered an olive branch of sorts to the Jewish community and at least to an extent, liberal Jews (including the somewhat left of center "Jewish establishment") have accepted. However, whether or not Jews will ever fully forgive him for his past remains uncertain.

1985: Nation of Islam leader Louis Farrakhan emerges on the national scene and holds a rally, filling up Madison Square Garden. The event is characterized by antisemitic rabble rousing. Later, Farrakhan would seemingly imply that Judaism is a "gutter religion."

1986: Steven Cokely, an aide to Chicago mayor Eugene Sawyer charges that Jewish physicians have been injecting African American infants with the AIDS virus.

Louis Farrakhan: The Nation of Islam's leader has become practically synonymous with black antisemitism. Farrakhan infuriated Jews when he appeared to call Judaism a "gutter religion" and leveled vague threats of another holocaust if Jews did not get their act together. Despite his antisemitism, Farrakhan continues to receive high marks from blacks (as well as some whites) for his message of black self-reliance and economic empowerment. Remarkably, in the last couple of years, Farrakhan—who revealed that he has minute traces of Jewish blood—has made halting concilliatory gestures toward Jews—albeit on his own terms.

1991: Crown Heights Riots—Interracial Brooklyn neighborhood explodes after seven-year-old black boy, Gavin Cato, is accidentally struck and killed by the Lubavitcher rebbe's motorcade. Disturbances rage for four days and three nights and anti-Jewish violence results in the death of Yankel Rosenbaum, a rabbinical student. Some Jews refer to the riots as a *pogrom*.

1992: Anti-Defamation League study reveals that African Americans are almost twice as likely as whites to harbor antisemitic views.

1992: New York City Mayor David N. Dinkins Is Defeated in His Bid for Reelection—The defeat of African American mayor Dinkins, at the hands of Republican Rudolph Giuliani, is partly atributed to the fallout from Dinkins's alleged mishandling of the Crown Heights affair.

1993: Khalid Abdul Muhammad, a Farrakhan deputy, delivers an address at Kean College in New Jersey in which he refers to Jews as, "bloodsuckers of the black nation."

1993: Leonard Jeffries is demoted from his position as chairman of the Black Studies Department at City College of New York, amid controversy over his alleged antisemitic teachings.

October 1995: Farrakhan's Million Man March in Washington was a day of celebration and solidarity for black men. To many Jews, it represented the national legitimation and star power of an antisemite. Months later, Farrakhan's attempt to establish himself on the international scene by meeting with Libya's Muammar Gadhafi drew intense criticism from many.

1995: Freddy's, a Jewish-owned retail store in Harlem, is firebombed by a black neighborhood activist.

1997: Lemrick Nelson Conviction—Youth accused of killing Yankel Rosenbaum during the Crown Heights riot is sentenced to thirty years in prison on a civil rights charge, three years after his initial murder trial resulted in an acquittal.

June 1997: Betty Shabbaz, widow of Malcolm X, is burned in her apartment by her own grandson. She would die from her wounds three weeks later. The funeral reunites black and Jewish luminaries from the civil rights era, and former Mayor Koch delivers a memorable speech invoking biblical psalm, "A Woman of Valor."

Fall 1997: *Amistad*, Steven Spielberg's film about an uprising aboard a transatlantic slave ship is released. The film, on a sensitive topic so dear to African Americans, directed and conceived by a Jewish filmmaker, provokes continuing dialogue on black-Jewish relations.

WHAT NOW? The Crown Heights riots, coupled with the ascendance of Louis Farrakhan and other racial demagogues are ominous developments for black-Jewish relations. In some ways, things have never before been as bad. The days when blacks and Jews coalesced to help this country realize its most noble ideals, are nothing more than a wistful memory. But the silver lining is that things may have gotten so conspicuously bad that people cannot help but take notice. Among those perking up appear to be intellectuals in both communities, and the result has been a flurry of literary output on the subject of black-Jewish relations. Works included in this genre are Paul Berman's anthology, *Blacks and Jews: Alliances and Arguments* (1994); *What Went Wrong? The Creation and Collapse of the Black-Jewish Alliance* by Murray Friedman (1995); Michael Lerner and Cornel West's collaboration, *Jews and Blacks: Let the Healing Begin* (1995); *Struggles in the Promised Land: Toward a History of Black-Jewish Relations in the United States,* edited by Jack Salzman and Cornel West (1997); and Seth Forman's *Blacks in the Jewish Mind: A Crisis of Liberalism* (1998). The present volume is, of course, the latest addition to this collection. Hopefully, when all is said and done, these literary endeavors will not be merely so much intellectual ax grinding, but viable and effective steps on the road to alleviating black-Jewish conflict.

2

Black-Jewish Conflict and the Regions of the Mind

ALAN HELMREICH AND PAUL MARCUS

One of the singular characteristics of the black-Jewish conflict is that, for the most part, it is not really a conflict *over* anything. In contrast to other group conflicts, which often hinge on matters of territory, economics, or clearly delineated political issues, the black-Jewish conflict has largely played itself out in the more intangible and emotional realms. At the heart of the dispute are feelings of insecurity and mistrust, competing claims to greater suffering, and issues of envy, resentment, and otherness. While certain practical concerns, such as economic exploitation in the ghettoes and racial quotas have at times played a role, mainly, the battleground between Jews and African Americans has been in a somewhat different place. To borrow from James Baldwin, the primary territories contested in the black-Jewish conflict have been "the regions of the mind" (Baldwin 1962).

It is not surprising, then, that the conflict has escalated with an analogous shift in the orientations of one of the principals in the conflict, the African American community. Over the last three decades, the primary focus of the black struggle has shifted from the realization of practical legislative measures toward issues of meaning and identity. This trend may have had its roots in the heady days of the black power movement of the 1960s. However the outlook developed and crystallized in subsequent years and in many ways continues to characterize the dominant mode of expression of the African American community today. This is not to say that more tangible concerns, such as economic empowerment and community development, have not played a significant role, particularly in recent years. But even these concrete agendas have been pursued against the backdrop of a landscape increasingly defined by issues of dignity, pride, and self-determination.

Much of this development is, no doubt, linked to the increasingly apparent practical limitations of what the civil rights movement was able to achieve. While significant gains were made in the areas of voting, employment opportunities, and desegregation, many blacks continued to languish in poverty and despair, long afterward. The shortcomings were apparent as long ago as the late 1960s, when race riots ravaged the country, and they are even more glaringly evident today. However the shift toward the emotional and intangible can also be seen in terms of an emerging stage in the collective emotional development of African American people. Having been liberated, at least in a certain sense, from the legislative and practical constraints of a severely racist society, African Americans were now free to explore the next frontier. With the noose of oppression considerably loosened, black people began moving into the realms of ideology, personal experience and self-expression, and the project of refashioning their group narrative of self-identity.

The shift toward this intangible terrain of meaning and identity has had important implications for black-Jewish conflict. On a concrete level, it likely paved the way for the breakup of the black-Jewish civil rights organizational and political coalition. With the emphasis less and less on the realization of practical legislative goals, the presence of Jews may have been increasingly superfluous, as it was chiefly in the practical realm where Jewish assistance was valued. In addition, with the increasing focus on the emotional and the psychological, the emasculating specter of the entire black-Jewish alliance, with its overtones of dependence and paternalism, came off as more and more distasteful.

But perhaps just as important, the increased emphasis on meaning and identity may have shifted African Americans' psychological focus to the symbolic ramifications of what Jews represented.

In many ways, it was this fact that bode most ominously for black-Jewish relations, for it was primarily on the symbolic and emotional plane where Jews posed the greatest threat. If examined psychoanalytically, we begin to see that the upsurge in black-Jewish conflict has stemmed largely from African Americans' efforts, both conscious and unconscious, to come to grips with the uncomfortable symbolic realities embodied by the Jewish experience. These efforts were increasingly mandated in an era in which blacks began focusing on issues of self-constitution and self-identity as the subjective and intangible became magnified. In an important sense, it has been African Americans' efforts to undo, deny, and, increasingly, reconstruct to their own liking, these difficult symbolic realities, that have been fueling the conflict that arose out of the ashes of the heralded black-Jewish alliance, now some thirty years in the grave.

A BRIEF HISTORY

The civil rights era was one of the grandest time periods in American history. On some levels, it was an era that proved that America actually "worked." A number of milestone civil rights endeavors were passed, both with congressional as well as popular support that brought America that much closer to reconciling its troubled reality with its hallowed ideals. Included in the impressive legislative legacy of the time were the 1954 *Brown v. Board of Education* decision that deemed the principle of "separate but equal" public schools unconstitutional; the 1964 passage of the Omnibus Civil Rights Act, and the accompanying establishment of the Equal Employment Opportunity Commission. And in what may have been the climax of the era, the landmark Voting Rights Act, which ensured broad protection for blacks exercising their tenth amendment right, was enacted in 1965. Furthermore, the period saw the gradual crumbling of the system of segregation that had been a cherished Southern institution up until that time. Adding to the heroism of the period was that the change had been realized the "right" way, not through violent uprisings, but rather through an enchanting mix of legitimate political action and peaceful civil disobedience.

And yet, despite the impressive gains of the era, the actual economic situation of blacks was slow to improve. In 1968, four years after the Civil Rights Act, median black income remained less than two-thirds that of whites (Sitkoff 1993). Inequality was even greater in urban areas. It was the tremendous frustration and anger emanating from this urban poverty that resulted in the eruption of the 329 race riots in 257 cities that broke out between 1964 and 1968 (Friedman 1995, 213). These riots, violently cathartic events in which blacks typically ravaged their own neighborhoods, reflected the belief that despite the civil rights gains, there was really little to be hopeful about.

In many ways, these feelings of despair were vindicated by the events of later decades. Despite the legacy of the civil rights revolution and two decades of affirmative action, by 1991, the median income of African Americans was actually lower than it had been at the time of Martin Luther King Jr.'s death in 1968, at 57 percent that of whites (Sitkoff 1993). The already significant inequality between blacks and whites that had existed in this country had actually grown. While large segments of the black community, often with the aid of affirmative action policies, have sprung into the middle class, what has been referred to as the black "underclass" has grown. One can argue that, on the whole, the economic and social problems of the black community have intensified.

Somewhat incongruously, and in many ways significant to the psychological outlook of African Americans, these developments had coincided with favorable trends on both the legislative and political fronts. It is worth noting that the years of the urban riots, a time period in which the despair of urban blacks was sufficient to trigger an explosion, had coincided with the years of the greatest advances on the civil rights front. And deflatingly, the years that saw the greatest intensification of problems for African Americans in the inner cities, corresponded rather directly with the time period in which affirmative action made its greatest inroads into the institutions of American society. Furthermore, even as African Americans continued to languish economically, they saw a tremendous increase in their political representation. In 1965, few blacks held political offices throughout the country and in the entire South the number of black elected officials was less than fifty. By 1992, however, the number of blacks holding political offices of all types throughout the nation would exceed seventy-five hundred. And in a figure which, in truth, may say as much about black political leverage as the degree to which African Americans have been unable to escape troubled inner-city areas, blacks have served as mayors of nearly every major American city (Friedman 1995, 203).

As these troubling and sometimes perplexing developments increasingly took on the form of inescapable realities, the sad message began to sink in: African Americans could not win. The economic and social windfall expected to correlate with the significant legislative and political achievements, was proving all too elusive. Sadly African Americans were beginning to see that it was not particularly fruitful to devote their efforts and energies in the practical, political, and legislative realms. As their harsh reality illustrated, advances in this realm were much too disconnected from attaining the social and economic goods of American life.

REGIONS OF THE MIND

At the same time, something else was beginning to occur, a subtle development taking place in the inner consciousness of African Americans, one that seemed to stem as much from the positive upshot of the civil rights era as its all too apparent disappointments. A new era in the psychological outlook of African Americans was getting under way. Up until this moment in history, African Americans had labored under the emotional weight of a severely racist and oppressive society. With the liberating events of the 1960s, African Americans were beginning to enter psychological terrain that had previously been unexplored. The legislative gains allowed African Americans to increasingly view themselves on equal footing—at least officially—in the great arena of American group existence. The accompanying sense of empowerment was, in many ways, a mandate for African Americans to turn their attentions to their own thoughts, feelings, emotional experiences and, in general, onto issues of self-reconfiguration. We can link this development to African Americans' dramatic intensification of activity in the realms of identity and ideology on the heels of the civil rights revolution, manifested in the emergence of the black power era, black nationalism and, ultimately separatism and doctrines of racial pride. Having already, in a sense, mined the political, legislative realm, African Americans were now engaging the next frontier.

As much as their new state of liberation was critical in bringing African Americans toward the intangible, psychological realm, the economic despair in their communities likely played an important role as well. African Americans could not simply rest easy with the implications of their bleak economic fate. To do so would have entailed a concession that they had somehow "failed" in the great American quest toward material success. Narcissistically, this would have been unbearable. One of the fundamental assumptions of group psychology is that ethnic, national, and racial groups must view themselves in a heroic and triumphant light. This is not only the case on the collective level, but inasmuch as individuals evaluate their own sense of self through the prism of the group reality, its ramifications affected discreet African Americans as well. To some degree, one can argue that African Americans needed a distraction from their painful economic reality. Comforting narratives of self-identity and more generally, the entire psychological and emotional plane, were fertile ground for this sort of "distraction." Furthermore, the concentration of energies in these intangible domains is potentially more gratifying than the concrete, practical struggle since, in a certain sense, the possible yields here are limitless.

Beginning with the onset of the "black power era" in the 1960s, the battle for the regions of the mind began to be waged. Many of the most significant social and historical developments affecting the black community over the last thirty years can be seen in this light. The emergence of black nationalism during what Friedman terms "the race revolution" (ibid., ch. 10) is certainly tied to the shift in emphasis toward the subjective and emotional. Though one component of the emerging ideology of black nationalism and separatism was that militant independence was the most *practical* way for blacks to move ahead in this country, a more essential component of black nationalism may have been how it reconstructed African Americans' emotional universe. At a time when blacks were seeking to repair their severely damaged collective ego, along came a perspective that stressed themes of group superiority, self-reliance, dignity and, indeed, manhood. In many ways, it was just what the psychoanalyst ordered. Hence the emergence of the thought and ideology of a series of confrontational "race men" such as Malcolm X, Eldridge Cleaver, Stokely Carmichael, and Amiri Baraka. According to Friedman, these individuals "articulated the anger that was building up in black neighborhoods and transformed the civil rights movement into a race revolution" (ibid., 218).

In addition, the time period saw the emergence of a new black literature that stressed militant themes. A number of seminal literary works burst onto the scene during these years, including *The Autobiography of Malcolm X*, Eldridge Cleaver's *Soul on Ice*, and Harold Cruse's *Crisis of the Negro Intellectual*, which argued that white, largely Jewish scholars, through their patronage, had stifled the development of black intellect. The new literature revealed that, now, the thoughts, ideas, and emotions of American blacks were beginning to take center stage, right alongside the organizations, coalitions, and legislative accomplishments that had defined the civil rights scene up to that point.

In the early seventies, the concrete issue of affirmative action consumed the black cause for a while. But in subsequent years, more intangible identity-related concerns moved to the forefront. Afro-American studies emerged as a legitimate—albeit controversial—part of the American academic landscape. In addition, Afrocentrism, an even more radical offshoot of Afro-American studies came into the picture. Afrocentrism fancied itself not so much as objective scholarship, but as a "corrective" of sorts, and even a "weapon" in addressing African Americans' feelings of cultural inferiority. In this sense, Afrocentrism embodied African Americans' burgeoning orientation in a highly concentrated form.

Through the eighties and up to the present, the emphasis on subjective issues of identity and racial dignity has taken on even more significant dimensions as many of the conditions apparently fueling the trend since its earliest days—poverty, unemployment, crime, and drugs—have intensified. The development is reflected to a degree in the rejection of the ideal of integration in many black quarters (including within the NAACP) and the nationalist impulses that characterize increasingly large sectors of the black community. It can be seen in the often surprising militancy and separatism of African American college students and the virtual mainstreaming of the tenets of Afrocentrism. It is also evident in the increasing popularity of Louis Farrakhan and the Nation of Islam. Though Farrakhan's message does have an economic, practical component, in the form of a certain muscular black capitalism, without the backdrop of his nationalistic-and pride-based message, it is unlikely that Farrakhan's ideas would have the kind of appeal that they appear to enjoy.

All of these developments are representative of a significant shift that has come to define the African American community over the past thirty years. Gone are the days when the African American story was being written in the courthouses, congressional chambers, and malls of Washington. In more recent times the story has been written in somewhat more rarefied territory: It has been narrated, mainly, in the regions of the mind.

IS IT GOOD FOR THE JEWS?

Where do these developments, which have been shaping the dominant mood of the black community for the greater part of the last four decades, leave the Jews? In many ways, at least as far as their place in the African American psyche is concerned, it leaves Jews clutching on for dear life.

There are many reasons for this troubling state of affairs. However, to begin to get a hold on this issue, which is central to the main concern of our anthology, we must travel back in time to the heady days of the black-Jewish civil rights coalition. This coalition, which encompasses the apex of the black-Jewish relationship also, in important respects, contains the relationship's downturn. In many ways, the label "coalition," which is frequently applied to the black-Jewish relationship of the fifties and sixties, is a misnomer, for the black-Jewish civil rights alliance—which was well in place since the earliest years of this century—was a highly uneven partnership. Though in the common mythology, the two groups banded together in a unified fight against racism and discrimination, what the coalition essentially amounted to was Jews, with their greater educational attainments, legal, and political expertise, as well as financial might, banding together to help blacks. Though this idea does not fully conform to the much cherished sentimental view, if examined more dispassionately, one is obliged, we think, to conclude that this was the reality.

A relationship that is so heavily characterized by themes of dependence and altruism usually carries within it the seeds of future problems. In the case of the black-Jewish civil rights coalition this was particularly so, since the areas where Jews were able to make the greatest contribution—primarily areas that required educational attainment and financial resources—were traditionally areas of narcissistic vulnerability for blacks. In addition, it was essentially understood throughout, by both parties involved, that the assistance blacks were receiving from Jews could not really be repaid. With African Americans' lack of practical resources and social position and power, what tangible benefits would they really be able to offer in return? In addition, Jews' needs were hardly as glaring or as pressing as those of African Americans, so the prospect of Jews being reimbursed, as it were, was not really a prominent area of concern. It is reasonable to suppose that such unequal power dynamics were breeding grounds for, at least subliminally, feelings of guilt and debt, exacerbating the already tense and ambivalent nature of the relationship. We may go so far as to say that the nature of the relationship, while perhaps ego-enhancing for some Jews involved, was emasculating for the African American beneficiaries of Jewish largesse. It also probably did not help that some Jewish civil rights workers comported themselves in a manner that did not exactly serve to obscure these unequal power dynamics. As Andrew Hacker reports, in reference to the Freedom Summer volunteers of 1964: "The problem was not a lack of fellow feeling, but the condescending tone. One only had to look in on meetings to hear the new arrivals doing most of the talking" (Berman 1994, 161).

In a climate of pragmatism and technique, such difficulties might have been overlooked in favor of an emphasis on the ultimate prize, the passage of civil rights legislation. And indeed, in many ways it was the temporary placing aside of the problematic and potentially incendiary issues alluded to above, that may have allowed the coalition to survive as long as it did and achieve tremendous gains. But a new age was now under way, and in a time when the symbolic and emotional loomed ever larger, such an emasculating and narcissistically injurious partnership, increasingly, had to be exorcised.

The most efficient thing to do, on the part of African Americans, to achieve this end may have been to sabotage the partnership. Of course, prior to the passage of the most important civil rights legislation, there was great disincentive on the part of most blacks to undermine the alliance, which was so clearly beneficial, at least on the practical plane. But with the passage of the Omnibus Civil Rights Act in 1964 and the Voting Rights Act a year later, Jews, whose primary utility was in the practical sphere, were no longer such a hot commodity. The tremendous benefits derived, largely, from the black-Jewish partnership had now, it seemed, rendered this very alliance increasingly disposable.

The emergence of anti-Jewish sentiment around the time following the passage of these legislative acts can be seen in this context. The decreased necessity of practical gains (with the most important ones already realized) combined with underlying feelings of black resentment and narcissistic injury, to form a fertile breeding ground for anti-Jewish expression. Thus, we see a number of instances of hostility toward Jews emanating from the black community, and particularly from civil rights quarters, as the sixties wore on. During a public forum on the highly charged issue of busing, the head of the Mt. Vernon chapter of <u>CORE</u>—an organization whose very existence was a legacy of the black-Jewish alliance—remarked that Hitler's mistake was not killing enough Jews. In another incident, Cecil Moore, head of the Philadelphia chapter of the NAACP essentially told Jews to "back off" from the civil rights movement (Friedman 1995, 227). This last sentiment was increasingly typical among black activists. And, in a particularly disheartening episode, Rabbi Jacob Rothchild, whose Atlanta synagogue had some years earlier been firebombed by a white supremacist objecting to the rabbi's outspoken civil rights stance, was jeered by an audience of blacks while giving a lecture—on the importance of Jewish involvement in the civil rights cause (ibid., 291).

The appearance of rabidly anti-Zionist sentiments, particularly in the more radical segments of the civil rights community, while a separate development in its own right, can also be linked to the general anti-Jewish hostility overtaking the movement during this period. Examples of this anti-Zionism include the resolutions passed at the infamous Palmer House Conference in 1967 that referred to an "imperialist Zionist War" and a series of anti-Israel articles published in the Student Non-Violent Coordinating

Committee's (SNCC) newsletter around the time of the Six Day War (ibid., 230–33). While much of this anti-Zionism may have been an outgrowth of the general Third World(ist) ideology that was enveloping the movement at the time, a good deal of it can also be seen as a specifically anti-Jewish gesture.

These developments can all be viewed as part of a campaign, both conscious and to an extent, unconscious as well, to dismember an alliance whose psychological drawbacks, by this point, may well have begun to outweigh its practical benefits. The campaign, as subliminal as certain elements of it may have been, seems to have worked. A close analysis of the breakup of the black-Jewish partnership, yields the inescapable, though admittedly contentious, conclusion that at least to a significant extent, the collapse can be traced to the antisemitic and anti-Zionist rhetoric of the "black power era." This is not to say that other events did not play a role in the alliance's demise. These include the Ocean Hill–Brownsville conflict over community school board control; Jews' vocal opposition to racial quotas in the early seventies; and, at least in intellectual circles, the related emergence of the Jewish-dominated neoconservative movement and, what some have argued, its race relations fallout. In addition, the increased prominence of Israel in the psyche of American Jews may have diverted a degree of Jewish energy and romance from the civil rights struggle. After all, there is only so much emotional fuel to go around. And, while operating mainly on the fringes, Jewish militant urban warfare outfits, notably Meir Kahane's Jewish Defense League, certainly fanned the flames of racial conflict.

Still, while the cumulative effects of these developments cannot be ignored, the most straightforward and, we think, psychologically compelling, analysis suggests that the open rejection of Jews on the part of black activists, coupled with the virulent antisemitic rhetoric and anti-Zionism that began to appear in the wake of the civil rights revolution, played the premier role in souring the already complex and ambivalent relationship between these two communities.

This is not to say, of course, that the conflict is strictly a one-sided affair. Historically, there has certainly been a fair amount of Jewish wrongdoing toward blacks. This includes the economic exploitation that took place in urban ghettoes in past decades; the racist fare emanating from Hollywood, particularly in the earlier days of film, often under the stewardship of Jewish studio executives and filmmakers; and, some feel, the Jewish community's increasingly detached manner regarding the plight of African Americans in recent times. These factors have, quite plausibly, played some role in creating and escalating black-Jewish conflict. Nevertheless, they do not represent what we think are the most important concrete, as well as psychological, issues that have generated the problem. And hence we have concentrated, mainly, on black antisemitism.

SITTING DUCKS

The black-Jewish alliance collapsed at the time and manner in which it did, largely, because in an age when African Americans' issues of self-constitution and self-reconfiguration took on greater primacy, the discomforting and emasculating conditions that the black-Jewish partnership posed, were increasingly unendurable. However, there were also a number of other reasons why African Americans' new emotional and psychological agenda spawned an increase in black-Jewish tension. In the new psychological climate there was an increased emphasis on the part of African Americans on actions and positions with symbolic resonance. This new orientation, however, put Jews in a particularly vulnerable position: In a time of heightened symbolism, a rejection of Jews—a group with whom African Americans had previously enjoyed a close and intimate bond—was among the most powerful symbolic gestures of independence and liberation that African Americans could have made.

While on the one hand, a generic rejection of whites by African Americans would have certainly yielded some psychological as well as symbolic benefits, it would not have really packed the full punch. It is basically taken for granted, by both victim and victimizer, as well as any third party, that a desire exists on the part of an oppressed group to reject their prior oppressors. Thus, when such a desire is actually expressed, it is really just a matter of favorable circumstances presenting themselves. For blacks to vent their fury at "white America," their former generic oppressors, then, would not have been a particularly symbolically potent event. But if Jews, perhaps the only white group that had befriended blacks, were spurned, people were bound to take notice. In rejecting Jews, the segment of the white population most benevolent toward blacks, African Americans were able to convey the message that, regardless of one's "credentials," merely being white made one abhorrent and unwanted. In the new radicalized age, the opportunity to convey such a message may have been irresistible, justifying perhaps the subversion of what may have otherwise been a stance of gratitude toward Jews. Ironically, then, the very significance of the role that Jews played in the civil rights struggle was a motivation for anti-Jewish outbursts, many of which explicitly denied the actual value of this role.

But not only was it important for African Americans to symbolically express their rejection of and separation from the white community, it was also essential at the time for this disenfranchised and victimized group to vent its previously pent-up narcissistic rage. The venting of narcissistic rage seems to realize its maximal yields when it actually results in the inflicting of pain upon another and hence a feeling of superiority and power over the other. Thus, we can surmise that at a time when African Americans were looking to let out their anger on the road to healing their severely damaged group ego, they were searching for a group upon whom to exact injury. With the exception of perhaps the most militant elements, African Americans were not about to wage a violent physical war, so the sort of pain we are dealing with here is emotional and symbolic. However, generic white America would not have been the optimal choice of target for this sort of pointed psychological aggression. There was nothing to indicate that whites generically, who had historically exhibited supreme callousness toward African Americans in the form of racial oppression, would have been especially emotionally receptive, for good or for bad, to any sort of verbal or symbolic gesture that African Americans would have made. They had failed to demonstrate the requisite sensitivity. Jews were a different case. If nothing else, Jews, with their steady commitment to civil rights causes, had demonstrated a basic emotional and moral commitment to African Americans' affairs. Such an emotional stake, however, betrays susceptibility to pain. So, if the objective was inflicting pain, Jews were a particularly appealing target. Much like close friends and relatives are frequently the targets of one's anger, Jews, because of their prior intimate involvement, were sitting ducks for African Americans' expressions of this sort of rage, as soon as the need to express it presented itself.

In a number of ways, then, expressions of antisemitism yielded significant psychological benefits for African Americans. Black antisemitism was instrumental in eliminating the emasculating and uncomfortable realities of the black-Jewish alliance by essentially serving to sabotage and tear this alliance apart. In addition, antisemitic rhetoric was used to make a powerful statement of collective racial independence. Furthermore, antisemitism was utilized both as a vent for narcissistic rage and to maximize the yield of narcissistic gratification by inflicting harm upon Jews, and thus exploiting Jews' special vulnerability to African American aggression. These sort of emotional benefits were very much in demand at a time of heightened emphasis for African Americans on the intangible realms of subjectivity, meaning, and refashioning an acceptable narrative of group and self-identity.

Antisemitism of this nature was an everpresent menace in the waning moments of the black-Jewish civil rights alliance. However, with the coalition essentially ripped apart by the close of the 1960s, black antisemitism began to take on a slightly different use. In the past, anti-Jewish hostility served to derail an unwanted coalition, maximize a statement of group independence, and achieve optimum utility from the venting of narcissistic rage. In the new mode, the likely motivation for black antisemitism becomes even more deeply embedded in the symbolic and psychological realms. Increasingly, antisemitic rhetoric came to be African Americans' mode of grappling with the uncomfortable implications symbolized by the Jewish experience, both in the arena of public perception as well as the internal psychological sphere. No less than its previous permutations, the escalation of the new mode of black antisemitism is directly linked to the burgeoning subjective and ideological orientation of the black community. This incarnation of black antisemitism, serving to address the unsettling realities represented in the Jewish experience, has carried on through to the present and may well be the defining factor in black-Jewish conflict today.

THE NARCISSISM OF LARGE DIFFERENCES: NERDS, JOCKS, AND EVIL GENIUSES

We have suggested that in part, it was because Jews' assistance of African Americans revolved around areas that were narcissistically vulnerable for blacks, namely areas of educational attainment, social status, and economic and political power, that feelings of tension and resentment were magnified. However, African Americans' apparent discomfort at the perceived bookishness as well as considerable accomplishments of Jews in American society seems to be part of a larger divide between blacks and Jews that is likely playing a significant role in the conflict. Throughout history, African Americans have been racially maligned through assertions that they are somehow baser and more primitive than whites. Implied in these assertions—and often stated explicitly as well—are attendant notions of intellectual inferiority. Yet it is precisely in the realms of intellect as well as to a degree "civilization" where Jews have been frequently exalted. Not only is Jewish "genius" much heralded, but, as Ellen Willis points out, Jews are also considered harbingers of the moral order of civilized society (Willis 1979). If African Americans have been accused by racists as dwelling in the territory of the id, Jews are more often considered to be a sort of ethnic embodiment of the superego. This sort of symbolic rift does not only manifest itself in feelings of insecurity and inferiority on the part of African Americans, it also comes into play through Jewish feelings of discomfort emanating from the specter of black physicality, athletic prowess, masculinity, and sexuality, a phenomenon chronicled by Norman Podhoretz in his landmark essay, "My Negro Problem and Ours" (Podhoretz 1963).

While much has been made of the narcissism of small differences as it relates to Jews and African Americans, it seems that here it is the very magnitude of perceived difference that is fueling the conflict. The symbolic polarity between the two groups suggested above, on a certain subliminal level, sends off signals of enmity. Both groups view the other as sort of cosmic opposites. The dynamic can be likened to the way in which psychic battle lines are drawn between "nerds" and "jocks" in adolescence: Each side represents the extreme embodiment of otherness. Of course, Podhoretz's insights notwithstanding, in our culture there are probably more grounds to be threatened by notions of another group's perceived intellectual superiority, than with notions of another group's sexual and physical prowess. Indeed, physicality and sexuality have definite derogatory connotations as well. This may help explain why evidently the above dynamics have more frequently led blacks to resent Jews than the reverse, as the demonstration of significant Jewish racism is somewhat elusive.

There are other ways in which the fallout from this rift has led to black-Jewish conflict, particularly, black antisemitism. One way for African Americans to deal with the "messy" emotions emanating from the perception of Jews as superachievers on the cerebral plane, is to lower Jews' moral status. If Jews, with all of their special acumen and advancement, are somehow perversely evil, then their achievements are suddenly much less threatening. In effect, they are removed from the realm of comparison, their significant intellectual accomplishments relegated to the doings of some caste of evil geniuses. This may be the impetus for much of the black antisemitic rhetoric that portrays Jews as "bloodsuckers," racial exploiters, and behind-the-scenes manipulators of American society: Jews' accomplishments and aptitude become much easier to stomach since, by and large, people are not prone to compare their own achievements to the accomplishments of evil geniuses. At the same time, however, contentions of Jewish evil also serve to undercut the other threat that Jews symbolize: They directly contradict the notion of Jewish moral elevation. In a rather efficient way, then, claims of Jewish wrongdoing in the extreme, claims that characterize the Jews as demonic, allow African Americans to address the threatening symbolic implications of the Jewish reality—though in a manner with highly destructive ramifications for the black-Jewish relationship.

THE FANTASY OF JEWISH OPPRESSION

There are other ways in which black antisemitism serves to address the unsettling symbolic implications of the Jewish reality. If we start to assess the actual content of black antisemitism, we begin to see that the great bulk consists of assertions of Jewish oppression of blacks. This fact all but cries out for a psychoanalytic interpretation since, historically, Jews have been the group *most favorably* disposed toward blacks. In the past, the theme of Jewish offenses toward blacks tended to be more subtle, characterized by assertions such as Harold Cruse's charge that Jews had thwarted the development of black intellect; Malcolm X's contention that Jewish claims of friendship toward blacks were only designed to focus prejudice upon blacks and away from Jews (Friedman 1995, 220); and perhaps the insinuations prevalent during the black power era that U.S. involvement with Israel was connected to American imperialistic designs on Africa (ibid., 230). As time went on, however, the charges became bolder. The new, more strident, accusations of Jewish oppression of blacks are embodied in a number of more recent incidents: the 1985 assertion by a New York City black activist that Jewish teachers are to blame for the problems of inner-city black youths; Steven Cokeley, an aide to Chicago mayor Eugene Sawyer, charging that Jewish physicians were deliberately injecting the AIDS virus into black babies (ibid., 338); and, more recently, Khalid Abdul Muhammad, a Farrakhan deputy, referring to Jews as "bloodsuckers of the black nation" (ibid., 346). In addition, the new fashion of charges of Jewish oppression is represented in Al Sharpton's charges in the wake of the Crown Heights riots that Jews "took my brothers to the Persian Gulf and trained them how to kill" (Goldberg 1996, 308). Furthermore, blatant claims of Jewish oppression are found in the pseudo scholarly assertions of a "planned and plotted and programmed" project by Hollywood Jews to defame blacks through the dissemination of racist images (Friedman 1995, 110), as well as crusades to demonstrate that Jews played a preeminent role in the slave trade.

Previously, assertions of Jewish wrongdoing enabled African Americans to come to terms with the specter of Jewish intellectuality and moral elevation. Here, too, these assertions of Jewish oppression of blacks are useful in enabling African Americans to build a symbolic and emotional universe much more to their liking. The roots of this phenomenon may be found in the vital role that group heroism plays in the African American psyche. Indeed, every group must latch on to—or create—a heroic element in their history. Some groups, such as the Jews, have a glorious biblical narrative to serve this end, a fact alluded to by Lawrence Thomas (Thomas 1994). Others, such as the Germans, have an exalted intellectual tradition. More generally, Americans can look to their pioneering role in founding a society based on civil libertarian principles as a source of historical heroism. However, African Americans, because of slavery and the overall obscurity surrounding their African roots, have very few such narrative goods to latch on to. Sadly, where other groups can turn to a rich and far-reaching historical tradition, African Americans have something of a void, at least according to the standards set forth by Western society.

However, there is still one "good" that African Americans can grip in building a heroic and valiant group narrative and that is the specter of victimization. The sense of victimization can itself provide much of the heroism and valor that African Americans may be unable to derive through other means. In a paradoxical way, it is the very degree of marginalization in African Americans' history that is able to provide them with collective ego gratification. But because of just how precious this posture of victimization is, African Americans must guard it jealously—warding off all potential symbolic threats from the outside. The need to do so is magnified in a time when other avenues toward ego gratification—such as economic and educational attainment—appear to be cut off, or greatly curtailed.

In many ways, Jews are the group that represents to African Americans the most conspicuous threat to this all important status of victimhood. While the perceived victimization of Jews, though perhaps receding ever so gradually from the collective consciousness, does not directly undercut African Americans' own claims of victimization, at the very least it poses a challenge to black claims of uniqueness in this realm. Furthermore, competing claims for "most victimized group" by Jews and African Americans causes further problems for blacks since by appearances, and certainly by comparison, Jews have "overcome" their history of oppression through tremendous economic and cultural success. Hence, they are not even real victims, but imposter victims, as it were, with blacks being the "real" Hebrews. The role that Jews played in assisting blacks during the civil rights struggle presents a further threat to blacks' sense of historical heroism. The fact that at least somebody, namely Jews, was there to help African Americans in their hour of need, undermines to a degree the heroism of the narrative by detracting from the completeness of black victimization. Simultaneously, of course, the specter of Jewish assistance also raises the stock of Jewish heroism, making it all the more threatening a notion for blacks.

By perpetuating the view that Jews oppressed blacks, African Americans, in an efficient manner, can address the symbolic threats that Jews pose to their own sense of historic heroism and valor. The matter now gets turned completely on its head. In the role of victimizers of blacks, Jews are no longer competitors for the status of exclusive victimhood, but, rather, they are facilitators of African Americans' very own designation in this role. The symbolic role of Jews, rather than detracting from black victimhood, is actually now being used to confer it. Simultaneously, Jews' own association with victimhood and heroism is undermined since, as oppressors, they can neither be true victims nor heroes. Charges of Jewish oppression can also go a long way toward mitigating the threatening image of Jewish benevolence toward blacks during the civil rights struggle. If such charges do not necessarily refute specific claims of Jewish assistance, at the very least, they obscure and confuse them. In one fell swoop, then, charges of Jewish oppression of blacks can bring African Americans a considerable distance toward reconstructing a symbolic universe much more to their emotional specifications.

Charges of Jewish oppression have tremendous utility for African Americans, both on the level of perception, as well as for the internal psychological benefits that they provide. They serve as great propaganda in the symbolic war with Jews over victimhood and heroism. At the same time, to the extent that African Americans can internalize messages of Jewish oppression, dubious as they may be, black people are aided in their ability to bask in the glow of a glorious and valiant historical narrative. And, as the basic orientation of the African American community has shifted from a practical and legislative thrust to a more intangible and psychological mode, these sorts of emotional benefits have been increasingly in demand. The rise in black antisemitism following the civil rights era and the mounting intensity of charges of Jewish oppression can thus, in many ways, be seen as symptomatic of the escalation of the battle over the regions of the mind.

FANTASY REALIZED

The need for African Americans to assert their own unique heroism and victimhood continues to be of central importance and, in many ways, has carried us into the current stage of the psychic territorial war. As we have seen, antisemitism has tremendous value in helping African Americans deal with the psychologically unsettling ramifications of the Jewish reality. But in many ways, the benefits of black antisemitism do not stop there. Beyond helping African Americans to cope with some of the disturbing symbolic implications of the Jewish group narrative outlined above, antisemitism can be used as a catalyst to actually change and redefine these symbolically threatening realities. Increasingly, this seems to be what is happening.

Historically, black antisemitism has usually produced some sort of backlash among Jews. Thirty years ago, the anti-Jewish hostility and attendant anti-Zionism of the black power movement caused many Jews to recoil from the civil rights struggle. Of course this withdrawal was not merely a voluntary response to perceived antisemitism—frequently Jews were actually evicted from the movement by disgruntled and embittered black activists. As time went on, however, Jewish response to black antisemitism became not only alienation, but verbal retaliation. In recent years, the trading of recrimination between the two communities has become a ritual of sorts: Jesse Jackson's infamous "Hymietown" utterance was greeted with a full-page ad in the *New York Times* entitled "Jews Against Jesse," while, as J. J. Goldberg reports, "Jewish leaders began speaking out against Jackson at every opportunity" (Goldberg 1996, 325). The incendiary antisemitic rhetoric of Louis Farrakhan has been met with even more vociferous outcries. Following a particularly venomous speech given by Farrakhan lieutenant, Khalid Muhammad, both the Anti Defamation League and the American Jewish Committee took verbal and printed action. And the aftermath of the Crown Heights riots saw the launching of the Jewish Action Alliance, an organization whose entire purpose was, arguably, to fight black antisemitism.

In a bizarre sort of way, with the increasingly vocal and public nature of the Jewish backlash, blacks were getting exactly what they wanted. If filtered in a certain selective and decontextualized way, it could be argued that with the hostile, aggressive stance Jews were taking, African Americans' historical fantasies of Jewish oppression could be construed as coming true! While without this sort of response, African Americans would perhaps have had to rely on historical revisionism and demagoguery to paint Jews as the "oppressors," now all they had to do was consider the prospect of hordes of Jews who, in the wake of the latest antisemitic incident or lecture, were out for blood. It does not matter terribly that this hostility was merely a response to prior aggression on the part of blacks. What matters is the immediate, visceral sensation of being attacked. Regardless of the overall context of these Jewish attacks, if there is a will on the part of African Americans to internalize such attacks as oppression, this could certainly be done. Unbeknownst to Jews, who were probably reacting in a fairly reasonable and self-preserving manner, Jewish reaction to black antisemitism was actually serving African Americans' psychological needs—at Jews' own expense—and likely reinforcing the phenomenon that it was decrying. One can further surmise that it was not merely the very public and vocal Jewish hostility emanating from the likes of the ADL and the American Jewish Congress that served these needs; even the hypothetical knowledge of unvoiced feelings of hostility emanating from Jews in response to antisemitism would probably have triggered feelings of heroic victimization among African Americans.

The intensification of this sort of black antisemitism, arguably fueled and reinforced by the Jewish response, has not taken place in a vacuum. This dynamic must be seen in terms of an overall shift in the African American community in recent decades to the intangible and emotional realms. Much like the earlier manifestations of antisemitism and charges of Jewish oppression, this more current phenomenon represents the fallout of African Americans' reconfiguring of their narrative of self-identity and, more broadly, the reclamation of the regions of the mind. It remains the challenge for both African Americans and others to explore ways in which the noble project of self-reconfiguration can be pursued with less divisive ramifications.

WHERE DO WE GO FROM HERE?

Throughout, we have argued that black antisemitism, the main component of black-Jewish conflict, which we have addressed, is tied to African Americans' increased emphasis on the intangible and emotional realms and issues of self-constitution. It would be wrong to downplay the importance of these realms to human well-being. It is primarily matters of identity, meaning, self-worth and dignity that shape the very quality of our existence, in many ways, much more than material factors. However, there is also ample space to misuse these domains. It seems that African Americans have all too often drawn on these intangible realms to motivate and fuel the anti-Jewish hostility that, we feel, has played the primary role in destroying the black-Jewish alliance.

We have illustrated a number of ways in which this has taken place. These include the way in which narcissistic resentment led to the sabotaging of the black-Jewish civil rights alliance through expressions of antisemitism and anti-Zionism; the manner in which African Americans, in effect, "sacrificed" Jews in the name of symbolic racial statements and the inflicting of emotional injury; the way in which the two groups' mutual polarity, or, the "narcissism of large differences," has led to black antisemitism; and the dynamics by which the symbolic threat posed by Jews to African Americans' sense of heroic victimhood, has led to charges of Jewish oppression. As we have also argued, these developments have been reinforced and, to a degree, perpetuated by the Jewish response, which allows African Americans to bask in the sensation of Jewish oppression.

These phenomena can be linked to other ways in which African Americans have inadequately dealt with narcissistic rage and have addressed issues of low group self-esteem through unsatisfactory means. These include aggression turned in on the self, manifested in recurring instances of rioting and looting, in which African Americans have wrought destruction upon their own communities. In addition, the, at times, seeming need of African Americans to traffic in fantasies of omnipotence, can be seen as a response to feelings of narcissistic rage, low self-esteem, and even self-hatred. This urge to feel omnipotent, and even to a degree superhuman, is evident in the rhetoric of black demagogues, which is often characterized by intense grandiosity and frequent references to royal ancestry. It also seems to infuse much of Afrocentrist writing, with its exaggerated claims of African contributions to world scholarship and civilization. One further way in which African Americans have inadequately dealt with issues of self-constitution is through projection and externalization, that is, hurling accusations against others that reflect one's own perceived shortcomings.

We wish to briefly suggest more fruitful, less divisive, as well as more psychologically "reasonable" means through which African Americans can address their emotional needs and through which, ultimately, both communities can begin to overcome the psychological issues that divide them. First, we believe it is crucial for African Americans to develop positive avenues toward boosting self-esteem and strengthening their collective ego, ones that do not traffic in the realm of bringing others down. Such compensatory structures can be accessed both on the tangible, concrete level as well as in the psychological sphere. More concrete means of establishing such compensatory structures include the strengthening of the economic infrastructure of black communities. This is already being pursued, as both politicians and community leaders have come to see the tremendous value in developing sustainable, that is, self-sufficient, economies in the inner cities. Included in this realm are economic empowerment zones, tax incentives, as well as the establishment of black-owned credit institutions and small businesses. Unfortunately, however, many of the more vociferous advocates of this kind of economic empowerment harbor separatist and even antisemitic impulses. The paradigmatic case is Louis Farrakhan whose defiant ideology is, as we noted earlier, enmeshed with messages of economic enterprise. Thus, often such economic empowerment endeavors, which can go a long way toward laying the groundwork for reducing black-Jewish tension, can intensify the problem as well, because of the incendiary rhetoric that often surrounds them. Arguably, the recent bombing of Freddy's, a Jewish-owned business on 125th Street in Harlem, is an instance where antisemitism and black economic empowerment became destructively intertwined. It remains the challenge to separate the valuable ideal of black economic empowerment from the antisemitism and militant separatism that can accompany it.

Central to reducing black-Jewish conflict and building compensatory structures is also alleviating the social malaise that plagues much of the black community. In many ways these social problems, which are inseparable from the economic issues as well, are fertile breeding grounds for antisemitic expressions since, for example, they intensify narcissistic rage. Obviously, these social problems, along with the economic ones plaguing the black community, are extremely complex and in some ways are more elusive and intractable than the psychological issues we have been addressing. However, they cannot be ignored by anyone seeking a complete and effective solution to black-Jewish conflict. Furthermore, addressing these issues is not simply mandated in the name of reducing black-Jewish conflict: It is, quite simply, the right thing to do.

However, there are also more directly psychological ways in which self-esteem can be boosted and the conditions that breed narcissistic rage can be alleviated. These too are already being stressed by influential figures in the black community, with the increased emphasis on themes of dignity, "manhood," and racial pride. Nevertheless, much like the economic empowerment endeavors, which stem from the same basic perspective, these themes are also frequently infused with messages of separatism and antisemitism. Some of the biggest purveyors of "self-esteem"–oriented rhetoric are radical Afrocentrists as well as Nation of Islam figures. In this regard, the forces working to boost African Americans' self-esteem, a goal that is in many ways integral to reducing black-Jewish conflict, frequently are the same forces perpetuating the conflict. The mandate lies with members of the African American community to separate the valuable messages of self-esteem, dignity, and self-determination from their sometimes attendant antisemitism and militant separatism. Exactly how this can be accomplished is not altogether clear. But, at least in part, it would seem to involve African Americans' recognition of some of the psychological functions that antisemitism serves for their community, such as the ones discussed in this chapter. The endeavor of separating the good from the bad and divisive will also hinge on African Americans' strengthening of their self-critical ego functions. Developing these crucial capabilities should give African Americans both a greater ability and inclination to discern positive means of boosting self-esteem from negative ones.

Thus, in order for black-Jewish conflict to be alleviated, African Americans must, to some degree, turn inward and address the problems within their own community, both tangible and psychological. There are some fruitful, psychoanalytically informed modes of improving the dialogue between the two groups that needn't wait until everything is all right on the home front. Some of these are discussed in the editors' conclusion, where we describe the dynamics of small, psychoanalytically informed intergroup workshops. These interventions are predicated on the "contact hypothesis," which contends that personal contact between groups reduces stereotyping and demonization. It is believed that social interaction and favorable mutual experiences between members of groups thwart the conditions that breed such stereotyping and demonization, including the reliance on externalization and projection in managing internal conflicts and anxieties, both on the individual and the group level.

These workshops will enlist clinicians and others sophisticated about group psychological dynamics from each community and hopefully improve the mode of dialogue and communication between the rank and file as well. However, the political and organizational leadership must also be at the forefront of improving dialogue and communication. While, quite obviously, black leaders who traffic in antisemitic rhetoric are very much at fault, as we have argued, the flamboyant denunciations emanating from Jewish leadership quarters may in some ways be reinforcing elements of the conflict as well. While it is clear that Jewish leaders and organizational officials should not be silent in the face of black antisemitism, perhaps it is time to reassess the effectiveness of the current mode of response. All the while, those with positions of power within the Jewish community should welcome those members of the black community who are transcending the tendencies toward projection and externalization, and are actually seeking alliances with Jews. Among their ranks are "moderates" such as Henry Louis Gates Jr., Cornel West, Cynthia Tucker, Roger Wilkins, and, yes, Jesse Jackson. For some time, Jews have already been enjoying the sympathy of renegade black "conservative" types such as Stanley Crouch, Michael Meyers, Roy Innis, and Armstrong Williams. But to make the fledgling "realliance" go even further, Jews must seek to build relationships with figures who enjoy credibility among the black grass roots as well, lest the African American friends of Jews become merely exceptions that prove the rule.

Of course, here one runs the risk of encountering figures who may not be quite vociferous enough in their denunciation of black antisemitism. However, on this issue, too, Jews may want to reassess their previous stance. While it is important to help facilitate a climate within the African American community that is intolerant of antisemitism, some ways of doing this might be better than others. It is questionable whether or not insisting that any African American who wishes to join forces with Jews must denounce the latest antisemitic incident, is the best way to achieve this end. Even the most eloquent and condemnatory denunciation cannot address the psychological forces that lie at the root of black antisemitism. Indeed, at least on a certain level, such demands on the part of Jews can foster even more resentment and discord. Blacks start to view it as a sort of challenge to resist these requests, another way of asserting black muscle and independence—perhaps a residual protest to the paternalistic relationship of the past. It is probable that the reservoirs of good will produced by the establishment of dialogue with moderate members of the African American community can do more to defang black antisemitism than the most pointed tongue lashing.

While we have placed some of the burden of alleviating black-Jewish conflict on the shoulders of the Jewish organizational leadership, the bulk of the emotional and psychological onus has been placed on the black community. This flows from our perspective that it is chiefly black antisemitism that is responsible for the rift. However, Jews have a role to play in the emotional sphere as well. There is sometimes a tendency on the part of Jews to qualify their emotional response to African American suffering. There is a sort of unstated question that goes something like, "We have suffered and overcome, so why can't you?" This sort of thing must be put to rest. What is needed in its place is unqualified and genuine empathy. African Americans must feel that Jews, when addressed with the subject of African American suffering, are completely validating their pain. This means that Jews cannot use African Americans' suffering as a springboard to comparisons with their own group's historical misfortune. Since, as we have stressed, a good deal of the conflict is linked to issues of historical heroism and victimhood, a truly empathic response on the part of Jews might be both a disarming, as well as morally mandated gesture, and certainly one in the interests of black-Jewish reconciliation.

The alleviation of black-Jewish conflict, however, is not merely a psychological issue. In many ways black-Jewish conflict is a social and symbolic crisis that raises serious questions about the political and ideological underpinnings of American society, though this is perhaps another discussion. But even using a largely psychological approach must look somewhat beyond the regions of the mind. For psychoanalysis as applied to black-Jewish conflict to be worthwhile, it must acknowledge and grapple with the social and economic realities in which its praxis resides. We feel it is largely the poverty, hopelessness, and despair of wide segments of the African American community that provides the impetus to indulge malignant narcissistic group tendencies. In many important respects, these factors are no less significant in fueling black-Jewish conflict than the psychological issues that we have addressed. Therefore, blacks, Jews, psychoanalysts, and other concerned Americans should get to work addressing these troubling economic and social realities. A comprehensive and workable solution to the problem demands nothing less.

REFERENCES

Baldwin, James. 1962. "Letter from a Region in My Mind." *The New Yorker*, November 17.

Berman, Paul, ed. 1994. *Blacks and Jews: Alliances and Arguments*. New York: Delacorte Press.

Friedman, Murray, 1995. *What Went Wrong? The Creation and Collapse of the Black-Jewish Alliance*. New York: Free Press.

Goldberg, J. J. 1996. *Jewish Power*. New York: Addison-Wesley.

Podhoretz, Norman. 1963. "My Negro Problem and Ours." *Commentary*, July. Cited in Berman, 1994, 76–92.

Sitkoff, Harvard. 1993. *The Struggle for Black Equality: 1954–1992*. New York: Hill and Wang.

Thomas, Laurence. 1994. "Group Autonomy and Narrative Identity." In *Blacks and Jews: Alliances and Arguments*, edited by Paul Berman. New York: Delacorte Press.

Willis, Ellen. 1979. "The Myth of the Powerful Jew." *The Village Voice*, September 2. Cited in Berman, 1994, 187–203.

3

If I Am You,
Then You Are . . . Fake

C. FRED ALFORD

There is something almost oxymoronic about doing psychoanalysis at a distance, for psychoanalysis is knowledge of the most intimate sort. Still, it may make more sense when we are talking about groups rather than individuals, for groups lack certain of the rich particularities of individuals, though only a fool would deny that groups have their idiosyncrasies. In fact, that is probably the best place to start—with a puzzling statement made by someone about his group and another, one that does not quite make sense.

Consider the claim by Khalid Abdul Muhammad, a representative of Minister Louis Farrakhan, to a group of largely black students at Kean College in New Jersey on November 29, 1993. Blacks, he said "are the true Jew. You [speaking to a black audience] are the true Hebrew."[1] Think about it for a moment. What a strange thing to say, especially for a Muslim. Instead (or rather, in addition to) excoriating Jews, Khalid Muhammad claims to be them. Would a member of the Irish Republican Army say "we are the true British?" Would a Palestinian say "we are the true Israelites?" Presumably not, or is this secret identification with the enemy more universal than we know?

One who is neither black nor Jewish like myself has a certain advantage, an advantage of a little distance, the chance to be curious. Outrage and hurt are the great enemies of curiosity, virtually guaranteeing that we shall not puzzle about why someone said something. We know he did it because, at best, he does not understand, and at worst hates us. Or perhaps they go together. The troubling thing about Khalid Muhammad's statement is that it claims a type of understanding that must result in obliteration. If I am you, then you have no right to exist. Or as Khalid Muhammad put it, Jews are "imposter Jews."

Psychoanalytic group psychology has a limited number of insights to offer. Perhaps the most important concerns how much we need our enemies. We need our enemies to know ourselves, to give meaning to our lives. We need enemies in order to disown the bad parts of ourselves. Frequently, these parts are those deemed closer to nature in some way, which is why the stereotype of the enemy, be he black or Jew, has a certain monotonous sameness. The enemy is greedy, hypersexual, cunning, and desirous of our women. René Girard, who studies scapegoating, argues that the actual qualities of the scapegoat are unimportant, with one exception: The scapegoat is always marginal, on the edge of society.[2] What happens when two scapegoats are at each other, what seems to be happening among blacks and Jews? Is it a fight to see who is the real scapegoat, or is it over something else?

To say that we need enemies to define ourselves is not incorrect, but it neglects the degree to which the enemy becomes a reservoir for unintegrated, unacceptable parts of ourselves, alienated aspects of our own existence. We do not just need enemies to define ourselves. We need enemies to *be* ourselves. Vamik Volkan, author of "The Need to Have Enemies and Allies: A Developmental Approach," in his presidential address to the International Society for Group Psychology, explains the origins of the need for enemies this way. "We know that the infant develops mental images of himself and others in a *bipolar* way; the second task he must perform is to try to integrate the opposing images and to get rid of the bipolarity of his images of himself and others."[3]

For example, a baby awakens and is hungry. He becomes fearful and angry, until suddenly his mother appears with food. He is satisfied. Volkan holds (his reflects the majority view in developmental psychoanalysis today) that the infant experiences himself as two separate people: the angry fearful infant and the satisfied one. More precisely put, he experiences no connection between these two self states. Similarly, he experiences the mother who frustrates him, and the mother who satisfies him, as virtually two separate mothers. Development is about the integration of these split experiences. In other words, development is about the toleration of ambivalence.

This, though, puts it a little ideally. The integration is never complete. Some images of bad self and bad other are so totalistic and threatening that they never find an integrated place in the psyche. The more absolute and saturated with primitive experience the image is, the more difficult and incomplete the integration will be. Volkan argues that culture helps keep us sane (albeit at a price—the price of enemies and conflict) by finding "suitable targets of externalization," reservoirs in which we may put these bad, hurtful, and unacceptable experiences that are at the same time bad, hurtful, and unacceptable parts of the self. They are both because many occurred before the self was fully differentiated from its world, so that bad experience, bad other, and bad self were indistinct. These targets or reservoirs are extensions of the self, containing the most powerful and unmelded experiences of our lives, which is why they are hated so passionately.

Enemies, it is apparent, are as important as allies in defining the self, perhaps more important, as they contain the most threatening parts of the self, parts we would have to live with if the enemy did not exist. It is, from this perspective, no accident that the rise of the militia movement in the United States has come about as the "evil empire" disintegrated. If the evil empire is not outside, over there, then it must be inside, over here, in the black helicopters that carry the UN troops that will inflict a one-world government on us all. One-world government is, of course, an image of the dissolution of boundaries, precisely the terror evoked by the loss of the enemy: the dissolution of the boundary between good and bad.

Volkan's theory, probably the single most influential in psychoanalytic group psychology today, connects individual and group psychology. We join a group by sharing the same "suitable targets." Conversely, to share these targets, which have the quality of what D. W. Winnicott calls a transitional object, self and other at the same time, is to be a group member. The result is the creation of what Erik Erikson calls a pseudospecies—tribes, clans, classes, and ethnic groups that behave as if they "were separate species, created at the beginning of time by supernatural intent."[4]

BUT IT DOES NOT QUITE FIT BLACKS AND JEWS

It is a powerful theory, explaining the origins of much group conflict, including the almost unknowable sadness we feel when we lose an enemy. But it does not quite fit the relationship of blacks and Jews. It does not explain Khalid Muhammad's claim that blacks are the real Jews. Is he really saying "We are our own 'suitable target of externalization?' " Not quite. Somehow the "suitable target," at least when it comes to blacks and Jews, is not so polarized as Volkan makes out, the Jew containing for Kahalid Muhammad both desirable and undesirable aspects of the unmelded self. It is as if the primal splitting got confused, not following the primal fault lines of good and bad, both good and bad aspects of the nascent self becoming projected into the other, who is both enemy and ally.

Unintegrated aspects of the self are by no means always bad. They are aspects that for whatever reason are so raw with feeling they are almost impossible to integrate, especially when neither parents nor culture offer a model of integration, what the cliché "role model" actually refers to. A stereotypical example would be a young girl locating her feelings of competence and assertion within men, as these feelings contradict the only role she sees available for herself. What good aspects of the self have blacks, and Jews, been tempted to locate in each other, unable to acknowledge in themselves? This must be the case, or otherwise the enemy-ally would not be such a complex, confusing, and ambivalent figure.

"Enemy-ally": it is the term I shall use to capture not just the ambivalence, but the confused and confusing boundaries between self and other, that lies at the heart of relationships like that between blacks and Jews in the United States today. Though it implies that one group admires as well as hates another, it is not a relationship we should be too sanguine about. The combination enemy-ally may actually be more explosive, more intransigent, precisely because it is so mixed up. History is replete with former enemies becoming allies, and vice versa. The history of World War II and the cold war provide at least a dozen examples, our wartime enemies now among our closet allies. The complexity of the relationship between one enemy-ally and another may actually be more difficult to come to terms with.

One might argue, as Laurence Thomas does, that blacks envy Jews, which is why they want to be them.[5] Certainly it works the other way around, as Norman Podhoretz recognizes in "My Negro Problem and Ours," originally published in 1963. "Yet just as in childhood I envied Negroes for what seemed to me their superior masculinity, so I envy them today for what seems to me their superior physical grace and beauty."[6] But envy puts it too harshly. As the psychoanalyst Melanie Klein points out, jealousy and envy are not the same. In envy we want to deprive the other of the good, spoiling the good just because the other has it. In jealousy we want to have the good for ourselves. Envy cannot bear to desire what it cannot have; jealousy can.[7] The relationship of the enemy-ally is one of jealousy, not envy, admiring aspects of the other so much one wants to be them. It is perhaps equally destructive. If I am you, then you must disappear. But it is also something to work with, the possibility always existing that we might admire someone at a distance, even if it still hurts. Says Podhoretz, "I am now capable of aching with all my being when I watch a Negro couple on the dance floor, or a Negro playing baseball or basketball. They are on the kind of terms with their own bodies that I should like to be on with mine, and for that precious quality they seem blessed to me."[8] To be willing to live with the ache is progress in separation, even if the subsequent history of Podhoretz's "Negro Problem" is not unproblematic.

In an article in *The New Yorker*, Paul Berman calls the enemy-ally "the other and the almost the same," capturing well the richly paradoxical relationship between people whose bipolar minds are more complex than they know. What is the attraction?[9] Cornel West puts it this way.

When you have a culture that has put such a premium on critical intelligence—what Freud would call the ego—then you get a preoccupation with the id: the irrational, pleasure-seeking forces of the body and sexuality. Jewish culture has revolved around education to which Blacks often were denied access. There's no doubt that in American culture there has been a certain Jewish preoccupation with the id in a variety of forms, one of which is a fascination with Black culture and the Black body. A special relationship has evolved between the two groups, which functions on a deep cultural psychosexual level. It's not rational; it's to do with need. The Jews need to feel they have a special relationship with the people associated with the id. The Black community needs to have a special relationship with the people associated with ego.[10]

The most important term here is "need," the need to have a special relationship with the other group, in order to retain access to parts of oneself that have been lost or rather split off and denied.

It is worth emphasizing that much—though not all—of this need has a fantastic, irrational quality. Or rather, what is irrational is its location of self in the other. Jews will not find their lost desiring selves by embracing blacks or by rejecting them. Nor will blacks find their critical intelligence in Jews or in hatred of Jews. It is such an obvious point, perhaps, but one that is too often overlooked. It is natural to alienate parts of oneself in the other, but it is not good, and it will not be solved by idealizing these aspects in the other, or devaluing them, but only by reclaiming them.

One reason it is not good is because it is not only these presumably good aspects that are alienated but their dark twins. The graceful physicality of blacks easily slides over into the hypersexuality of blacks. The intelligent Jew readily becomes the cunning Jew. The projection is all mixed up, and the first step in recovering it and sorting it out is to withdraw the projection. How this might best be encouraged on a social level is the topic of the conclusion. It is the most important thing a psychoanalytic approach to group conflict can teach us.

The point for now is that part of the problem of blacks and Jews is a tendency to overidentify with each other, an enmeshment that can encourage its opposite—denial of the other's humanity. If I am really you, then you must be fake. Or worse, you must be the usurper of my real identity so that I will regain mine only when you lose yours. Cornel West does not seem to see the full implications of this reasoning and, in fact, begins to be carried away by the fantasy. It may seem like a nice fantasy, an admiring fantasy, but it is not. I quote West at length to convey a feeling for the deep identification involved.

There is a real sense in which Black people are profoundly Jewish people, just as Jews are profoundly Black. . . . This is part of the irony of Farrakhan. One of the reasons why he is so obsessed with Jews is precisely because of the profoundly Jewish nature of modern African-American peoples as well as the profoundly Black nature of modern American Jewry. There is a kind of symbiotic relation owing not just to the focus around certain stories in the

Biblical text . . . about who sides with the oppressed and the tragic peoples who cry and bleed and are scarred and so forth. These are real. But there is also this sense of being a perennial people on the move, having to make and remake themselves. . . . These are deep, very deep, elective affinities. . . . There is a sense in which Black and Jewish folk are almost stuck together, either at each other's throats or embracing one another, but that is still a kind of family fight.[11]

West is mistaken. It is not a family fight. Blacks and Jews were never family, which is not to say that they were not allies at certain points. That both groups were despised by the white Christian majority is not the same as being family. Even if they were not family, you might reply, is it not a nice ideal?

No, because it denies the reality of separateness, leading to fantasies of usurpation, the fantasy of Khalid Muhammad. At the conference that inspired this volume, several speakers and audience members (it was hard to tell who was who at points) waxed poetic about the fact that blacks and Jews both lived in ghettoes. But they did not. The Warsaw ghetto is only remotely similar to Harlem, and in any case this does not make blacks and Jews family. Instead, it is more likely to lead to a competition in suffering, as when Khalid Muhammad toured the Holocaust Museum, only to conclude that his people's suffering was worse—as though there were a shortage of suffering. There is, but only when the other becomes a virtual part of oneself, so that his suffering must detract from yours, because you are really one, two halves that don't make a whole.

My analysis may not seem rigorously psychoanalytic, but in one respect it is. I take the fantasy seriously, what all good analysts do, be they psycho- or social. I assume that neither Muhammad nor West are engaging in mere rhetorical excess, but that they are expressing a fantasy of union that, by its own internal logic, becomes a fantasy of unity and usurpation. From this perspective, Khalid Muhammad, so angry with the Jews, is also saying something about his disappointment.

"I'm you, and you're me, and we're all together" is the idea behind an old rock song. It is a fantasy of union, presumably a nice sentiment. But consider what happens when the fantasy no longer persuades. Not "I am me, and you are you," but rather "I am you, and you are fake." The fantasy of union becomes one of usurpation, not separation, as in the "imposter Jew." You are a fake insofar as you pretend to be like me but are not. Instead, you are like the other, the enemy, the worst enemy there is, the enemy who pretends to be me.

It is not entirely false. In the United States, there is a sense that Jews have gone over to the majority, voting more like Protestants and Catholics than ever before. The Jewish neoconservative movement is real. Though it hardly represents a majority of Jews, it makes an appeal to this majority that was widely heard, an appeal couched within an ambitious intellectual framework the likes of which conservatism had not seen for years. Berman tells the old Alfred Kazin joke. "What's the difference between the International Ladies Garment Workers' Union and the American Psychiatric Association? One generation." It is more true than false, for Jews that is. There is no comparable joke for blacks. Or if there is, it would be the "joke" told by Malcolm X at Harvard. "What do they call a Negro with a Ph.D. in Mississippi? Nigger." Only it is not just about Mississippi, and it is not very funny.

Consider the possibility that the alliance between blacks and Jews was never as deep and profound as all that, a fact always known to blacks somewhat better than Jews. Driving Miss Daisy always looked different to the chauffeur than the passenger. But both imagine, and grieve (more in anger than in sorrow in many cases) a unity that never existed in the first place. Over fifty years ago, Ralph Bunche wrote the foreword to a book analyzing black reaction to German antisemitism, stating that "it is common knowledge that many members of the Negro and Jewish communities of the country share mutual dislike, scorn, and mistrust."[12]

Blacks and Jews worked together best during the era of assimilationism: the years immediately preceding World War II, interrupted by the war, and running until the early 1960s. It was an era in which the denial of differences between blacks and Jews was coincident with the rhetoric of the movement at the time, a denial of difference overall. "One day we will all be light brown," is how one of my high school teachers, advisor to the Civil Rights Group (we first called it a club, like all the other clubs, from drama to chess, but soon changed its name) of all white, mostly Jewish students, put it. None disagreed with the ideal, or perhaps I should say denial. A denial, by the way, that lacked psychological depth even then; Cornel West's comment about the appeal of intellectual Jews to desiring blacks, and vice versa, was more true then than now.

What strained the relationship between blacks and Jews was not just black's rhetorical alliance with the Third World but the assertion of difference and the denial of assimilationism: that blacks and Jews had different histories and different futures. The rift between blacks and Jews would have happened with or without the intervention of the black nationalists, or rather, black nationalism expressed in dramatic form differences present all along.

Jews in the United States are generally white Europeans. They are white Europeans with a history of persecution, but a history of persecution is better, or at least different, than no history at all, the consequence of slavery for blacks. As James Baldwin put it,

the most ironical thing about Negro anti-Semitism is that the Negro is really condemning the Jew for having become an American white man—for having

become, in effect, a Christian. . . . The Jew does not realize that the credential
he offers, the fact that he has been despised and slaughtered, does not increase
the Negro's understanding. It increases the Negro's rage. . . . The Jewish tra-
vail occurred across the sea and America rescued him from the house of
bondage. But America *is* the house of bondage for the Negro, and no country
can rescue him.[13]

One might argue whether America rescued the Jew, but Baldwin's point is
clear. Jews and blacks are not only not in the same boat, but they never
were, not even—or especially—when they crossed the Atlantic to the
United States.

Freud wrote of the narcissism of small differences, the way in which small
differences among people who are otherwise so alike makes for especially
long-lasting and acrimonious quarrels, particularly among people who live
closely together, such as the Portuguese and the Spanish, or the English
and the Scots.[14] Freud's formulation is readily interpreted in terms of Volkan's theory of the need for enemies: We accentuate small differences to
create enemies who are enough like us to hold convincingly, or represent,
our bad parts, but just different enough to hold them at a distance. It is
a great theory, and it is in effect the theory to which Berman subscribes in
his *New Yorker* article, which concludes with a reference to Vladimir
Jankélévitch, who holds to a version of Freud's small differences theory.
"Jankélévitch knew this. His idea of almost-the-same populations pictured
'spouses who can neither live together nor live apart.' "[15]

It is a great theory, but it does not fit blacks and Jews, or rather it fits
a fantasy of their relationship but not their reality. For all his considerable
insight, Berman too idealizes a relationship that never was. We need a term
almost the opposite of the narcissism of small differences to describe the
relationship of blacks and Jews—or at least to have a complete understanding of it, for something like the narcissism of small differences is not entirely
false, which is what makes it entirely wrong, a part of the story transformed
into deep insight into the whole.

"The manic denial of big differences" is my nominee for the opposite
term, though it quite lacks the pizazz of Freud's term. In any case, it is the
idea that is most important, the tendency of two heavily scapegoated
groups to deny their differences so that they might mourn, and fight over,
a lost unity that never was—a lost unity that is better than no unity at all.
It is touching really, and it raises the interesting point that groups, as well
as individuals, need to mourn relationships that never were, as well as ones
that are no more. It is helpful, however, to know the difference. The opposite of Erikson's pseudospeciation is not, after all, nonspeciation. It is
genuine speciation, neither creating false differences nor denying the reality
of real ones.

When I say the lost unity among blacks and Jews, I mean just that. Blacks and Jews have at various times been allies in a common struggle, and it is this that is important to remember, for this is reality. If the tendency with the enemy is to exaggerate the differences, the tendency with the ally is to deny the differences. And the tendency with the enemy-ally is to do both at once, the result of which is Khalid Muhammad's I am you, and you are fake logic, which is another way of saying "we are so exactly alike that your very existence must obliterate mine. One of us must die." Here is the idea of the enemy-ally taken to its extreme and logical conclusion, which is why the enemy-ally is a dangerous relationship. Enemies can come to a *modus vivendi*, but the enemy-ally must die for me to live.

All this is quite illogical, you might respond. I would reply that it is extremely logical, the logic of unconscious group fantasy, for it is the nature of fantasy that it has a borderline quality about all or nothing at all. In fantasy, as in the unconscious generally, we do not have moderate relationships or ambivalent ones. We fuse, we separate, we are all, we are nothing. The enemy-ally, apparently a moderate, modulated relationship containing elements of both enemy and ally is actually a confused fantasy, which means that it contains the extremist elements of both enemy and ally, the extremes of total difference and absolute identity.

Fortunately, social relations are not always logical, which means that they do not always go to their psychological extremes. Nevertheless, the tendency exists, insofar as social relations are based on fantasies that one group has about another. Or rather, fantasies that one group has about itself, what it is and is not, projected into the other. The statement by Khalid Muhammad that blacks "are the true Jew," initially so curious, upon consideration actually taps the psycho-logic perfectly, opening the door to the extremes of psycho-logic. Once inside, we see that the psycho-logic is shared, albeit in less extreme and dangerous forms, by such reasonable men as Cornel West and Paul Berman.

It may seem nice, even cozy, in this moderate form, but it is not, for it too is a way of not seeing. One of the reasons blacks hate whites, James Baldwin argues, is that whites frequently refuse to look at blacks. This is the topic not only of much of Baldwin's work, but one of the finest novels of the twentieth century, Ralph Ellison's *Invisible Man*. In fact, there are two ways not to look. One is not to get close enough, the relationship to which Baldwin and Ellison refer. The other way is to get too close. The primary defensive function of identification is to get so close to the other, one does not *have* to look, to see, to know. To look takes a little perspective, and perspective means distance. We do not, and cannot, really know those we identify with. All we know is our own projections.

Though I have eschewed comparing black and Jewish relations with family, there is one respect in which it may be useful. Of all the traits that mark so-called dysfunctional families, the most striking is "pathological certainty," the absolute conviction of family members that they know who the other family members really are, where they are coming from, and what they are thinking.[16] Dysfunctional families get better when family members start to become curious about one another, curious about the differences, willing to be surprised. It would be progress if blacks and Jews were less certain of each other and more curious.

THE IDEAL OF CONVERSATION

Knowing the dangerousness of the extremes, the tendency of psycho-logic to go all the way to the end and beyond, should we strive for moderation? No, we should strive to emancipate the extremes from their confusion so that they can be seen, known, and lose some of their power in the light of day. The analyst does not say to the troubled patient "think moderate thoughts." He or she encourages the patient to think extreme thoughts but in such a way as to put into words what is already there, so that exposed to the light of consciousness the logic of extreme fantasy might lose some of its power. The task of psychoanalysis is to drive the demons in, not out: into contact with the rest of the psyche so that the realms of the mind might become acquainted with each other so that the alienated parts of the self devoted to enemy and ally might talk to each other.

My proposals are all directed at those who talk about relations between blacks and Jews and particularly those who encourage students and others to talk about their experiences, feelings, and attitudes. These talks are going on all around us: in conferences such as the conference that inspired this volume, in classrooms, in lecture halls, in the workplace, dorm rooms, and on the street corner. We are all participants, and many are leaders and consultants as well. The principles of psychoanalytic practice are as relevant here as on the couch, if only we can be a little flexible with them.

Psychoanalysis is in many respects a dark teaching as far as group psychology is concerned, having much to say about what compels groups, but little to say about what to do about it. This is realistic, the need to have enemies so overwhelmingly powerful that no amount of insight will change it. While knowledge is not power, it can still help, and here is one area in which the knowledge of psychoanalytic group psychology may be especially helpful, suggesting strategies to drive the demons in, so that they do not remain alienated parts of ourselves, but partners in conversation: conversation that begins with others and ends somewhere deep inside ourselves.

What is conversation? Let us consider what it is not. "How can I listen when I'm trying so hard to be heard?" said *one*. "I have enough problems of my own," replied another. "I don't have any room for yours too." Conversation requires a room, and it requires an antiroom: place to hold ideas within ourselves without becoming the idea. A place to hold and evaluate what we take in from others, without having immediately to accept or reject it. The primary contribution of teacher, facilitator, leader, and therapist is to function as this antiroom, modeling what it is like to hold, contain, and consider an idea, representing what it is to entertain an idea without becoming or obliterating it. The antiroom is the parlor where we entertain ideas. Conversation takes place between rooms and antirooms, and its main virtue is a willingness to suspend judgment and be surprised. In a word, the main virtue of conversation is curiosity.

There is not much conversation these days, and some environs are so hostile to conversation that it is not worth trying. The street corner is one, but so is much so-called "talk radio." The term is just right: everyone talks, no one listens, and the premium is on the most outrageous statement. In such circumstances, it is probably best not to participate.

Four principles of conversation are especially important. They apply not only to actual spoken conversation, but to all who write, read, lecture, and listen in the spirit of conversation, in the spirit of the antiroom, which is willing to play host to ideas, entertaining them without immediately judging them. In the language of psychoanalysis, the antiroom is a transitional space, like Winnicott's transitional object, representing self and nonself at the same time.

1. The fantasy is unity, not just with the ally, but with the enemy-ally. We should be gently critical of all who suggest that behind the strife and conflict of everyday life lies a hidden unity with our apparent opponent, a shared history of struggle, and the like, if only we can recover it and bring it forth. While the claim is not simply a lie, it is not true either. It is an idealizing fantasy that generally suppresses real differences as well as real bases for alliance.

The goal of conversation is to recover lost projections, parts of the self alienated in the other. Fantasies of lost unity are unhelpful, creating the confusing enemy-ally that actually makes it more difficult to recover the projection. If we do not know who is who and what is what, we cannot reintegrate it. [This is the unconscious aim of confusion, mixing things up so much that we do not know where we end and the other begins.]

2. Confusion is the great ally of change: Without passing through confusion there can be no change. Confusion is also the great enemy of change. If we consider that people hold the beliefs they do in order to keep themselves from being overwhelmed by anxiety and depression, we will understand the need to tread gently and go slowly. Hot, intense exchanges may be exciting, they may be cathartic, they may even foster intense feelings of love for the enemy-ally, but they do not last, and little is changed in the long run. I am thinking here of "race relations weekend encounter groups" and the like, but each reader will have his or her examples.

Only if we understand how confused people are, and how this confusion it built into the self so that it becomes the self, will we appreciate how long it takes to change and how gently those who would foster change must tread. People generally do not believe half the things they say; the trouble is, they generally do not know which half. Nor do we. Appreciating confusion is also a matter of respect. A person does not "have" beliefs; the person *is* his or her beliefs, the point of Volkan's theory. It is worthwhile to respect even odious beliefs—not because they might just possibly be true (it was never true, and never will be true, that Jews were leaders of the slave trade, for example), but because the belief is held by a self who needs it. Our task is to help the self find another belief, one that depends a little less on the enemy.

3. Political correctness is repression. People must be free to be "incorrect" in order to change. To state in advance that any topic is acceptable, as long as the discussion "is conducted within the framework of mutual respect," is guaranteed to chill discussion. As a teacher who discusses race relations in class, I know that no one ever says what he or she is really thinking. Everyone lies, and everyone is scared to death of saying the wrong thing. In fact, people lie so much they do not even know what they think anymore, which means people have to be free to try ideas out, to listen to themselves say things to see if they believe it in the cold light of day. In therapy, a patient might say the same thing a thousand times before really hearing what he says. People do not always believe the terrible things they say, but they cannot know this unless they hear themselves say it.

People must also be protected in discussion. This is the function of the antiroom that becomes the holding environment for conversation. People can say what they will, they can hurt others' feelings, but it is important for the discussion leader to prevent scapegoating, the isolation and sacrifice of one or several participants. The topic of this chapter has been the need for enemies, for scapegoats. The discussion leader must be careful not to let this be enacted in the group. In general, the best way of dealing with it is to interpret it. There is nothing like learning from within the transference of the moment.

4. "Give it a rest." The relationship between blacks and Jews is characterized, I have suggested, by pathological enmeshment, "stuck together" as West puts it in a conflict that never dies. Not every racist or antisemitic remark needs to be confronted, nor does every conflict need to become the subject of a conference. Sometimes it is good not to talk about it, though of course this can readily slide over into denial. There are no rules here, only a feel for the feelings involved. If it feels like the friction is itself the goal, it might be wise to back off and wait.

NOTES

1. Paul Berman, "The Other and the Almost the Same," *The New Yorker*, February 28, 1994, 61–71.

2. René Girard, *The Scapegoat*, trans. Yvonne Freccero (Baltimore: Johns Hopkins University Press, 1986), 17–23.

3. Vamik Volkan, "The Need to Have Enemies and Allies: A Developmental Approach," *Political Psychology* 6, no. 2 (1985):219–47, quote on 232.

4. D. W. Winnicott, "Transitional Objects and Transitional Phenomena," in *Collected Papers* (New York: Basic Books, 1958), 229–42. Erik Erikson, "Ontogeny of Ritualization," in *Psychoanalysis: A General Psychology*, ed. K. M. Lowenstein et al. (New York: International Universities Press, 1966), 606.

5. Lawrence Thomas, "Group Autonomy and Narrative Identity: Blacks and Jews," in *Blacks and Jews: Alliances and Arguments*, ed. Paul Berman (New York: Delacorte Press, 1994), 286–303, quote on 288–89.

6. Norman Podhoretz, "My Negro Problem and Ours," in *Blacks and Jews: Alliances and Arguments*, ed. Paul Berman (New York: Delacorte Press, 1994), 76–96, quote on 88.

7. Melanie Klein, "Envy and Gratitude," in *The Writings of Melanie Klein*, ed. R. E. Money-Kyrle, 4 vols. (New York: Free Press, 1975), 4:176–235.

8. Podhoretz, "My Negro Problem and Ours," 88.

9. Berman, "The Other and the Almost the Same," 62.

10. Michael Lerner and Cornel West, eds., *Jews and Blacks: Let the Healing Begin* (New York: G. P. Putnam's Sons, 1995), 137–38. The book is a conversation; the passages quoted are all from West.

11. Ibid., 221.

12. Bunche, quoted in Clayborne Carson, "The Politics of Relations between African-Americans and Jews," in *Blacks and Jews: Alliances and Arguments*, ed. Paul Berman (New York: Delacorte Press, 1994), 131–43, quote on 131.

13. James Baldwin, "Negroes are Anti-Semitic Because They're Anti-White," in *Blacks and Jews: Alliances and Arguments*, ed. Paul Berman (New York: Delacorte Press, 1994), 31–41, quote on 37.

14. Sigmund Freud, *The Standard Edition of the Complete Psychological Works of Sigmund Freud, Volume 21: Civilization and Its Discontents*, trans. James Strachey (1930; New York: W. W. Norton, 1961), 59–145.

15. Berman, "The Other and the Almost the Same," 71.

16. Edward R. Shapiro and A. Wesley Carr, *Lost in Familiar Places* (New Haven: Yale University Press, 1991), 11–15.

4

Black Liberation and the Jewish Question

E. VICTOR WOLFENSTEIN

Although the problematics of the African American liberation struggle have been one of my major preoccupations for over a quarter of a century, I've not given any special attention to the relationship between Blacks and Jews. I cannot, therefore, claim any expertise on the matter, but can only offer a few thoughts in response to this question: How might we understand the relationship of Blacks and Jews *if* we view it from the perspective of the struggle against white racism? The answer, I will suggest, is that the focus on this relationship—whether originating with Jews or Blacks—is for the most part a displacement from the primary locus of conflict. It is, in this quite psychoanalytic sense, symptomatic. The main reason for analyzing Black-Jewish relationships is to dissolve the symptom and undo the displacement so that the central conflict can be forthrightly confronted.

In the first part of this chapter I contend that the formulation "Blacks and Jews" is misleading and disturbingly asymmetrical. It is symptomatic, in the sense just noted. I therefore attempt to reframe the issue within the problematics of white racism and black liberation. In the second part I present a psychoanalytic-Marxist model of American race relations within which to analyze Black-Jewish conflict and collaboration. The third part of the chapter is an application of the model. I briefly examine the civil rights movement of the 1950s and 1960s, before turning to the symptomatic encapsulation of Black-Jewish relations in our present historical situation. In the latter regard I contend that, for many Jews, the remembered trauma of the European Jewish religious-*racial* past distorts perception of the American Jewish religious-*ethnic* present.[1] The consequence is a certain blindness to the continuing traumatic impact of white racism on black people and a corresponding tendency to misinterpret black attitudes toward white people, Jews included.

One preliminary point: It requires binocular vision to see race relations clearly. If we reduce race to attitudes and beliefs, we fail to recognize the objective interests (advantages and disadvantages) that structure racial interactions. Conversely, if we reduce race to objective interests, we fail to recognize the affective and attitudinal investments that impinge so markedly on our individual and collective consciousness. The trick, then, is to use a double optic—but also to avoid double vision.

THE JEWISH QUESTION

Here is an anecdote that helps to define if not to justify my approach to the question of Blacks and Jews.

When I was about twelve years old, several of the Jewish students in a shop class were being disruptive. The teacher chastised them and, in the course of so doing, said something like, "The Jewish race thinks it has it made." We were taken aback at this statement, but my classmates were pretty much reduced to silence. Speaking of displacement: I protested that Jews were not a race. This secondary issue became the focus of a not very useful discussion.

This incident took place in the midwestern United States in the early 1950s. If it had occurred in Germany in the 1930s, my deflection of the issue would not have been possible. In that historical context Jews were a race. Which is to say, they had been racialized, constructed as the racial other to the equally constructed Aryan self. Culture, custom, language, and belief had become signifiers of biology and bloodlines; and on this pseudobiological basis Jews were persecuted, oppressed, and, in time, destroyed en masse. By contrast, the racialization of Jews in the United States, although fairly pronounced as a response to the great waves of Eastern European immigration in the early 1900s, was far less thorough; and by the 1950s it was giving way to less virulent forms of ethnic and religious prejudice. Indeed, by that time Jews were fast becoming white people, who walked on the right side of the color line, and for whom the racialized other was (most important) black people. This is not to say that, as individuals, Jews were notably racist. It is to say that they lived their lives as white people for whom Blacks were structurally defined as the racialized antithesis.

So, albeit a displacement from the issue of prejudice, my protest to the shop teacher had an empirical warrant. In the contemporary United States, Jews are not a race. Whites are a race, Blacks are a race, Jews aren't. Jews are white people. Hence there is an unfortunate asymmetry and even presumption when we talk of Black-Jewish relationships.

Think of it this way. We could construct a matrix with two dimensions. One would be racial—let's say White, Black, and other. The second would be religious—let's say Buddhists, Christians, Jews, and Muslims. Using this simple schema we could investigate a variety of relationships: for example, Black Jews with White Jews, Black Muslims with White Christians, Black Christians with White Christians, and so forth. In this way we would generate a categorization of major social actors and collectivities, one that is especially useful for analyzing the phase in the black liberation struggle extending from the early 1950s to the early 1970s. We would be putting Jews into an appropriate political perspective. And we would not be reducing Black Jews to invisibility.

In other words, it is certainly legitimate to analyze the role of White Jews in the American racial drama. There really are such people, they really constitute an identifiable presence, one can look at the racial scene from their perspective(s), and assess how they are perceived by others—in the present instance, by black people of whatever religious orientation. The formulation "Black-Jewish relationships" is at best a poor approximation to this more complex framing of the issues.[2]

Instead of analyzing the relationship of Blacks and Jews from the perspective of race, one might approach it from the standpoint of identity politics and multiculturalism. Here the principal social actors are defined by land of origin (African American, Asian American, European American, Latino, Native American, etc.) and/or gender and sexual orientation (male, female, gay, lesbian, bisexual). Jews seem to have disappeared. Still, nothing prohibits us from reintroducing a religious dimension. We then have Jewish Americans, Christian Americans, and so forth. But if we were now to juxtapose African Americans and Jewish Americans, we would be replicating the asymmetry noted above. For most American Jews remain, despite the more recent immigration of Middle Eastern Jews (Persians, Israelis, etc.), European American. Hence we should not be surprised if most African Americans place Jews into this cultural category. Moreover, although our increasingly multicultural society presents us with novel problems and opportunities, it has not eliminated the either/or of white racism: White or Not-White, with the position of negation anchored by Black people. There are gradations in between and other axes of discrimination and even domination. But White over Black—in Winthrop Jordan's phrase (Jordan 1969)—has proven to be remarkably durable.

So what is a Jew? The least problematical answer to this question is that a Jew is someone who is identified with Judaism as a religion—as a set of beliefs and rituals. Further, Judaism, like other religions, has a history and generates a web of social relationships. Religion thus overlaps in meaning with culture or way of life. Hence the common sense notion of cultural Jews, people who are not observant but whose identity is Jewish. Finally, the term, "the Jewish people," can be used to cover this set of meanings and to emphasize the affective bonds that often accompany Jewish identity.

Each of these three meanings can be prejudicially transformed. At the religious level, there is the long-standing Christian heritage of the Jews as murderers of Christ. Culturally, Jews are negatively characterized as shy-locks, the tribe of the avaricious (sometimes wealthy and powerful, some-times petty, stingy, and money-grubbing). And peoplehood can be perverted into race—into bloodlines and mystified essences.

Taken singly or together, these prejudices can be and have been used as motives for and vehicles of oppression. This has not, however, been the American Jewish experience. Unlike Blacks, Jews have not been the victims of white racism. But a kind of homogenizing ethnic identity has been cre-ated for them. Stereotypically, Jews have been cast in the images of the eastern and middle European immigrants of the early twentieth century. They have been, so to speak, *ethnicized*. Along with the outward signifiers of religious identity, this imposed ethnicity makes Jews visible as Jews. Hence, in its negative dimension, I characterize the American Jewish ex-perience as one of religious-ethnic prejudice.

In sum: Black people are the victims of white racist oppression; Jews are white people who are, often, the objects of religious-ethnic prejudice.[3]

Thus far I have attempted to place Jewish identity within the proble-matics of American race relations. So doing both calls into question the equation of Blacks and Jews and narrows the scope of the issue. The issue is narrowed still further when we consider the variety of positions that comprise the two sides of the postulated equation.

On the Jewish side, we again might think of a matrix with two dimen-sions. Along one axis we would have the nature of one's Jewish self-identification, along with the other attitudes toward black people and/or white racism.

As to the first axis: At one extreme we might find Jews who don't really think of themselves as Americans—people whose Jewishness goes very deep and excludes any other major self-identification. Somewhat less stri-gently, these might be people who view themselves as Jews who happen to be in America. Then come Jewish Americans, who experience a version of the two-ness W. E. B. Du Bois ascribes to African Americans—a dual, at least partially conflicting, identity, in which one is always uncom-fortably hyphenated and self-divided (Du Bois 1903, 1990). Next there are Jewish Americans/American Jews, people who experience their Jewish and

American identities as equally important but not conflictual. Approaching the other end, we have people who think of themselves as Americans who happen to be Jewish. Jewishness is not denied, but it is no longer a central component of personal identity. Finally, there are those who have left their Jewishness behind or at least have attempted to do so.[4]

As to the second axis, we might simplify matters by defining three positions: sympathetic to the claims of Blacks and strongly opposed to white racism in its many forms; unsympathetic to the claims of Blacks and white racist in their attitudes; not particularly concerned with race matters, one way or another.

Now it seems clear that, from the Jewish side, the question of Blacks and Jews is limited to self-identified Jews who are either markedly in sympathy or markedly out of sympathy with the struggles of black people. The former, for example, are the kind of people who participated in the civil rights movement as Jews—whose participation followed from their Jewish identity and values.[5] The latter group is harder to characterize. It consists partially of Jews who are simply white racists, partially of Jews who have been negatively impacted by direct experiences of conflict with black people. Importantly, people can slide over from the first group to the second when certain issues—most notably attitudes toward Israel—are brought into play.

What about the black side of the matter? So far as I can tell, most black people are not especially concerned with the Jewish question; and even those who do address it do not typically initiate the discussion. Rather, it seems that some black people, characteristically in positions of intellectual, political, and/or religious leadership, respond to three kinds of Jewish initiatives: attempts at dialogue aimed at interracial progressive action, attacks on perceived black antisemitism, or attempts at "healing dialogue" about perceived antisemitism. Which is to say, the Black-Jewish question is, pragmatically, the concern of the self-identified Jews who initiate these three kinds of contact and the Blacks who respond to them.

In sum: Black-Jewish relations are a rather small piece of a quite large interracial puzzle. They can be usefully considered within this larger frame. When the larger frame is excluded from the discussion, its exclusion becomes the appropriate analytical issue.

WHITE RACISM

In order to analyze black liberation and the Jewish question, we require a working model of white racism. This section provides one that is based on my own research. Other approaches to the subject are, of course, available.

My work in race matters has centered on the black nationalist tendency in the black liberation movement, with special emphasis on the role played by Malcolm X (Wolfenstein 1981/1993a). In the course of this work I've developed a class-group interpretation of white racism and the struggle against it. Originally this involved setting Freud's group psychology within the problematics of Marxist class analysis. More recently I've recast the psychoanalytic component of the model in terms of Bion's group psychology (Bion 1959; Wolfenstein 1993b).

For simplicity's sake we begin with the assumption that American society is structured vertically by the opposed interests of the bourgeoisie (capitalists) and the proletariat (workers)—those who own and control the major means of social production and those who work for the owners of the means of social production. This assumption is empirically based, as any review of ownership and income statistics reveals. But the bipolarity of class structure is only part of the story. There is also a petty bourgeoisie consisting of relatively small-scale independent entrepreneurs and upper-level employees in corporate and other bureaucracies. There is, further, a tripartite structural division within the working class between (1) workers in relatively protected forms of employment with relatively good wages; (2) underemployed and vulnerable workers (Marx's industrial reserve army of labor); and (3) the chronically unemployed. This last segment is also the basis of the lumpen-proletariat, who are the members of what Malcolm X termed the hustling society.[6]

Workers in the first category, when looked at from the perspective of socioeconomic status (or capacity to consume), are middle class. So, too, are many members of the petty bourgeoisie. The middle class, which cuts across class lines in the structural sense, has been a major stabilizing force in American political life.

Race cuts across class lines in both of the preceding senses. We are, indeed, so strongly divided by race that class distinctions sometimes almost disappear (about which more in a moment). Nonetheless, there are class distinctions in the black community as well as the white. Malcolm X liked to distinguish between house Negroes and field Negroes when characterizing black class relationships. The black middle class, he claimed, consisted of modern house Negroes, who were interested in being close to their masters—that is, who aimed at racial integration. The masses were field Negroes, who were interested in escaping from the plantation—that is, who were separatists and black nationalists.

This characterization is both too simple and polemically charged. But it accurately reflects the enduring tension in the African American community between assimilationism and separatism; and it usefully correlates these tendencies with class divisions (see Halisi 1996). Moreover, between Malcolm X's time and our own, these class divisions have become more pronounced, as an enlarged middle class has become more sharply differentiated from the masses.

Here is a simplified picture of class/race relations in the United States:

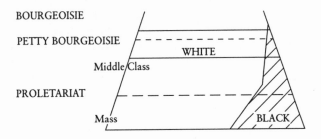

From a purely class-analytic perspective, the black and white sectors of the proletariat have a common interest. The lower the class position, the more unified the interest. There is a cross-cutting racial interest, insofar as black and white workers could be competing in the same labor markets. The racial division of labor markets provides some protection for white workers. The advantage gained from the racial segmentation of labor markets is, however, minimal in comparison to the disadvantage of all workers, relative to the advantages of the bourgeoisie. And this differential intraclass advantage hardly accounts for the ferocity of white racism and the willingness of white workers to substitute racial struggle for class struggle. For black workers, on the other hand, the racial struggle unambiguously takes priority. As the preceding analysis suggests and as Malcolm X so often emphasized, black people are oppressed on the basis of race, oppressed by white workers as well as white capitalists. They have a common enemy, and this enemy has a variety of resources at its disposal: territorial segregation (no longer de jure but persisting de facto), job discrimination, unchecked police brutality, prejudicial imprisonment, and pervasive white racist attitudes facilitating and legitimating these various modalities of oppression. Thus, where for white workers white racism involves a displacement of class struggle, for black people black racialism is a rational—indeed, vital—response to the existing situation.[7]

In the first instance, black racialism does not require psychological analysis. It is comprehensible from the perspective of interests. But the phenomenon of white racism cannot be comprehended on this basis alone. Moreover, white racism is not just, or even primarily, a matter of individual attitudes. It is a collective mentality. Indeed, its hold often weakens at the level of individual interaction. Hence, the analysis of white racism requires a group psychology and not just an individual one.

For clarity's sake, let's briefly rehearse the central features of W. R. Bion's theory of groups. Bion recognizes, first of all, that human beings are group animals: "No individual, however isolated in time and space, can be regarded as outside a group or lacking in active manifestations of group psychology" (Bion, 132). Within organized groups he distinguishes two interpenetrated levels of functioning: that of the work group (which is instrumentally rational) and that of the basic assumption group (which is not). He identifies three such basic assumptions: dependency, in which the group exists "in order to be sustained by a leader on whom it depends for nourishment, material and spiritual, and protection"; fight-flight, in which the group exists to "fight something or to run away from it"; and pairing, in which the group exists to witness (especially the imagined sexual) interaction of a couple, from whose union a messianic leader is expected to be born (146–53).[8]

Bion views the basic assumptions as having the "characteristics of defensive reactions to psychotic anxiety" (189). Hence they have something in common with "mechanisms described by Melanie Klein . . . as typical of the earliest phases of mental life" (141), most notably the paranoid-schizoid position. This does not mean, however, that groups function at a preoedipal level. Indeed, there are at least traces of a developmental line from the dependency situation, for which the prototype is mother and infant, to the pairing situation, for which the prototype is witnessing the primal scene.

Psychologically, the white race is an emotional group in the Bionian sense, with the black race as its protectively split-off counterpart:

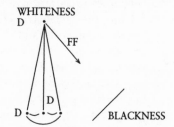

Whether or not embodied in an individual leader, whiteness is idealized, indeed, fetishized. White people identify with each other on the basis of their common identification with the racial fetish. Internally, the group is governed by the dependency basic assumption. Whiteness is the source from which all goodness flows. Correspondingly, blackness is the source of all evil. Black people are demonized, and all the anxiety-producing contents of the collective unconscious are split-off, projected, and displaced into them. Thus at the intergroup level, the fight-flight assumption governs, with the consequent legitimation of hostility in thought and action. Finally, in this relationship black people are projectively sexualized. They function as the containers for white people's fantasies of uninhibited, animal-like and violent sexuality. In short, they become hated and desired through the same projective mechanisms.

Bion emphasizes that the basic assumptions are developmentally primitive. Following Freud (1921), I would note that they are also essentially hypnotic. For both reasons, they are substantially immunized from rational criticism. Moreover, because social destabilization increases anxiety, their hypnotic and paranoid-schizoid quality intensifies during times of rapid social change. In these circumstances the more fascistic potentialities of white racism become manifest.

If we now combine our prior analysis of interests with our briefly formulated conception of group emotion, we conclude that working-class white racism is a case of *mass motives serving ruling class interests*. This may be pictured as follows:

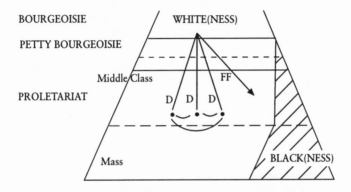

White workers are united with their class oppressors in a dependency group formation. Black people are experienced in terms of fight-flight. Whatever their social class position, they are the recipients of the repressed, projected, and displaced contents of the white racist group mind. Consequently, they must struggle against the pressure to introject this projected white racism. More generally, they must free themselves from the tendency, common among oppressed peoples, to identify with their oppressors. This may require a reactive mobilization of group emotional potentialities. And they must find ways of organizing themselves to fight for the realization of their racial interests.

I term a collectivity that is organized on the basis of its interests and that is capable of overcoming or at least containing its group-emotional tendencies a progressive movement. Conversely, a collectivity that is not organized on the basis of its interests and that is dominated by group emotion I term a regressive movement. Even progressive movements, however, must contend with regressive tendencies, while regressive movements may have their progressive aspects.

Because this psychoanalytic-Marxist model of white racism in the United States is highly general, it can be applied across a wide historical span. It can be used to chart demographic movement, interclass mobility, changes in legal and political relationships, and so forth, as long as White over Black characterizes race relations in this country. Regrettably, the model retains its applicability.

TRAUMAS: PAST AND PRESENT

Using this model, let's briefly consider the relationship of Jews and Blacks during the formative 1950s and 1960s before turning to our own historical situation.

In class terms, Jews had been and were continuing to be upwardly mobile. This upward mobility was accompanied by a progressive whitening of racial identity. Blacks by definition were Not-White and, despite the pattern of upward mobility during and after World War II, were more mass than middle class. Thus Jews and Blacks were in an inverted, mirror-image relationship to each other. They had opposed racial interests, and the bond of common middle-class interests was tenuous at best.

Jews did have a distinctive pattern of contact with Blacks during this period. On the one hand, a part of the Jewish petty bourgeoisie operated businesses and/or owned income-producing property in black areas. Here the racial other was typically a member of the black masses. On the other hand, Jews were characteristically liberal in their political and social orientation and were strongly represented in racially progressive organizations. Here, the racial other was typically a member of the black middle class. Thus, Jews were situated along the Black-White boundary in two quite different class locations.

Although this mapping of Jewish racial presence is extremely simplified, certain features of Black-Jewish interaction are intelligible in its terms. First, Blacks properly perceived Jews as white people, with characteristically white attitudes and interests. Liberal Jews could legitimately differentiate themselves from more conservative white people; but racially speaking, they were simply white liberals. Second, the black response to the white Jewish racial presence split rather sharply along class/ideological lines. The middle-class Blacks who predominantly constituted the leadership cadres of the civil rights movement recognized the necessity and even desirability of working with white liberals. Although they were sensitive to the many ways in which white racist attitudes continued to manifest themselves even here, they acknowledged shared values, and so the possibility of productive collaboration. And because black and white religious leaders were also important leaders of the movement, Jews who participated as Jews were recognized as such.

This is not to say the civil rights movement was one big happy interracial and interfaith family. But it did effectively embody interracial and interfaith middle-class interests. By contrast, the interests of the black masses were not adequately represented by the movement's leadership. Politically and culturally, mass interests were much better articulated by the black nationalists. From this perspective, white liberals were enemies, not friends—deceitful foxes, as Malcolm X characterized them, in comparison to the segregationist wolves. The role played by Jews as ghetto businessmen and landlords could be brought forward as evidence of their white liberal deceitfulness and hypocrisy. Hence Malcolm X was notably effective in using the economic role of Jewish middlemen as a vehicle for undermining the political legitimacy of Jewish white liberals. No doubt, ethnic stereotypes of Jews were mobilized in these polemics. But, I am suggesting, their mobilization was determined by a quite specific constellation of class, racial, and political forces.

From this perspective—and not only this perspective—the question becomes: How does such a complex play of forces and issues get reduced to the encapsulated asymmetry of Blacks and Jews?

The answer to this question is essentially political.[9] Blacks and Jews were uneasily held together by the tradition of emancipatory struggle that culminated in the civil rights movement. When that movement came to an end, the matrix of Black-Jewish cooperation dissolved.

The great accomplishments of the civil rights movement (properly so called) were the passage of the Civil Rights Act of 1964 and the Voting Rights Act of 1965. As their names indicate, these enactments concerned social and political rights, that is, the rights of citizens in a democratic society. They did not address economic and class issues. Which is also to say, they did not directly address the issues of greatest pragmatic concern to the black masses. Beginning in 1964, however—in part as a result of spontaneous ghetto insurrections—the movement was reoriented around mass interests. This had three major consequences. First, black nationalism, especially in the form articulated by Malcolm X, increasingly constituted the ideological matrix of black liberation politics. Second, in its most radical form, black nationalism involved a "black awakening in capitalist America" (Allen 1970). Put simply, black mass interests could not be realized within the limits of a capitalist system. If they were to be realized, the system would have to be transformed—hence the emergence of revolutionary black nationalism. Third, revolutionary black nationalism easily passed over into Third World internationalism. With the war in Vietnam on the one side and the emergence of Africa from colonial rule on the other, one could plausibly conceptualize an international power structure (white racist, capitalist, and imperialist) as the common enemy of oppressed Third World people.

Revolutionary black nationalism did allow for alliances with white people, but—unlike the civil rights movement—not on the basis of Christian or Jewish religious affiliation. To the contrary: insofar as the emergent movement had a theological orientation, it was Islamic. This partially reflected the influence of Elijah Muhammad's Nation of Islam. But Muhammad apart, Islam was viewed as an African and Third World religion. It was taken to be the religion of the colonized. It breathed the spirit of rebellion. Christianity, by contrast, was viewed as the religion of the European or American colonizer. It functioned hegemonically to pacify the colonized native. This is not to say that the struggle was defined in religious terms. When these terms were introduced, however, they precluded the previous patterns of interfaith collaboration.

From within this political-religious perspective, the Jewish occupation of Palestine, with the subsequent establishment of the state of Israel, was necessarily viewed as an instance of imperialism. Whatever its relationship to the Holocaust, it functioned as an outpost of European and American interests. Analogically, Israelis were white, Palestinians were black. Consequently, if American Jews identified themselves with Israeli interests and actions, they were now triply—as white, as imperialist, and as Jewish—on the other side of the political line from the leadership of the black revolutionary movement.

Although the revolutionary black nationalist movement faded away in the early 1970s, black nationalism and Third World internationalism lived on as ideological tendencies. Needless to say, not all black people identified themselves with these orientations. Nor were all American Jews uncritical supporters of Israel. And at the local level, alliances between liberal Blacks and liberal Jews sometimes endured.[10] But, in the absence of a politically liberal, integrated, middle-class social movement, the terms of Black-Jewish discourse were increasingly set by Jewish nationalists (Zionists), on the one side, and black nationalists, on the other. Within this structure, Jews who were not nationalists tended to become invisible, while Blacks who were not nationalists were forced into being either critics of or apologists for black nationalism.

How, more concretely, did the Israeli-Palestinian conflict come to structure Black-Jewish interaction?[11]

In 1979 Andrew Young, U.S. ambassador to the UN, had a brief meeting with a member of the PLO. He was summarily forced to resign his position. His resignation was widely and, I believe, correctly seen to be the result of pressure from the Israel lobby in U.S. politics. Jesse Jackson expressed the views of many African Americans when he commented: "When there wasn't much decency Jews were willing to share decency. But when there is power they don't want to share power" (Kaufman 1988, 233).

Later that year Jackson traveled to the Middle East. Prime Minister Begin refused to meet with him; Arafat embraced him. Thereafter he was the object of unremitting hostility and attack by many Jews—including highly orchestrated attacks from the Anti-Defamation League during the months leading up to his 1984 presidential campaign. Jackson was publically restrained in his response to these attacks, but let his irritation show in an off-the-record comment to a black reporter: "Complaining about the attention his positions on the Middle East were getting, Jackson told the reporter, 'All hymie wants to talk about is Israel; everytime you go to hymietown, that's all they want to talk about' " (ibid., 256).

The public outrage was immediate, the provocations that led up to the comment were completely ignored. Jews could criticize Jackson, but he could not criticize them. Humiliatingly, he was forced to bury his anger and apologize.

Jackson's friend Minister Louis Farrakhan of the Nation of Islam was not similarly politically constrained. He said what many black people thought: "I say to the Jewish people who may not like our brother, when you attack him you attack the millions who are lining up with him. You are attacking all of us. If you harm this brother, I warn you in the name of Allah, this will be the last one you do harm" (258). The ADL reacted by accusing Farrakhan of "beerhall demagoguery," an obvious allusion to Hitler (Magida 1996, 146). Farrakhan responded to the insult in its own terms: "The Jews don't like Farrakhan, so they call me Hitler. Well, that's a good name. Hitler was a very great man. He wasn't great for me as a black person, but he was a great German. . . . He rose up Germany from nothing. Well, in a sense you could say there's similarity in that we are raising our people up from nothing" (Kaufman, 231).

If I am correct, the terms of Black-Jewish conflict were crystallized in this series of events. Broader social forces lie behind them. But it was at this time that Farrakhan became identified with black antisemitism and so took his place at the center of Black-Jewish discourse.

From their own perspective, the Jewish critics of Jackson and Farrakhan were defending Israel in the Middle East and warding off the threat of antisemitism in the United States. But viewed from a black perspective, the critics were attempting to tell black people what they could or could not do or say: "You [black people] are not permitted to address the plight of the Palestinians or reply in kind to Jewish insult and attack." It is hardly surprising that the response to this arrogance of power would be, "who in the world do you think you are?" But when Farrakhan responded in this quite predictable fashion (i.e., his first comment in defense of Jackson), he was accused of being a Hitler.

No doubt, at that juncture Farrakhan had the option of not escalating the controversy. He could have rejected this characterization as ridiculous and let it go at that. But there is a certain logic to his responding as he did. In a private conversation with Arthur Magida, he said: "Jews got a hell of a nerve asking me to apologize. . . . Jews are too arrogant, too proud of their power. They want everyone to bow down to them, and I ain't bowing down to nothin' or nobody but God" (Magida, 150). And in a 1994 speech he commented on the way in which accusations of antisemitism can be used to silence criticism: "Nobody talks to the Jews the way they should be talked to. When somebody says something that might upset the Jews, they say, 'Don't say that because it's anti-Semitic.' So you run up a tree and shut your mouth. But Farrakhan ain't running nowhere" (ibid., 153).

In other words, the logic behind Farrakhan's Hitler remarks might be articulated this way: "Jews are forever invoking the Holocaust to direct attention away from their own use and abuse of power. Mention Hitler and the Holocaust, and critics are forced into silence. Well, just for once this tactic isn't going to work. I am not fooled or intimidated by your accusations. You want to call me Hitler, then call me Hitler." The deployment of this logic does not mean that Farrakhan is not also antisemitic and inflamatory. But Farrakhan is who he is. If we (white people, white Jews) are genuinely interested in dialogue, then it behooves us to focus on the situational logic as well as the manifest content of his remark. To say it once more: When Israel enters the picture, Jews attempt to control the discursive space. Blacks, believing that they have the right to think and speak for themselves, struggle against being controlled in this fashion. For them, the situation is all too familiar: Jews are white people and, as with all other white people, "when there is power they don't want to share power." Hence, when Jews don't recognize that power is the central issue and when they reduce black self-assertion to black antisemitism, meaningful discussion is precluded.

Here is a more general way of approaching the matter. Black people in the United States must, in their own interest, continue to struggle against white racism. Black nationalists like Farrakhan are vital to that struggle, both because they speak to the needs of the black masses and because they are often willing to speak bluntly to the powerful. Jews are white people— very white indeed, when whiteness is measured in terms of economic and social class. But they also have a distinguishable religious-ethnic identity and a religious-racial past. Their affiliation with Israel signifies the Holocaust and, more generally, the Jewish experience of racial oppression. Hence, when Israel enters the discursive picture, the ghosts of the Jewish racial past walk again, and the Jewish ethnic present fades from view. Jews are mobilized into a fight-flight group, with its accompanying fantasies. Black people then find themselves behind yet another veil (Du Bois): The Jewish racial past renders the black racial present invisible.

Let's take up one example of how this process plays out. As is well known, Cornel West is one of the leading black public intellectuals of his generation. His politics are broadly social democratic, but he is also notable for his attempt to narrow the gap between the separatist and assimilationist positions in black cultural life. Michael Lerner could also be characterized as a social democrat and certainly as a progressive. He is also what might be termed a Jewish public intellectual, in the sense that his politics and his sense of Jewish identity are fundamentally intertwined. He is not, however, a hard-core Jewish nationalist. Given these features of the two men, the

Lerner-West "dialogue on race, religion and culture in America" (1996) can be read as a latter-day version or as a remnant of the so-called Black-Jewish alliance of the civil rights movement.

The published record of this dialogue contains various points of mutual respect and understanding. But mutual recognition ends when it comes to black nationalism and Louis Farrakhan. Lerner begins with the belief that Farrakhan is a "racist dog" and a "pathological anti-Semite" (191) who is to be judged on the basis of his attitude toward the Jews. West, he claims, should condemn Farrakhan and disassociate himself from him. West, with remarkable patience, attempts to justify his interaction with Farrakhan, and to offer Lerner another image of him. West notes first that there is a difference between black mistrust of whites and Jews and Jewish mistrust of Blacks: "We have a history of white supremacy and oppression. There is not a history of Black supremacy and oppression" (188). Black fears of white people are historically warranted. Except in local instances, white Jewish fears of black people aren't historically warranted. Hence, West seems to be implying that Farrakhan must be seen in context. And, in context and from the perspective of black people, Farrahkhan certainly isn't a "racist dog, but a xenophobic spokesperson when it comes to dealing with Jewish humanity—but who, in his own way, loves Black folks deeply, and that love is what we see first" (191). Moreover, Farrakhan expresses the black rage that grows out of white racist oppression: "What is at the core of Farrakhan, though, is a manifestation of Black rage articulated in a bold and fearless message vis à vis the white power structure" (203).

West has here articulated three of the core elements of the black nationalist position: black nationalism is a response to white nationalism, that is, to the white racist oppression of black people; it affirms the value of black people; and it directs situationally appropriate anger toward the white power structure. In the latter two regards, it helps to transform identification with the oppressor into racial self-identification and self-destructive aggression into self-productive aggression (Wolfenstein 1981/1993b).

But Lerner will have none of it. He rejects West's historically grounded analysis in favor of paranoid fantasies:

> Someday in the future, when ruling elites in this country have decided that the way to maintain power is to manipulate anti-Semitic sentiment amongst both Blacks and whites to deflect their anger against the system, this guy can play the role of being a representative of Black outrage against Jews. In that circumstance, Farrakhan would become, not the leader like Hitler, but an important element in an anti-semitic, fascist front in America. (205)

Lerner produces two other fantasies along similar lines: America becomes dominated by German and Japanese interests, and Farrakhan is used to deflect rage against the ruling classes onto Jews (205); Farrakhan stirs up

black ghetto antisemitism, which spreads to and infects white youth (208).
What is striking about all three fantasies is: (1) that they invert the facts
of American experience, in which black people, not Jews, have played the
role of racial scapegoat and (2) that they mirror with great precision the
experience of Jews in Nazi Germany.

West responds to Lerner's fantasies empathically and rationally. He does
not deny the historical basis for Lerner's anxieties, only the plausibility of
the scenarios he has articulated. Blacks simply don't have the power, he
insists, that these fantasies assume. To the contrary: Black people are the
ones who have been the victims of the powerful in this country. But try as
he will, West is unable to break through Lerner's disavowal of present-day
reality. Rational argument, as Freud recognized long ago, is powerless
against emotionally driven psychological defenses.

I believe that the Lerner-West interaction speaks to more general tendencies. If so, we might summarize its lessons as follows.

Many Jews carry with them, in their individual and/or collective memories, the traumatic experience of antisemitic persecution that culminated
in the Holocaust. This remembered trauma creates a hypersensitivity to
anything resembling antisemitism—whether or not antisemitism is the core
issue and whether or not there is a real danger of persecution. When,
therefore, this sensitive area is approached, group psychological defenses
take over and complex issues are reduced rapidly to a binary Us versus
Them. In this simple splitting of the non-Jewish world into friend or foe,
the possibility of thinking through, evaluating, and differentiating among
criticisms is foreclosed. Criticism directed at white racism, justified criticism
of specifically Jewish actions, and statements reflecting religious-ethnic prejudice are (1) collapsed into each other and (2) reduced to Nazi-style, racial
antisemitism. Consequently, blacks find themselves in a discursive situation
in which meaningful communication is impossible.

For black people, this situation is distressingly familiar. It's been over
thirty years since Malcolm X pointedly analyzed the ways in which communication between Blacks and Whites is falsified when the former say
only what the latter want to hear. White people, he argued, demanded that
black people provide them with a mirror of their benevolence. Many black
people felt constrained to comply with the demand. Honest communication
required, however, that black people break the mirror and speak plainly
about the evils of white racism.

I trust the continuity is evident. White Jews demand that black people
reflect back to them their essential goodness. Blacks are to be grateful for
Jewish contributions to black liberation, mindful of the horrors of the Jewish racial past—and silent about Jewish insensitivities and abuses of power.
Once again, therefore, honest communication requires a lifting of a discursive veil.

If Cornel West can be seen as an heir of W. E. B. DuBois and the other great humanist leaders of the black liberation movement, Farrakhan is the heir of Marcus Garvey, Elijah Muhammad, and Malcolm X. There is more than a little irony in this lineage. Farrakhan, who was recruited into the Nation of Islam by Malcolm X, was also one of those who condemned Malcolm X to death. And, speaking personally, I much prefer Malcolm X to Farrakhan as a messenger of black nationalism. Malcolm X, while never compromising on his criticism of white racism and his affirmation of black people, outgrew the mystigogy, biologism and, to a certain extent, the patriarchalism of Muhammad's teachings. He was a shrewd critic of capitalism, colonialism, and neocolonialism; and he was unswervingly dedicated to the liberation of all black people. Farrakhan is mystigogical, biologistic, patriarchal, and homophobic. He is also what Robert Allen (1970) characterizes as a bourgeois black nationalist. But like his black nationalist forefathers, Farrakhan effectively articulates the strivings of, especially, the black masses. Hence, his influence on Blacks in the inner cities, on black mass culture generally, and hip hop music in particular.

At one point in his attack on Farrakhan, Lerner claims that the black leader "misdirects anger toward a safe target, rather than the ruling elites, who are the real source of our problems" (203). This ignores the fact that Jews are overrepresented, not underrepresented, among the ruling elites, so that—from this perspective—Jews are part of the problem rather than part of the solution. And it is not clear to me that Farrakhan *substitutes* the one for the other. But I would agree that focusing on Jews *as Jews* is a deflection away from the central issue and that black interests are not advanced when the Nation of Islam promotes the *Protocols of the Elders of Zion* and other mystifications of Jewish power. Whatever the cause of these political choices, they do play into Jewish paranoia and thereby help to keep the sideshow going.

Yet it would be a mistake to reduce black nationalism to the Jewish question. As already noted, fundamentally black nationalism is about selfhood, identity, and pride. In these terms, Farrakhan's Million Man March was profoundly affirmative. As Angela Davis, bell hooks, and others pointed out, it was highly problematical from the perspective of gender. But it was simultaneously an important statement of national identity, as well as an attempt to address—if only symbolically—the continuing and pathologizing effects of white racism on black people, black men in particular.

The tendency of black people to identify with the oppressor is one of these pathologizing effects. For this disease, there is no more effective remedy than black nationalism. Black nationalism does involve fighting fire with fire. Group psychological defenses are mobilized to defend against group psychological intrusions; and this defensive process is not without its risks, including the distracting mystification of Jewish power. It is quite pointless, however, to wish that things could be different. Only if things actually *were* different, that is, only if the mass of black people were no longer victimized by white racism, would it be realistic to hope for a fading away of group psychological states of mind. And, unfortunately, the prospects for the black masses are increasingly bleak. One cannot anticipate, therefore, that black nationalism will either disappear or lose its group psychological edge.

The last point can be stated in nonpsychoanalytic terms. Sometimes black nationalists are accused of being essentialists. They transform the cultural fact of being black into an essence or substance, it is claimed, into a kind of racial thing-in-itself. In so doing they are mirroring the essentialism of white racism.

I'm not sure that essences are always figments of the metaphysical imagination, nor am I convinced that we can live without them. Be that as it may, in the American racial situation it is evident that white racism does the essentializing. That is, racialization (psychologically speaking) results from the group psychological dynamics depicted above. White people racialize black people. Counterracialization, that is, an affirmation of blackness, then becomes necessary for psychical survival.

Is it asking too much that Jews, whose essentialism contributed so much to their own survival, make the attempt to see themselves from the perspective of their essentialized racial other?

I have tried to provide an historical and theoretical context for the analysis of contemporary Black-Jewish conflict. Seen through my analytical lenses, its significance is reduced and our attention is drawn back to directly racial issues. But what, pragmatically, can we say about the relationships of Blacks and Jews? First, the aim of a renewed Black-Jewish alliance is unrealistic. It is no longer sustained by a situational play of power and interests. Second, as long as Jews allow their attitudes and actions in the American present to be determined by their persecution in the European past—and as long as past persecution is used to cover over present power—they will consistently overstate and misunderstand black criticism of white Jews. And, third, productive interracial discourse requires taking black nationalism seriously. Consequently, we might be grateful to people like Cornel West, who work so hard to keep the lines of communication open for all the involved parties.

NOTES

1. The idea of Jewish ethnicity is not unproblematical. See pages 67–68.
2. In what follows, the reader should be able to tell by context whether white Jews or Jews more generally are being discussed.
3. As long as the differences signified by these terms are kept in mind, the terms themselves are a secondary matter.

4. As to these last two categories: just because they have moved away from Jewish identity does not mean that they will cease to be categorized by others as Jews.

5. One could broaden this category to include all Jews who hold progressive/ liberal racial views. But people who fall into the category of weakly self-identified Jews would be likely to object that their liberalism and racial progressivism is not distinctively Jewish, but rather broadly humanitarian, etc. They would not, to put it another way, be likely participants in Black-Jewish dialogue, but rather in Black-White dialogue.

6. In *Victims of Democracy* (1981, 1993a, 184–91) I argue that there is a shadow economy in the United States, class structured like the legitimate economy, with the lumpen-proletariat at the bottom and corporate crime syndicates at the top.

7. We will add American Jews to the model below.

8. For subsequent elaborations of Bion's analysis see Alford (1994) and Lawrence, Bain, and Gould (1996).

9. The recent discussion of Black-Jewish relations has focused on the slide from uneasy cooperation in the 1950s and early 1960s, to mutual suspicion and even outright antagonism in the 1980s and 1990s (see Kaufman 1988; Berman 1994). My own interpretation of these events is close to those of Clayborne Carson (1994) and Andrew Hacker (1994). For a notably fair-minded analysis of Black-Jewish relations in the early 1970s, see Labovitz (1975). On black attitudes toward Jews, see Cohen (1988) and Locke (1994).

10. This was notably true in Los Angeles. See Sonenshein (1993).

11. A more complete analysis would have to include the question of affirmative action as well as that of Israel and the Palestinians.

REFERENCES

Alford, C. Fred. 1994. *Group Psychology and Political Theory*. New Haven, Conn.: Yale University Press.

Allen, Robert. 1970. *Black Awakening in Capitalist America*. Garden City, N.Y.: Anchor Books.

Berman, Paul, ed. 1994. *Blacks and Jews: Alliances and Arguments*. New York: Delacorte Press.

Bion, W. R. 1959. *Experiences in Groups*. New York: Basic Books.

Carson, Clayborne. 1994. "The Politics of Relations between African-Americans and Jews." In *Blacks and Jews: Alliances and Arguments*, edited by Paul Berman. New York: Delacorte Press.

Cohen, Kitty O. 1988. *Black-Jewish Relations: The View from the State Capitols*. New York: Cornwall Books.

Du Bois, W. E. B. 1903, 1990. *The Souls of Black Folks*. New York: Vintage Books.

Freud, Sigmund. 1921. *The Standard Edition of the Complete Psychological Works of Sigmund Freud. Volume 18: Group Psychology and the Analysis of the Ego*. Translated by James Strachey. London: Hogarth Press.

Hacker, Andrew. 1994. "Jewish Racism, Black Anti-Semitism." In *Blacks and Jews: Alliances and Arguments*, edited by Paul Berman. New York: Delacorte Press.

Halisi, C. D. 1996. "Dividing Lines: Indigenous Polarities in African-American Thought." Paper presented at the 1996 meetings of the Western Political Science Association.

Jordan, Winthrop. 1969. *White Over Black: American Attitudes Toward the Negro, 1550–1812*. Baltimore: Pelican Books.

Kaufman, Jonathan. 1988. *Broken Alliance: The Turbulent Times Between Blacks and Jews in America*. New York: Charles Scribner's Sons.

Labovitz, Sherman. 1975. *Attitudes toward Blacks among Jews: Historical Antecedents and Current Concerns*. San Francisco: R and E Research Associates.

Lawrence, W. Gordon, Alastair Bain, and Laurence Gould. 1996. "The Fifth Basic Assumption." *Free Associations* 6, no. 37.

Lerner, Michael, and Cornel West. 1996. *Jews and Blacks: A Dialogue on Race, Religion, and Culture in America*. New York: A Plume Book.

Locke, Hubert. 1994. *The Black Anti-Semitism Controversy: Protestant Views and Perspectives*. London: Associated University Presses.

Magida, Arthur. 1996. *Prophet of Rage: A Life of Louis Farrakhan and His Nation*. New York: Basic Books.

Sonenshein, Raphael. 1993. *Politics in Black and White: Race and Power in Los Angeles*. Princeton, N.J.: Princeton University Press.

Wolfenstein, E. Victor. 1981, 1993a. *The Victims of Democracy: Malcolm X and the Black Revolution*. New York: Guilford Press.

———. 1993b. *Psychoanalytic-Marxism: Groundwork*. New York: Guilford Press.

5

Black Myths and Black Madness: Is Black Antisemitism Different?

MORTIMER OSTOW

The recent eruption of black antisemitism has surprised and shocked many Jews. Examining the situation at this point with an understanding of the psychodynamics of antisemitism (Ostow 1996), the observer finds little reason for surprise. The conditions for the development of antisemitism in the black community have been growing in recent years, and one should have predicted the current situation.

Accusations of Jewish misconduct toward blacks have elicited incredulousness and dismay because of their obvious falsity and outrageous nature. However antisemitic accusations have always been false. What distinguishes antisemitism from competitiveness or rivalry has been its reliance upon fantasy. In fact the more fantastic the accusation, the more readily it is believed by the greatest part of the population that is targeted for antisemitic propaganda.

That Jews, more than any other segment of the American population, have been more friendly to blacks and have tried, sometimes at great cost, to support their demands for fair treatment, should, in retrospect, not have been expected to deter antisemitism. The history of antisemitism offers a number of examples of shifting attitudes toward Jews. Not only do former allies become enemies, but former enemies sometimes become allies. Evidently the dissemination by blacks of antisemitic canards has been intended, not only to demonstrate the dangerousness of Jews, but also to break the bonds of friendship and even appreciation that had existed hitherto.

Antisemitism as expressed by individuals differs from the same phenomenon expressed by groups, and I shall present them separately.

Since Louis Farrakhan is the best known, if not virtually the quintessential black antisemite, it will be of some interest to examine his antisemitism
and its relation to what we may infer about his mentality from published
statements. I shall base my remarks primarily upon a perceptive appraisal
of the man, his attitudes, conduct, and influence, by Professor Henry Louis
Gates Jr., that appeared in the *New Yorker* of April 29–May 6, 1996 (116–
31), and upon Arthur Magida's biography, *Prophet of Rage* (1996).

Gates registers his surprise at encountering some paradoxes. At the outset
he observes that his subject is intelligent, curious, and charming, and yet
"deeply strange." He is educated and enlightened, yet credulous; he believes
that he has experienced true revelations from a supernatural source. He
credits bizarre myths about the origin of the human race and that white
people were created by the genetic experiments of a wicked scientist called
Yakub seven thousand years ago, so that whites are really blacks that are
drained of color and humanity. This myth had been created by Farrakhan's
predecessor, Elijah Muhammad, and is accepted by Farrakhan. "Personally," said Farrakhan, "I believe that Yakub is not a mythical figure—he
is a very real scientist." Farrakhan expresses great and presumably sincere
admiration for Jews, both individuals and the community; and yet he contends that there are very wise scoundrels among the Jews whom he feels
obligated to condemn not only as scoundrels but as Jews. His paranoid
myths about Jews alternate with expressions of admiration and affection
and wishes for reconciliation. Indeed, he expresses desire for reconciliation
between blacks and whites and between blacks and Jews and yet he does
not alter his belligerent stand that he illustrates by pugilistic metaphors and
by assuming pugilistic postures.

I assume that Gates has not studied the psychology of antisemitism. If
he had, he would recognize that these paradoxes are commonly found
among antisemites, that they betray strong ambivalence. Gates calls Farrakhan's preoccupation with Jews, both positive and negative, a "psychological obsession." He quotes Farrakhan: "But it's like I am locked in a
struggle. It's like both of us got a hold on each other, and each of us is
filled with electricity. I can't let them go and they can't let me go." Parenthetically, I believe that the Jewish community would be happy "to let"
Farrakhan "go" if he would stop harassing them. We shall explore these
paradoxes.

True antisemitism can be distinguished from dislike of individual Jews
or even small groups of them or even hostility or attacks upon them. Intergroup rivalries have always been common among neighboring communities. Antisemitism is characterized by the following circumstances and
conditions. The antisemite expresses hostility to all Jews as a worldwide
community even though he may retain his friendship with individual Jews.

Antisemites themselves will sometimes call attention to this paradox. The true Jewish miscreants are a mythic community while the Jews who are targeted for abuse or death are the very real Jews who are visible and available.

Briefly, I contend that antisemitism appears when there is a need for a principle of evil to account for serious distress. The distress may arise from either an external source or from disturbance of the normal process of affect regulation. Nevertheless, whatever the actual source of the distress, most of us, and especially antisemites, attribute it simultaneously to two sources. One is a visible source, which may indeed be real. The second is a virtual source, an ultimate source, a cosmic principle that accounts for the first. Generally, the idea of a principle of evil is invoked to explain the feeling that the individual is separated from his God, that a malignant influence has come between them, and that he no longer enjoys the radiance of God's beneficence. Usually a myth is then contrived to bridge the gap between the real and the mythic. The myth assigns the cosmic source of evil to a visible enemy, an enemy who may indeed exert a real adverse influence, but who more often than not is quite innocent. In 1348 it was known that the plague was spread by contagion and that Jews suffered along with everyone else, but yet the Jews were accused of poisoning the wells. Since the virtual enemy cannot be attacked, the attack is displaced to the visible but mythic source of distress. This mythic enemy, in the past two thousand years in Christendom, has been the Jew. Let me develop this argument in somewhat greater detail.

Usually, antisemitic accusations partake of the mythical. Classical anti-semitic canards include accusations that the Jews kill Christian children because they require their blood for their Passover observance; that Jews poison wells or food stores; that Jewish doctors deliberately kill Christian patients and especially children; that Jewish bankers have formed a con-spiracy to seize control of all the world's currency and gold in order to achieve political power. Behind these myths the individual who entertains them apprehends unconsciously and dimly that he is threatened or beset by some cosmic evil. How can he account for it? Many ancient and me-dieval Christians saw Satan or a low-level devil as the adversary, and even today, many individuals who would reject the idea of superstition, still cross their fingers or knock on wood in order to disarm or frighten away the devil. However, since the Christian Bible and the early Church fathers associated the Pharisaic Jews with Satan, Jews and devils were subsequently associated in the minds of credulous Christians. In graphic representations, Jews were represented with features of the devil such as horns, hooves, and tails, and conversely, devils were represented with a large, hooked nose and the stigmatizing special hats and badges required of Jews in the Middle Ages. This accusation that the Jews are satanic, that they were responsible for the crucifixion of Jesus, that they frustrate God's purposes, has been promoted as a basic myth of Christianity for two millennia. The ultimate basis of antisemitism is the identification of Jews as the source of cosmic evil. Since cosmic evil can find expression in any number of ways, the specific reasons given for antisemitism may vary widely, depending upon local circumstances.

Often the accusation relates to a real conflict of interest between the antisemites and the Jews, such as business rivalry, envy of success, envy of Jewish communal cohesion. The enmity based upon this competition differs from ordinary intergroup rivalry by virtue of the sense of cosmic hostility that is assumed to lie behind the real and immediate danger. That being the case, the truth of the accusation becomes irrelevant. To those who are trying to deal with what they perceive as a cosmic evil, veridicality proves nothing; the lie reinforces the validity of fantasy in general, and of the antisemitic fantasy in particular.

In some instances, the power of the belief that cosmic evil is attached to Jews, is exploited for political or other irrelevant purposes. In Russia, at the turn of the century, royalists associated the Jews with revolutionaries, and arguing from the *Protocols of the Elders of Zion* that had been created for political use, they promoted antisemitism to encourage popular hostility to anti-czarist forces. In his by now well-known op-ed piece in the *New York Times* (July 20, 1992) Gates describes the use and exploitation of antisemitism by black misleaders, but he does not acknowledge its ultimate sources and causes. To attribute antisemitism to a specific opportunistic exploitation of it or to a specific conflict of interest or a specific experience of disadvantage attributed to Jews, is to mistake the precipitant for the underlying cause.

But these considerations do not tell us what it is that generates this sense of cosmic evil rather than simply an appropriate feeling of distress or pain or unhappiness. In the absence of antisemitic agitation, antisemitism varies in prevalence and intensity. In a psychoanalytic study involving consideration of ten cases, we found that the only personality characteristic that seemed possibly connected with antisemitism was hostility.

It seems to me that what is important here is not the issue of the presence or the absence of distressing circumstances but rather each individual's personal response to them. Usually, in the absence of really severe stress, most people accommodate to whatever conditions they are compelled to endure. Increase in the level of stress will usually elicit a sense of increased misery and a response that is reasonably appropriate and characteristic of the individual. But sooner or later, adaptation occurs, and each individual reverts to his or her own characteristic mood despite a continuing feeling of injustice and perhaps momentary reflections of despair.

There are some people, however, whose mood is poorly regulated so that in the presence of discomfort of almost any degree, and especially increments of discomfort, they respond with mood disturbance such as inappropriate depression, or paradoxically inappropriate euphoria, or intense anger. Depression and euphoria, inappropriate in sign or degree, impair the function of the individual himself. But anger seeks a victim, an individual or group or force held responsible for the pain and available for revenge. While the immediate trigger is, from our point of view, nonspecific, it elicits in these people not an appropriate measured response, but rather a fury born of the inappropriate anger that has been generated by a defective mood regulating mechanism. The anger is displaced, but even when it is not, its intensity betrays its origin, not in veridical reality, but in misapprehended reality or fantasy.

We all know people whom we encounter in our daily life who respond to even relatively slight frustration with excessively strong responses and others who maintain a level of surly irritability under circumstances that those around them are able to tolerate with some degree of equanimity. That mood (or affect) dysregulation is responsible, can be demonstrated by the administration of antidepression medication; the inappropriate anger will usually disappear promptly. It is such individuals who are most likely to seek and to find and target victims in a paranoid way. And these individuals are susceptible to antisemitic propaganda and are likely to espouse and promote it.

According to Friedman (1995), low-level endemic antisemitism did not appear prominently among blacks before recent decades. In the South, both before and after the Civil War, Jews and blacks expressed no special antagonism to each other. Some Jews played active roles in the abolitionist movement, probably out of a sense of justice and morality. But many who did not go that far, were more friendly and generous as merchants dealing with the black community than other whites. By and large, antisemitism was not especially active among middle-class Southern whites, but Jews were always careful to avoid arousing hostility, which was apparently latent in some segments of the population, not far beneath the surface, as the lynching of Leo Frank in 1915 in Georgia revealed. Some blacks, under the influence of church teachings, hated Jews as deicides, but were no more antisemitic than the whites who taught them this wisdom. Nevertheless, as is often the case, suspicion, envy, and hostility were mixed with admiration and identification. Although Jews as storekeepers sometimes earned the gratitude of blacks for treating them better then whites did, when some evidence to justify antisemitism was needed, is was easy to find fault with the individual with whom one traded.

To this point I have tried to present the psychodynamics of individual antisemitism. There is no evidence that black antisemitism, on an individual basis, that is, on a low-level endemic basis, differs from white antisemitism; in fact it seems to have been learned from whites by a virtual transmission of white antisemitic myths.

Malignant antisemitism is group antisemitism. The term used in Russia for mob attacks on Jews is *pogrom*. It is *pogrom* antisemitism that is deadly.

Not all antisemitic groups are fundamentalist in nature, and not all fundamentalist groups are antisemitic, but the paradigmatic antisemitic group is the fundamentalist group. Fundamentalist groups usually exhibit the following characteristics. The members of the group tend to imitate and identify each other. They wear similar clothing suggesting a uniform. They adopt similar gestures, mannerisms, and rules of etiquette. They behave like clones of each other, more like ants than people. They assume identical forms of verbal expression. They also subscribe to a common scripture, usually religious, but not necessarily. They all subscribe to their own idiosyncratic interpretation of their scripture, rejecting even classical and traditional exegesis. They carefully distinguish themselves from the community within which they arose and avoid and disparage it vigorously. I have described this position as *zealous separatism*. They acknowledge the deity of the religion to which they adhere as modified or limited by their own doctrine, and they defer to the group's leaders. Some of these leaders are genuine; others have been unmasked as frauds.

Fundamentalists seem to become anxious in the presence of personal freedom: freedom from rules, conventions and laws, freedom for themselves and for others. Sexual freedom is especially troublesome. They can permit sexual activity only under the most conventional and regulated circumstances. When their beliefs, conventions, or practices are threatened, they can become violent. They tend to become violent even in the absence of such threat, merely when they feel they have become strong enough to impose their organization on others. Their doctrines are held not merely with vigor, but they are held with a certainty that is ordinarily reserved only for the multiplication table. Inappropriate certainty may be pathognomonic of a fundamentalist position. Everyone outside the group is considered the enemy, whether heretic or infidel, but often one group is considered the special, unredeemable enemy. Among most Christian and Moslem fundamentalists, the intolerable enemy is the Jew, although nonfundamentalists of their own religion, race, or community are seldom spared. Among Jewish fundamentalists, it is the nonfundamentalist Jew who is the enemy, whether secular or orthodox. The Christian or Moslem fundamentalist feels as though his universe is contaminated by the encounter with the Jew. My description applies to groups that can be recognized in the three principal monotheistic religions. I doubt that they look different in others.

The reader will recognize that this description applies to many of the religious cults and sects that we encounter in the modern world. Some militant groups like the self-styled Christian Patriots of the American Northwest, and the Nation of Islam, can be recognized as paradigmatically fundamentalist; that is, the description applies to them precisely. Others, like lynch mobs in the South, or Russian peasant mobs that executed *po-groms*, or the black mobs of Crown Heights who murdered Yankel Rosen-baum in the summer of 1991, were temporary, and though drawn from a population relatively homogeneous for social and political attitude, never-theless did not possess the organization and discipline characteristic of fun-damentalist groups. However, even in the absence of these qualities, the zealous separatism of these mobs expressed itself in a murderous xenopho-bia, usually antisemitic.

What can we say about the psychodynamics of these groups? I have to present here, however briefly, my understanding of the dynamic that I have called the apocalyptic complex. This is a product of the process of regu-lating mood or affect. In most individuals, the regulation is carried out precisely so that we see no evidence of it. However, in the patient with affect disorder such as manic depressive illness or borderline personality disorder or attention deficit disorder, we see relatively frequent oscillation between "high" and "low" moods. We see the alternation sometimes in waking life but almost always in the dreams of such individuals. Modern pharmacological therapy, by means of which we treat these disorders cur-rently, functions by influencing the homeostatic mood regulating mecha-nism. I associate this mood fluctuation with the apocalyptic complex because it reminds one of the phenomenon of apocalypse, a kind of relig-ious writing that first appeared in the Western world about 200 B.C.E. It anticipates a correction of injustice by means of alternation of episodes of death and rebirth in one or more sequences, usually associated with a rev-elation of some kind. The Revelation of John of the Christian Bible is known as the prototypic apocalypse. It envisages the utter destruction of Babylon, that is, Rome, and the vindication and rescue of the Christian saints.

I recognize three types of apocalypse. On the individual level, the first type of apocalyptic process is seen in depressed patients who expect death and hope to be rescued, reborn. The second type is encountered among patients who are too euphoric, that is too "high." Without realizing why, they anticipate a punitive downfall that they usually blame on some enemy in a paranoid way, in accordance with the process that I described above. The third type finds expression in an outburst of fury that responds to the conscious or unconscious perception that they are becoming depressed or that they are emerging from depression.

A parallel classification can be discerned in the group apocalyptic phe-nomenon. The first type can be recognized in suffering and demoralized, despairing populations that can only hope for rescue. We find hopeful prophecies of this kind in the various classical prophetic books of the Bible. The second type, expressed in Revelation, threatens the destruction of the triumphant "wicked empire" and vindication of the Christian saints. It is the third type that is relevant to our argument here. As is the case with individuals, the group that feels itself under threat, responds with immoderate fury. They attribute the threat to what they perceive as their cosmic enemy whom they proceed to attack. However the apocalyptic community organizes itself as a fundamentalist group with all the characteristics that I enumerated above. The struggle is imagined as a cosmic struggle between good and evil, between God and Satan, between Christ and the anti-Christ, between order and chaos, between the Christian or Moslem faithful and the Jew.

Black antisemitism as we see it now is group antisemitism, achieving its most malicious expression in the fundamentalist Nation of Islam. Murray Friedman (1995) writes that even before the Nation of Islam acquired a significant following, the Student Nonviolent Coordinating Committee (SNCC) had become increasingly radicalized in the early 1960s, the more militant members seeing themselves as "a band of brothers sharing a life of monastic simplicity and commitment." In 1967, at the onset of the Six Day War, SNCC openly attacked Israel and supported the Palestinians, thereby terminating the black-Jewish radical movement in favor of a black nationalist model. In other words, it adopted a classical fundamentalist position of zealous separatism.

In recent decades, black racialism and separatism have acquired many of the characteristics of fundamentalism. The members of this separatist group have displayed, to an increasing degree, the characteristic zealous—in fact belligerent—separatism. They have created their own set of myths. They misrepresent in a negative way the previous black-Jewish alliance and its accomplishments and accuse Jews of persecuting blacks and other Third World people, for example, by finding pseudoscholarly "evidence" that they had been the major movers in the black slave trade, a canard of major proportions. They contrive a mythical black history that has become a kind of scripture for the masses, alongside and quite the opposite of a more objective history that, I suspect, is studied only by serious scholars. The purpose of these myths is not only to legitimize their appropriation of dignity and power, but also to destroy any sense of attachment to the Jews specifically and to whites in general. They have designated whites and especially Jews as their cosmic enemy.

Many nationalist blacks adopted distinctive costumes and coiffures, thereby manifesting their group identity and identification. The separatist movement responded not to a sense of chaos in the world, but rather to a feeling of a growing power to achieve their own liberation, a "revolution of rising expectations." They have felt exuberant with their civil right successes and the vigor of their movement. In the aftermath of violent speech and action, they naturally anticipate some sort of punitive correction, and they attribute the expected attack to Jewish antagonism. When they speak of Jewish antagonism they are referring to Jewish self-defense activities that they themselves have elicited. They have resisted freedom from racism as a value, and they have embraced black solidarity. Black audiences, black university students, and black media continue to exhibit an intolerance and bigotry that they share with only the most extreme elements of the white community.

In the *New York Times* article to which I referred above, Professor Gates attributes the promotion and orchestration of antisemitism to the personal ambitions of black agitators and would-be leaders. His analysis sounds correct and reminds one of the political uses of the *Protocols of the Elders of Zion*. But he does not recognize the original sources of black antisemitism. The need for a cosmic enemy derives, as I noted above, from the impulse to rise above the real oppression visited upon blacks: slavery, exploitation, murder, denigration, deprivation of civil rights, and the opportunity for advancement; and also from the expectation that they will be punished for their intemperate, extreme, provocative, and violent behavior. The basic myths of black antisemites are derived from religious indoctrination by religious white antisemites.

Of course Louis Farrakhan's Nation of Islam conforms to all of the criteria of a fundamentalist group. It consists almost entirely of converts to Islam from Christianity, and in that sense must be seen as a deviant religious movement. It is a structured organization rather than an angry mob. The Nation of Islam shares all of the antiwhite and antisemitic mythology of black nationalists. It demands a discipline and self-control and compliance that turns its members into automatons and clones, and that is not achieved by the unorganized and noisy black street and campus mobs. It incorporates also all of the ideas and prejudices of black nationalists and unorganized racists. As a religious movement it evokes and seeks to satisfy the religious and spiritual quest of its members, their need for a sense of immediacy with the divine, their need for an inerrant scripture to dispel uncertainty and intimations of chaos in the universe. That it serves as an inspiration and as a crystallizing nucleus for almost the entire black community is demonstrated by the admiration and compliance that Farrakhan is able to command even among the black masses that have not joined his movement and from authentic black leaders who should know better. The provocative speeches that Farrakhan's lieutenants present to black students and angry black audiences elsewhere, betray in their viciousness and deliberate deviation from reality and logic, the true menace of the movement and its leadership.

Let us return to Louis Farrakhan to see how these dynamics apply to him. Farrakhan describes the personal experience of having been aboard a giant spacecraft. He also speaks of a "Mother Wheel," a heavily armed spaceship the size of a city, which he expects to rain destruction upon white America while sparing those who embraced the Nation of Islam. (Magida attributes this fantasy to Elijah Muhammad, the founder of the Nation of Islam.)

These spaceship fantasies incorporate two separate elements. First, they can be seen as variants of the Unidentified Flying Object fantasy. This particular idea is not found characteristically among antisemites, but it does represent a specific dynamic which, as we shall see, is not irrelevant to antisemitism. Flying objects that permit ascent to heaven, appear incidentally in early apocalyptic literature, but centrally in an early (several centuries after the Common Era and perhaps before) variety of Jewish mysticism called *merkavah* mysticism. The latter is based upon the image of God's chariot that Ezekiel described in chapter 1. The mystical practice consists of trying to induce the experience of being transported to the *merkavah* (chariot) in order there to visualize God in his glory. The *merkavah* myth tells us that unless the aspirant is utterly virtuous and properly prepared with magical formulas and seals, he is in danger of being destroyed by the gigantic angels who surround God's throne (Ostow 1995, see ch. 5). Current UFO myths speak of abduction by aliens into a spacecraft, often shaped like a wheel. David J. Halperin, in a recent paper compares the *merkavah* myths with the UFO myths, noting the special prominence of terrifying eyes in both instances. He also calls attention to the bodily invasions that appear prominently in modern accounts. Halperin also reminds us of the myth of the heavenly ascension (*mi'raj*) of Muhammad on his marvelous steed Buraq. He concludes that the ascension tradition, more than thirteen hundred years old, may provide a clue to the psychodynamics of the ascension "memories" of our own contemporaries.

From my own psychoanalytic explorations of the *merkavah* fantasy, I conclude that it represents a device by means of which the mystic enjoys the illusion of reuniting with his parents; God is seen as the father, and the vehicle as the mother. The attempt to induce a mystical experience derives from the mystic's aspiration to transcend the bounding reality of the real world, to regress, that is to travel backward to what he might remember or reconstruct of his sense of having been initially united with his parents, in order to achieve a desired bliss. I am proposing here that Farrakhan's giant spacecraft represents his version of Ezekiel's chariot. Gates (1996) associates it to the spiritual: "Ezekiel saw the wheel, way up in the middle of the air." One could equally well associate Farrakhan's fantasy to "Swing low, sweet chariot, coming for to carry me home," and the verse of that song "a band of angels coming after me, coming for to carry me home." This song seems to invoke the magic of Elijah's chariot. Note that Farrakhan's predecessor in the Nation of Islam was Elijah Muhammad, each of whose names represents a personality who claimed heavenly ascent. Farrakhan's term "Mother Wheel" confirms my interpretation of the vehicle as a representation of the mother, at least in his case.

On the basis of these considerations I conclude that Farrakhan exhibits a strong mystical tendency which, I believe, betrays an impatience with the world of reality and an openness to the fantasy of regressive reunion with the parents of childhood. This tendency of course reactivates archaic psychodynamic mechanisms. Farrakhan cultivates the fantasy that the Jew is his arch enemy, a cosmic enemy, who conspires to seize control of Farrakhan and his universe and will not let him go. Farrakhan is projecting and personalizing his own inner struggle.

Let me draw your attention to a second aspect of the Mother Wheel fantasy. The fantasy that the gigantic space battleship will rain destruction upon white America, but spare the Nation of Islam, reproduces in theme the prophecy of Revelation which is, of course, incomparably more elegant and imaginative in language imagery. I spoke above of the role of apocalypse and of apocalyptic thinking in antisemitic psychodynamics. Revelation and Farrakhan's spaceship fantasy both express hope for messianic or divine rescue from earthly oppressors, the Romans in the first instance, and white America and the Jews in the second.

Apocalyptic thinking appears especially prominently among individuals with poor affect regulation or when external circumstances drive people to extremes of affect. Gates (1996) reports that after the Million Man March, Farrakhan spoke of having suffered from "depression." I don't know whether that was a professional diagnosis or Farrakhan's own designation for a down mood. Magida (130) describes an episode of serious emotional distress that was followed by a rebirth experience and which might well have been a depressive episode. Whether or not these were actual depressive episodes or merely pronounced mood swings, such experiences could occasion apocalyptic fantasies—especially in an individual who tries to escape into fantasy from the frustrations and disappointments of reality. Every antisemite attributes his misery to the Jew, and to the Jew's alternate and ally in the Christian world, Satan. By fighting the Jew he is trying to drive away his inner demons.

Let us return to Gates's (1996) surprise at the paradoxes and inconsistencies in Farrakhan's presentation. Farrakhan speaks of a yearning for universal brotherhood. To quote Gates: "It turns out that there is in Farrakhan's discourse a strain that sounds awfully like liberal universalism; there is also, of course, its brutal opposite. The two tendencies in all their forms, are constantly in tension. . . .What you hear depends upon when you tune in."

Gates reports Farrakhan's charges of inauthenticity. This from a man who has changed both his name and his religion, and yet who maintains he never really left the church; who expresses in a short period of time views that are mutually incompatible with each other. Farrakhan speaks of the "oneness of God and the oneness of humanity." "Then," he says, "we can approach our divinity." Yet this universalistic aspiration does not prevent him from declaring that his enemies are "worthy of death" (121–24).

The ambivalence that Farrakhan exhibits toward Jews reflects his own alternating positive and negative internal feelings; when the positive feelings prevail, Farrakhan admires Jews and wishes to join them, and probably envies them; when the negative feelings prevail, they become his demons, the financier who plots against him, or the "agents" who condescend to him, or the Jewish liberals who are "too paternalistic," or the Jewish bankers who conspire against his financial universe. It was not surprising to read that an investigation reported in the *Chicago Tribune* disclosed financial disarray among the businesses owned by the Nation of Islam.

It is not uncommon to find, in people who exhibit the kind of affect volatility that becomes manifest in apocalyptic fantasies and in mystical tendencies, contradictory attitudes, sometimes simultaneous, at other times in quick succession. Each attitude is generated and governed by the affect prevailing at the moment. When depression is threatened, the individual may attempt to deal with it either by attaching himself to and pleasing a protector or by appeasing or fighting a real or hypothetical enemy. That is why contradictory efforts may prevail either concurrently or successively. Stevenson's characters, Dr. Jekyll and Mr. Hyde, dramatically exemplify the syndrome of multiple personality. In the classical multiple personality, the several affect driven faces try to remain distinct from each other, to remain disassociated. Given the affect volatility alone, without hysterical disassociation, most individuals try to minimize or deny inconsistency, to emphasize continuity. Farrakhan does not pretend to have multiple personalities, nor does he attempt to conceal inconsistencies. He seems to delight in the irrationality that he exhibits. Leaders of fundamentalist groups gain credibility by sanctioning the irrationality that their followers tolerate or perhaps enjoy.

Of course, there is a fine line between hypocrisy and multiple personality. I suppose that when the two faces exclude each other, we can speak of multiple personality. When the individual deliberately dissimulates, we speak of hypocrisy. The two may coexist.

Farrakhan complains, disarmingly, that "I haven't even been arrested for spitting on the sidewalk or doing anything violent to anyone. And now you are going to call me a Hitler, like I'm planning to do something evil to the Jewish people." In fact, encouraging his followers to hate Jews and to prepare the ground for *pogroms* is indeed doing something very evil to the Jewish people.

In his book, *Prophet of Rage: A Life of Louis Farrakhan and His Nation*, Magida tells the following story. On an airplane flight in 1994, Farrakhan responded graciously, if noncommittally when a Jewish man asked him to "tone down your rhetoric about Jews." After the plane landed one of Farrakhan's guards stalked him through the airport muttering abuses and threats. Is this emotional inconsistency or hypocrisy? And from the point of view of the victim, what does it matter?

What Gates and Magida tell us of the Nation of Islam confirms my conclusion that it is a fundamentalist group. The specific apocalyptic complex that presumably generates anger in Farrakhan as an individual, also gives rise to fundamentalism in the group. It combines anger directed at a mythic enemy or current adversary with an apocalyptic desire to reunite in a loving way with divine parental figures, or semidivine fraternal figures such as angels, or with individuals in the same community. The charismatic leader entrains the individuals to form a group and evokes feelings of love combined with obligation and guilt.

Gates tells us that

> The truth is that blacks—across the economic and ideological spectrum— often feel astonishingly vulnerable to charges of inauthenticity, of disloyalty to the race.. . . .Farrakhan's sway over blacks—the answering chord his rhetoric finds—attests to the enduring strength of our own feelings of guilt, of our own anxieties of having been false to our people, having sinned against our innermost identity. He denounces the fallen in our midst, evokes the wrath of heaven against us; and his outlandish vitriol occasions both terror and a curious exhilaration. (118)

An exhilarating thrill marks the response of the group to the leader's call for fraternal unity and hatred for the enemy. Identity and mutual identification reinforce each other.

Gates's essay is accompanied by a drawing depicting Farrakhan backed up by two of his followers and protectors, both dressed in their characteristic bow ties and dark suits, with menacing, set, and expressionless faces. Gates quotes Leon Forrest, black writer, novelist and editor, to the effect that the Nation of Islam "represents all the old American values of thrift and hard work, discipline, respect for the family and the women." However it extends respect and neighborliness only to fellow members. It does not represent the old American values of individuality, respect for neighbors and their opinions, tolerance, and intercommunal unity. The very particularistic way in which the Nation of Islam and most fundamentalist groups practice their so-called virtues does not square with ordinary definitions of virtue and morality.

In Elijah Muhammad's doctrine, "a woman's behavior was strictly circumscribed: She was not to let herself be alone in a room with any man who wasn't her husband; her dress had to be modest." Under Farrakhan, the Nation of Islam, continues to promote very conservative sexual politics and a strong antiabortion stand. However, Farrakhan repudiates domestic violence and has named a woman a Nation of Islam minister.

We find in the fundamentalist group the same dynamics that we find in the individual antisemite who is trying to ward off depressive influence: anger, the readiness to resort to myth to account for frustration and disappointment, to designate the Jew as the principle of evil. But the dynamic of the group emphasizes for us the importance of love that complements the hatred, love only for literal and mythical members of one's extended family. The antisemite sees the Jews as someone who comes between himself and his God, interfering with the radiation of God's grace to him. He yearns for the comfort of the parent-child unity that he "remembers" or that he wishes he had experienced early in his childhood. This apocalyptic wish for the love of one's own real and mythical family members, and murderous impulses toward others, is revealed in both Farrakhan's mystical Mother Wheel fantasy and in the pseudomorality that he teaches his flock. It is not fortuitous that among the most consistent and prominent myths in the repertoire of antisemitism are those of the Jews as deicides, that is parent murderers, and as the murderers of Christian children. The mythic Jew prevents closeness between parent and child, between the individual and his God.

The readiness of so many blacks to rally around Farrakhan and his Nation, to credit their canards and myths, to follow on the Million Man March, reveals the strength of the anger that has been released by the combination of persisting discrimination by the white community, along with the many gains in civil rights, and genuine efforts by whites to build both equality and fraternity. There is much to wish for and correct within both the white and black communities, but an apocalyptic "revolution of rising expectations," a zealous separatism, does not promise the hoped for rebirth.

On the contrary, since the diversion of apocalyptic fury outward serves as a defense against the inward directed apocalyptic death wishes, the campaign to eradicate others usually carries suicidal potential and as often as not ends in the defeat and destruction of the aggressor. In those instances, the leaders and many of the followers are destroyed by forces that they have themselves evoked, and they may die by an act of self-immolation. Hitler is the paradigmatic example, and David Koresh of Waco, Texas, and Jim Jones of Jonestown, are lesser but still momentous examples.

I have tried in this chapter to demonstrate the following:

- Black antisemitism in general, and specifically in Louis Farrakhan's fantasies about Jews, displays the paradoxicality, the ambivalence, the creation of and reliance upon myth, the fluctuating quality that has characterized antisemitism since the early years of the Christian era.

- The basic psychodynamic that determines antisemitism is the designation of the Jew as the cosmic principle of evil alongside Satan.

- The need for a principle of evil is created not only by actual experiences of hurt, but also by the need to project out and reify depressing influences that arise internally, often as a consequence of affect regulation and sometimes in response to actual external stress.

- To my knowledge, serious, consistent and widespread antisemitism did not prevail among blacks until recent decades, and what there was, resembles the endemic antisemitism of the white nonfundamentalist community rather than the epidemic antisemitism of fundamentalists.

- Fundamentalist groups come into being in response to actual privation and suffering, but also in response to individual freedom and prevalent repudiation of conventional morality, standards, and values. The truly murderous antisemitism is that of fundamentalist or fundamentalist-like groups.

- The intrapsychic apocalyptic attempt to defend against injury or perceived attack creates murderous anger in individuals and encourages the organization of zealous separatist and hateful fundamentalist groups.

- Current black separatism partakes of the nature of group fundamentalism and crystallizes out as the fundamentalism of the Nation of Islam.

In Professor Gates's essay and Magida's book on Louis Farrakhan we can recognize most of these elements and patterns and dynamics and, in addition, a significant mystical tendency that favors the crediting of religious myths and the fantasy of uniting with parent figures in the service of personal salvation and the destruction of one's mythical enemies. Farrakhan's literal and verbal pugilism betrays that dynamic.

I find no alternative to the conclusion that black antisemitism does not differ from white antisemitism either in principle or in practice. I believe that blacks have learned to designate the Jew as the principle of evil from their early church education, that is, from the white Christian community. Louis Farrakhan does not differ in his mode of operation, in his psychology, or in his mythology from the purveyors of antisemitism of the past two thousand years in the West, and the Nation of Islam does not differ in its basic dynamics from the many fundamentalist groups and fundamentalist-type mobs of white Christian Europe and America and of fundamentalist Islam.

It would be well if all fundamentalists, of whatever color and religion, remember that after initial victories and carnage, most fundamentalist campaigns manage, in the end, to destroy themselves, leaders, and followers alike.

DO JEWS ENGAGE IN ANTIBLACK, RACIST HOSTILITY?

Since my assignment is to discuss black-Jewish conflict, I am obliged to consider the attitude of Jews toward blacks as well as black antisemitism. I know that Jews are thought to harbor a reciprocal animus toward blacks. With respect to Jewish attitudes toward blacks, we do have some historical written records.

In the Bible, blacks are referred to only as *Cushim*. Cush is the son of Ham. The term "Cushi" (*Cushim* is the plural) was subsequently applied to Nubian blacks and more broadly to all blacks known by the contributors to the Jewish Bible, mainly Ethiopians and other North Africans. No directly disparaging comments are made about Ham or about his descendants. That there was a mythic disparagement of these blacks is implied in a story that appears in Numbers, chapter 12. Miriam was punished for speaking critically of Zipporah, the black wife of her brother Moses. The text does not tell us what the criticism was; it does not say that she was inappropriate because she was black. However, Miriam was punished for her slander by acquiring a skin ailment that turned it completely white. Presumably this disorder was an ironic variant of *lex talionis*.

We find two significant references to Cushites in the Prophets. Jeremiah (13:23) asks: Can a Cushite change his skin or a leopard his spots? There is no disparagement intended here; Jeremiah would seem to imply that since everyone agrees that black skin is undesirable, the Cushite would change it if he could. Amos (9:7) asks rhetorically: Are you, Israel, not like the Cushim to me? The implication is not pejorative; Amos continues to list God's favors to other neighboring peoples. He is saying simply that Israel is will not be treated preferentially by God over his neighbors including the Cushim.

Verse 1:5 of the Song of Songs deals with blackness explicitly: *Shhorah 'ani vena'vah*. I am black *ve* beautiful. The phoneme *ve* can be translated either *and* or *but*, and different scholars translate it differently. In either case, what is expected to be a negative quality is affirmed to be positive.

In the Talmud, I have found two references (BT Shabbath 31a and Sanhedrin 108b), both trivial and unilluminating. Post-Talmudic literature is vast and unindexed and therefore not accessible to amateurs. Rashi, the celebrated Jewish exegete of Troyes, addresses the verse that we noted, Numbers 12. He had trouble coming to terms with the idea that Moses married a Cushite woman and tries to find ways to interpret the verse as honorific. Plainly, he considers black skin a disadvantage, though, as in the previous literature, no comment is made about the character of black people. Presumably, he reflects the attitude of the French people among whom he lived.

Black antisemitic literature accuses the Jews of playing a large role in slave trading. The evidence is that even when Jews lived in slave-trading communities, they played a role considerably less prominent than their numbers justified. It seems to be well established that Africans themselves and Muslims were the most prominent in slave trade.

We cannot review here the history of Jewish relations to blacks in America. Suffice it to say that Jews, probably everywhere, have responded to blacks as did the majority community in which they lived, perhaps on the average, less harshly. The history of cooperation in the civil rights movement is too recent and too well known and well documented to require comment. It had to be denied, minimized, and distorted to justify the canards voiced by black antisemites.

The Jewish communities of Israel and America recently cooperated in a monumental project of moving Ethiopians who identified as Jews, from Ethiopia to Israel, to rescue them from starvation and persecution. Some who presented themselves for rescue were known not to be Jewish, but these too in most instances were welcomed.

I do not know of any majority attitude of American Jews toward blacks. From my own observation, both in practice and in personal relationships, I would guess that these attitudes resemble the attitudes of other Americans toward blacks, but perhaps they are more positive and liberal. To say that they are more tolerant is to imply condescension, which I believe, will not be true of most. Certainly American Jews are put off by black hostility and animus and also by the dangers presented by black crime. But I think that this defensiveness toward blacks is commensurate with the provocation in each case and does not assume a momentum of its own.

There are of course many individual Jews who hold strong antiblack sentiments and many who hold problack sentiments. But there are many Jews who hold equally negative views of one or another communities of other Jews, generally the more recent arrivals in America. I would guess that the current hatred and contempt shown by fundamentalist Jews toward other Jews greatly exceeds Jewish hostility toward blacks.

I know of no organized or coherent Jewish antiblack sentiment or movement. There are no antiblack radio or television speeches, no antiblack newspaper or magazine articles, no incendiary speeches on college campuses. The activities of the various Jewish self-defense organizations are purely reactive and commemsurate with the dangers that blacks pose.

Having said that, as a psychoanalyst, I must call attention to the well-known but seldom mentioned fact that blackness carries a pejorative valence in the unconscious. In dreams of whites, a black man always implies a negative quality, whether danger or degradation. When I worked as a psychiatrist in the back wards of a segregated mental hospital, I often heard black people refer to each other pejoratively as such. Is this association of blackness with negative qualities, the result of cultural prejudice or an expression of a universal association of black with darkness and evil, as opposed to light and good? I suspect that in most instances both influences are involved.

To conclude, I would regard the expectation of a Jewish animus, symmetrical and reciprocal to black antisemitism, itself a black antisemitic canard.

REMEDIES

Finally, I am expected to suggest some remedies, some ways of attenuating the current climate of hostility between the two communities.

The fact that antisemitism has continued to flourish unabated for two thousand years in Christian communities would seem to confirm Maimonides' (12th century) opinion that the advent of the Messiah will be marked by the termination of the persecution of the Jews.

We have no access to fundamentalist antisemites, whether the Christian right or white Islam or black Islam. To them, Jews are agents of Satan and are not to be believed, trusted, or even tolerated. Perhaps one could try to immunize those who have not yet been drawn into their *folie*. How? By exposing antisemitic myths as such; by tracing their origins and meanings and demonstrating the motivations of those who purvey them; by demonstrating that antisemitism is shameful and evil and reflects badly on its proponents; that it violates basic precepts of their own religion.

We try to engage the cooperation of the leaders of the antisemitic community itself in these demythologizing and shaming activities. However, we often find to our dismay that even those leaders who do not share antisemitic sentiments will not speak up against those who do for fear of alienating the loyalty and losing the votes of the antisemites.

It is important to avoid permitting the antisemites to elicit from Jews the type of irrational and immoderate hatred that they themselves harbor, that is, mythopoetic hostility symmetrical and reciprocal to their own antisemitism.

REFERENCES

Friedman, M. 1995. *What Went Wrong? The Creation and Collapse of the Black-Jewish Alliance.* New York: Free Press.

Gates, H. L., Jr. 1992. "Black Demagogues and Pseudo-Scholars." *New York Times*, July 20.

———. 1996. "The Charmer." *The New Yorker*, April 29–May 6.

Halperin, D. J. 1995. "UFO Abduction Narratives and Religious Traditions of Heavenly Ascent: A Comparative Study." Unpublished.

Magida, A. J. 1996. *Prophet of Rage: A Life of Louis Farrakhan and His Nation.* New York: Basic Books.

Ostow, M. 1995. *Ultimate Intimacy: The Psychodynamics of Jewish Mysticism.* Madison, Conn.: International Universities Press.

———. 1996. *Myth and Madness: The Psychodynamics of Antisemitism.* New Brunswick, N.J.: Transaction.

6

Ruptures in Time: The Branch That Holds the Fork in African American and Jewish American History

MAURICE APPREY AND HOWARD F. STEIN

Eternal vigilance is the price of civilization. . . .
Derepression is utterly dangerous unless civil society is strong.
—Robert M. Young

INTRODUCTION: HOLES, VOIDS, ABSENCES, AND CULTURAL HISTORY

All human individual and collective life is a jagged ebb and flow of continuity and discontinuity, of fabrics of time and holes in these fabrics, and of what happens to us—how we are part of what happens to us—and what we make of what happens to us. Even if this fabric is a continuous, and continuously revised, weave of fact and fantasy, it nonetheless feels real and essential to those for whom its warp and woof are life's very calibrations. For some groups, the discontinuities in time amount to gaping holes punctured during some natural or social cataclysm. Some groups feel entitled, if not divinely ordained, to punch vast ruptures into the line of other groups, to assault not only these others' physical being, but their historical lines as well. The holes themselves become both part of the fabric and permanent insults to it. Group "history" consists of both of

Note: An earlier and shorter version of this chapter was published as "Broken Lines, Public Memory, Absent Memory: Jewish and African Americans Coming to Terms with Racism," in *Mind and Human Interaction* 7, no. 3 (August 1996). This earlier version was originally written for the International Seminar on Racism and Anti-Semitism, in Istanbul, Turkey, January 1995 in the framework of the Council of Europe Plan of Action Against Intolerance.

these, and of attempts to resew, to repair them over and again—to turn absences into presences. Sometimes we do this even if it kills us, or our children, or our children's children—or others'.

Two interlocked groups whose separate and joint histories illustrate this process in the United States are African Americans and Jewish Americans. Both of these peoples dwell among that mythically self-made, new, ever-renewable people, "Americans," who pride themselves on voluntary uprootedness, freely willed re-rootedness, and the belief that they can transplant themselves again any time they wish. This chapter further contributes to our understanding of the interplay between inner and outer worlds and to understanding this boundary under prolonged circumstances in which enslavements, expulsions, exclusions, lynchings, and exterminations are historically "normal." Further, this chapter is no mere comparison between two separate pariah groups in America but about the collective sense of rupture, of brokenness, in time among two American groups whose histories in America have long been entwined in the larger national history. It is about the psychological symbiosis between blacks and Jews and the larger symbiosis between their duality and American culture—which process makes the conflict in fact triadic. If it is about slavery and redemption from slavery in historic time, it is also about mutual enslavement in psychological time—and the possibility of redemption from this mythic time.

Any comparison of African American and Jewish American experiences will be tempted to dwell on understandable but futile narcissistic competition for "Who suffered worse, your people or mine?" (Freud's concept of the "narcissism of minor differences" [1930].) At play in this "dual-unity" (a term originated by Margaret Mahler) and the struggle for distinctiveness are, among others, (1) a shared history of oppression; (2) a mirror-image projection of aggression; and (3) a containment of more mainstream, "white" American ambivalence toward dependency, aggression, authority, and tradition. It is a combat that tragically plays into the ongoing drama of two condemned peoples who perform others' heinous deeds and mischievous wishes on stage on their behalf. *The psychological polarity of blacks and Jews is thus not entirely a polarity at all, but a sacred triptych in which the main panel—mainstream "white" culture—does not and cannot acknowledge its crucial projective part.* American history—black, Jewish, white—is not only complicated but convoluted.

It is human to be threatened by the kinds of problems that racism, expulsion, and extermination offer. Under these circumstances, who wishes to remember what, and how do they (we) remember? Can compulsive remembering and memorializing of the holes in time also serve to make the groups themselves "stuck," so that the holes become not only what others have done to them, but how they live with the sense of assault? *The once and recurrently transgressed, become in turn transgressors to themselves. Baited by the larger society, blacks and Jews bait each other.*

To use a dramaturgical image, at one level, *blacks and Jews are the "stage," and white Americans, the "audience"; at yet a deeper level, all are "performing" roles for one another. The mutual recriminations between two despised "races"* (and in American folk biology, both African Americans and Jewish Americans are distinct "races") *make macabre, fascinating theater to the rest who do not dare recognize their own inner drama being played out on inner-city brutality and in the media. In the vernacular, the triangular conflict reads "Let's you and him [or her] fight."*

What possible solutions are there? How can the cycle of woundedness and the narcissistic infliction of woundedness be interrupted? *Only grief can heal narcissism,* just as (in the myth of Echo and Narcissus) the original narcissism was itself child of an intolerable loss and of its unbearable grief. *Such grief requires continuous vigil and conscious effort. Inner and social mending must be inclusive, not self-righteously exclusive. Old us/them splits cannot be healed by new ones. Alienation and marginalization are the problem, not its solution. And "marginal," as an adjective, is inseparable from the unconsciously laden process of "marginalization," a verb-become-noun.* Concretely, this means that *any negotiation that takes place to mend the hearts of blacks, Jews, and whites, cannot be limited to "mainstream," more civil and moderate blacks and Jews* (e.g., the NAACP or B'nai B'rith), *but must include splinter groups* (e.g., the Nation of Islam, the Jewish Defense League) *who tend to be less polite and circumspect. These latter are not merely statistical outliers and loud nuisances* (see Colvard 1996; Zulaika and Douglass 1996). *Rather, they are the storehouse and voice of historical grievances. The vulnerability of grief diminishes the magnitude of grievance. Instead of trading insults and building barriers, blacks and Jews could begin to let walls between them fall.*

The remainder of this chapter is devoted to understanding what keeps the walls so long and so firmly in place—which, in psychoanalytic language, is to inquire into the myriad of resistances and to the desires that lurk beneath them. This study, too, continues the work of the authors (Apprey and Stein 1993; Stein and Apprey 1985, 1987, 1990) in attempting to trace the role of projective identification as an organizing principle of "whole" families, workplace organizations, communities, ethnic groups, and nation-state societies, wherein identities are split-off and branded onto outcast groups.

One needs neither African American nor Jewish American history to recognize that in any organizing, remembering, or recovery of time, nothing is entirely what it seems. Groups create elaborate retrospective mythic continuities of history in response to vast ruptures of continuity. Likewise, stylized memorialization, the refusal to remember, compulsive remembering, and so on, can all serve as screen memories to reexperiencing collective events, their obligatory family meanings, their personal, unconscious significance, and what powerful emotions one would feel if one truly remembered. Continuity and discontinuity, then, are not simple or self-evident. A core principle of Jewish history, American and elsewhere, is the history of holes themselves, of repeated homelessness after being at home in host countries often for centuries. Discontinuity becomes a recurrent thread of continuity: from Babylonia to Nazi Germany. The very people so envied by blacks and others for their biblical "begats" and stubborn-seeming persistence, are also the people who have repeatedly suffered ruptures long before the World War II Holocaust. Indeed, many American Jews whose progenitors fled the *pogromchiki's* brutality in the late nineteenth and early twentieth centuries, find that their family ancestral suffering is berated if not ridiculed by fellow American Jews whose families were killed by brutal Nazi squads or by the bureaucratized manufacture of death at the gas chambers.

In short, continuity sometimes masks radical discontinuity; and sometimes the litany of savage ruptures constitutes one vital form of continuity. Among African Americans who have migrated from the Old South to north of the Mason Dixon Line, one form of continuity often overlooked by those attentive only to the chasm between Africa and the Americas, is the great migration during the first third of the twentieth century from the rural South to the urban North. For all of its disruptiveness in personal, family, and community life, migration was nonetheless far more voluntary than forced slavery. And for all peoples, migration whether over oceans or over land, creates holes in time.

THE CREATION OF PERMANENT RUPTURE

Genocide and other massive transgressions, like the enslavement and killings of African Americans or the attempted extermination of the Jews, create *permanent ruptures* amongst people in ways that can never be restored or repaired.

When families are killed off, when a family member is carried off or sold off, ties to others are severed, *gaps* are created in the lives of the living and even in the lives of future generations. How is the ancestral line broken by death and separation? What do survivors insert in the gaps? What links between grandparents, parents, and grandchildren foster the continuance of dysfunction in families? What are the structures of the experience of death and bondage long after the concrete historical events of genocide and racist killings and/or kidnappings of Jews during the Holocaust or African Americans during slavery? These are clearly overwhelming questions for scholars and clinical practitioners and require interdisciplinary groups of thinkers to come to grips with the historical antecedents and consequent issues involved. In a short chapter such as this one, only a discreet and circumscribed issue can be taken up with a view to suggesting how Jewish and African Americans can stay vigilant and continue with the process of transforming themselves after the massive transgressions in history that still greatly affect their lives.

The necessarily narrow focus of this chapter then is the issue of *gaps in memory* and *remembering in action*. Even here the focus will be to determine a way to think about gaps in memory in ways that would suggest possible solutions. To this end, we call upon literary theorists, J. Hillis Miller, Geoffrey Hartman, and Wolfgang Iser, in order to provide a heuristic strategy in the sense that these strategies for thinking about solutions will not be exhaustive but suggestive and experimental. Before proceeding with this task, there must be a disclaimer. The Jewish Holocaust of World War II and the massive killings and slavery of Africans in America are not interchangeable circumstances, but they are horizonal in the sense that both situations attest to what crimes humans can commit against their fellow humans. The solutions proposed here may be shared by both Jewish and African Americans. The shared solutions, however, will only be effective if the two groups refrain from the phenomenon that Freud (1930) called the "narcissism of minor differences" (wherein groups with cultural similarity go to great lengths to insist on differences) and thus do not engage in the futile moral relativism of considering which group suffered more than the other. We foreground the experience of African Americans to highlight the problem of *lost ancestry* and the subsequent communal injury of a people; however, many, if not all, of the issues and conclusions we draw relate to Jewish Americans as well. A further strategy here is that in following the French philosopher Marcel Mauss (1967), we are interested in an analysis of *concepts about gaps in a lineage* as opposed to facts that are here only used to illustrate formulations that are reached by inductive methods. We do not wish to address the local or particular contemporary issues of problematic relations between Jewish and African Americans, but rather address the generic problems that lie at the core of both groups, in the hope that resolving these internal griefs will facilitate meaningful dialogue about *common human interests* in their relations with each other. To get to that core we want to illuminate on one hand the tremendous desire for transgressors such as Nazi Germany or slave traders and their offspring to repress moments in history of human beings' inhumanity to their fellow but dehumanized human beings, and, on the other hand, the tendency for transgressed groups to fill in gaps in their collective memory with shared assumptive world-views.

LOST AND BROKEN LEGACY IN AFRICAN AMERICAN HISTORY

The literary theorist J. Hillis Miller (1992) expanded our understanding of cultural narratives when he adopted the following vocabulary to expatiate on his views of the storyline:"line," "character," "anastomosis," and "figure."

In an epigraph to the opening chapter of his book *Ariadne's Thread*, Miller quotes George Grosz: "Line is the thread of Ariadne, which leads us through the labyrinth of millions of natural objects. Without line we should be lost" (1). In classical Greek mythology, Ariadne was the daughter of Minos and Persiphaë who gave Theseus the thread by which he escaped from the Minotaur's labyrinthine den. The question of freeing oneself from the labyrinth, says John Ruskin in a second epigraph in Miller's chapter on "Line": "seems not at all to have been about getting in; but getting *out again. The clue, at all events, could be helpful only after you had carried it in; and if the spider, or other monster in midweb, ate you, the help in your clue, for return, would be insignificant. So that this thread of Ariadne's implied that even victory over the monster would be vain, unless you could disentangle yourself from his web also*" (2; emphasis in original).

The line, for Miller, analogously leads to all other conceptual problems in story lines and story making; these conceptual problems include those of character, intersubjectivity, time, narrator, and mimesis or representation. Shortly we shall return to this first rubric of the "line" as a broken line with a gap wherein dwells a phantom, in order to connect the idea of a broken line to the experience of African Americans with the absence created from disrupted lineages, the wound of an absence, as it were.

Under the second rubric of "character," Miller draws our attention to its Attic Greek etymology and implications of the older meaning of the word to story lines and story making. "Character" is from the Greek verb *kharassein*, which means to brand, to cut or to scratch, to engrave, to make a deep impression. What is involved, asks Miller, in using an old meaning to explain how we use an old word, a phenomenon Derrida called "paleonomy"? "What is involved in borrowing a word for a 'character' in the sense of a letter or incised sign to name 'character' in the sense of personality or selfhood?" (32). To this question, Miller answers that the word *character* presumes that external signs correspond to and disclose some otherwise hidden nature. In this vein, we shall appropriate Miller's paleonomy of "character as a brand" in order to reveal aspects of our thinking about the bondage of African Americans—a group hitherto branded and "charactered" as the property of slave owners. In a word, how does the African American shift from the concreteness of brandedness to the flexibility of rewriting one's destiny?

Yet another "branding" complicates the bondage. Jewish Americans, who are often regarded by mainstream "whites" as nonwhite, bear the burden of white-ness in their relationships with African Americans. To blacks, they are white, but even more so, enforcers of the white social order. But to whites, they are Jews, neither black nor white. All three groups share a deep branding from which they all could be liberated.

The third rubric of the intersubjectivity of "anastomosis," a connecting channel, will add to our knowledge of the phenomenon of transgenerational transmission of destructive aggression. Appropriating James Joyce, Miller describes the intersubjectivity of anastomosis as "a triple interpersonal linkage that makes and marks out past, present, and future as the three ecstasies of time and joins each person to all previous generations, such that each person is both a new self and continuation of ancestor selves, all the way back to Adam and Eve." Accordingly, "In anastomosis the self is always outside itself. The presence of the self to itself in the present is the presence within that self not only of the other person who invades the self as the vessel of the body is invaded in sexual intercourse but, by way of that invasion, the presence as absence, *'l'être là du pas-là,'* which that interpersonal relation repeats" (163).

The intersubjectivity of anastomosis then speaks to the idea and "substance of oneself or of one's self in the other" (163). The self-in-other is an introject and is experienced as a phantom whose presence haunts and possesses the self and its future; the introject creates an absence, drives out the might-have-been authentic self.

By the time we get to the fourth rubric of "figure," the line is recognized to be linking, circular or reflexive, charactered, engraved, branded or embedded as well as intersubjective and intergenerational. Under the rubric of "figure," Miller suggests that the word "figure" itself contains a strategy for constructing narratives by way of the science of tropes, a paradigm. From Latin we know that "fingere" signifies making, shaping, confecting, creating a schema. We shall use the figures of metaphor and metonymy to address the issue of slavery as the perversion of a metaphor. What happens in the minds of humans when they decide to give up the metaphor (whole for whole) of trading by bartering goods between nations or interest groups in favor of the metonymy of trading humans as visible goods, or classifying the natural world in favor of stigmatizing, branding, and eliminating members of it? This is a complex question and one that tempts us to posit the notion of evil in humans. Evil thus becomes Dehumanization, the perception and creation of the other as less than human, a part-object, a commodity, a thing. What concerns us here are the consequences with which we have had to live, once we created evil.

So putting the vocabulary of "line," "character," "anastomosis," and "figure" together in order to illuminate the African American experience, we can test the following formulation: The broken lines of ancestry point to the line as a recursive transgenerational figure where ruptures are linked by apposition or anastomosis, and these links continue to perpetuate. In the mental space of the link between generations there lie the charactered, branded wounds of bondage and yet the absence of a representation to describe that engraved injury caused by the perverse dehumanizing act of trading humans as goods or trying to annihilate them. Such is the wound of an absence that it hurts, but one does not always know where it hurts or how it hurts or, on occasion, who the enemy is. The closest approximation to a representation may be the following: the motor of destruction by the transgressor remains the same but the license plate changes from slavery and murder to suicide, black-on-black crime, child abuse, mental illness, and so forth.

The senior author has discussed this phenomenon of change of function elsewhere (Apprey 1993). Here, following Hartmann (1964), we want to mention that in the flow of transgenerational transmission of aggression, a form of behavior that originated in one generation may appear in the next generation in a changed form. Thus "institutions which are built on tradition, even when they can be historically traced entirely or in part to the psychological trends of preceding generations, impose themselves on the individuals of subsequent generations as realities" (Hartmann 1964, 53). Frequently those abiding institutions "continue to satisfy along broad lines the same psychological needs to which they originally owed their creation" (Hartmann 1964, 33). The novelist Carolivia Herron (1991) in her novel *Forever Johnnie* tells us that this transfer of destructive aggression from generation to generation is a "curse" according to which five way stations may occur: (1) the females shall be raped by slavemasters and the males shall be murdered by slavemasters; (2) the males who are not murdered shall be sold away; (3) the males who are neither murdered nor sold away shall marry the females who are not murdered or sold away; (4) in marriage, enslaved males or former slaves shall have revenge on females perceived to have consented to the destruction of the males; (5) women and their daughters shall, therefore, be raped over and over again by enslaved men or former slaves. In such a sequence, then, incest may be represented as a derivative of, and as continuous with, rape and murder. This involves a three-fold process of (1) a historical presentation of rape and murder in the first instance; (2) appropriation by an oppressed group of a transgressor's cruelty, to serve a secondary purpose of revenge by the indigenous people; and (3) ossification of a structure of experience that says that victims may heap cruelty that originated with external transgressors onto their own kind. An elaborate and complex drama occurs transgenerationally in that space of a broken line inhabited by one generation after another. The question of the wound of an absence is taken up by the literary theorist, Geoffrey Hartman (1994) in his essay on public memory and absent memory.

THE WOUND OF ABSENCE IN GROUP SUFFERING

How do groups remember and "forget"? What is the nature of the social construction of history when enforced gaps are made? Hartman (1994), writing on the vicissitudes of public memory, faces the challenge of reattaching imagination to collective memory, observing along the way the creation of a communal story under modern conditions. To this end, he makes a distinction between "public memory" and "communal story." He contrasts the instability of public memory—with its technological base and mass-media sound bites, its unstable shock value, its ratings-driven mode—with the relative stability of communal story as a living deposit of collective memory preserved outside academic or written history.

Recognizing an ethical link between how humans come to know what they know and the moral life they aspire to lead, Hartman observes further that the gap between knowledge and ethical action has not grown less wide for humans. The pressures to be politically correct have increased, but neither human thought nor human actions have adjusted to the challenge of generalizing knowledge from the massive inhumanity of the Holocaust to mitigate the global extent of political misery.

Following Terrence des Pres, Hartman seeks to conclude that "thanks to the technological expansion of consciousness we cannot not know the extent of political torment; and in truth it may be said that *what others suffer we behold*" (29; emphasis in original). To this Hartman poignantly adds: "the triumph of technology has created two classes: those who suffer, and those who observe their suffering. This fact cannot be touted as moral progress, but there is one gain from it: given our new eyes for the pain of others, and given that 'we cannot not know,' all monopolistic claims about suffering no longer make sense" (29). For Hartman, then, claims to innocence are no longer defensible. Further, just as indefensible is a refusal to look beyond a particular people's suffering to the global extent of political misery. There is a consensus, however, that a people may derive from their history methods of living that permit them to circumscribe their knowledge and to draw distinctions between those who know and those who do not. This distinction which Hartman, following Lyotard, makes to show us what constitutes the culture of a people needs further examination. It takes us beyond Hartman's plea for self-awakening and generalizing to the global extent—and to the temporal extent: the transmission of collective memory from one generation to another. Let Hartman speak to the issue of consensual and collective memory: "This consensus is recovered by each generation. We start indeed with a cultural inheritance, yet it cannot be fixed as immutably as doctrine is in theology. Memorial narratives asserting the identity of nation or group are usually *modern constructs, a form of antimemory limiting the subversion of heterogeneous facts. Invented to nationalize consensus by suggesting a uniform and heroic past . . . they convert 'great memories' into political ideology*" (31; emphasis in original).

The psychoanalyst Heinz Hartmann (1958) has also written about the transmission of collective memory, and he does so in a most telling passage:

Man does not come to terms with his environment anew in every generation; his relation to the environment is guaranteed by . . . an evolution peculiar to man, namely the influence of tradition and the survival of the works of man. We take over from others . . . a great many of our methods for solving problems. . . . The works of man objectify the methods he has discovered for solving problems and thereby become factors of continuity, so that man lives, so to speak, in past generations as well as in his own. (30; emphasis added)

Hartman (1994) and Hartmann (1958) have here taken us into the realm of remembering consensually, constructing new stories to preserve collective memory, inventing narratives to define the identity of a culture. In this respect, they are in the same horizon as the psychoanalyst Vamik Volkan (1992) who has coined the terms "chosen traumas" and "chosen glories" to capture the wounded or glorifying experience of a people who are motivated to tie their identity to historical events and do so in ways that preserve their historical grievance or success, thus defining their identity in ways that seek to successfully or otherwise position them to sequester or overturn their fate.

Hartman (1994), Hartmann (1958), and Volkan (1992) direct their hypotheses in different directions; however, something unites all these concepts: a phantom created by a people to memorialize, to remember, to preserve, and rewrite a collective communal story. When Hartman (1994) goes to Toni Morrison's novel *Beloved* to articulate his views of the African American experience, he comes to the issue that is at the heart of this chapter: the wound of an absence, the wound of an absent history, or to be precise, the wound of a broken line, indeed, the wounds of interrupted ancestral lines. Accordingly, Hartman (1994) pointedly asks: "Where in Black history is there something comparable to a genealogy of begats, or the millennia of myths, chronicles, scriptures, and the scriptural interpretations that characterize the collective memory of Jews?" (35). To this question he juxtaposes Julius Lester's note that "the ancestry of African Americans is to be traced to a bill of sale and no further" (35). Regarding the wound of an absence, Hartman (1994) is very apt:

African American memory remains to be recovered. But more important still, where is the conviction of being loved that makes memory possible? What kind of story could have been passed on, or who stayed alive long enough to remember a suffering that destroyed those who might have recounted it, a suffering that allowed no development of person, family, or ethnic group? "Anyone Baby Suggs knew, let alone loved, who hadn't run off or been hanged, got rented out, loaned out, bought up, brought back, stored up, mortgaged, won, stolen or seized." (36)

Given this tragic situation, how may we recapture the communal story of wounds suffered by African Americans in terms of the transgenerational transmission of received destructive aggression through slavery and its ac-companying killings? Hartman (1994) would rely on the field of literature to illuminate our understanding of collective memory. For him, literature "counteracts the impersonality and instability of public memory on the one hand, and on the other, the determinism and fundamentalism of a collective memory based on identity politics" (35). With literature, Hartman would attempt to discover the living deposits or sedimentation that exists as a tie between generations. For what he is trying to articulate, he is helped by his choice of novels. There cannot be a richer and more haunting story than that of Toni Morrison's *Beloved* in which an infant, killed by its mother to enable it to escape slavery, returns as an eighteen year old to its mother's house, talking and engaging others in conversations of the most affectionate kind, yet hauntingly expressing the unlived life and "a love that never could come to fulfillment except in this fantasy form" (36). Hartman colonizes Morrison's story to bring home his message that the wound of absent memory is the ghost America has not yet faced and needs to encounter.

If Hartman has colonized Morrison's story, we too have colonized his account of it to take us to the level of intervention. To that end, we have suggested below a series of heuristic steps to enable us to approach the trauma of massive killings and their sedimentation or concealment, recog-nize the staging or recovery of trauma and its derivatives, and discover motivations behind the transgressions so that their new derivatives do not continue to cause harm. We also set forth one approach for transforming the derivatives of the trauma.

BEYOND GROUP TRANSGRESSIONS: THE KEEPING OF VIGIL AS POTENTIAL FOR TRANSFIGURATION

The pall of racism can begin to lift only as awareness itself becomes transfigured—awareness of self and other, and of the common vulnerability and fate we all share. In a short essay entitled "Murderous Racism," in which Maurice Blanchot comments on the work of Michel Foucault, Blan-chot (1987) wrote: "Men are weak. They accomplish the worst only by remaining unaware of it until they grow accustomed to it and find them-selves justified by the 'greatness' of the rigorous discipline and the orders of an irresistible leader" (100). Blanchot, of course, was writing on the human weaknesses that led to the Jewish Holocaust by the Nazis. However, the weaknesses that allow humans to accomplish their worst deeds by re-maining unaware of them until they become accustomed to their heinous crimes also include rationalizations that supported the slave trade on the basis of the economic health of the South in the United States. In com-menting on heinous crimes perpetrated by humans on other humans, we must parenthetically state again that racist crimes are horizontal but not interchangeable. Thus, there are features that antisemitism shares with racism toward African Americans but there are also decisive contrasts between them. In this chapter we emphasize only those features shared by many a transgressed people as we suggest pointers toward their mental and concrete forms of emancipation.

Racism remains despite the most rigorous attempts to overturn its practices. What follows is an attempt to formulate strategies for overturning the effects of racism, and to do so first by suggesting a conceptual or theoretical basis of such strategies in order to avoid premature and precipitous foreclosure. In short, one can plunge into implementation without systematic thought and thereby possibly re-create the very circumstance of hurt and injury that one intends to correct.

Accordingly, we suggest four way stations for thinking about a plan of action against the impact of racism. The first way station has already been hinted at by Blanchot's identification of a human weakness; the first way station is to disturb the cunning naïveté that keeps humans in a fog as they practice racism or silently but complicity watch it practiced. In other words, humans accomplish their worst under both the willful direction of others and under the throes of unconscious repression, and they do so in order to remain unaware of, until they become accustomed to them, racist practices that are further justified formulistically as "simply motivated by economics," "honest mistakes," "orders from above," and so forth.

The second way station in this heuristic strategy is that even when humans repress their recognition of crimes committed directly or indirectly by their bloodied hands, they find a way to stage facsimiles of these crimes. These facsimiles often distort the circumstances of the crime. Witness the existence of museums and castles built in memory of colonists. Staging, the rubric of this way station, is best explained by Wolfgang Iser (1992), a reader-response critic whose work is partly shaped by the phenomenologists Edmund Husserl and Roman Ingarden. For Iser, staging—the distancing or extraction of a phenomenon from its natural place, its simulation and then its completion—provides a way to reincorporate an event into a different context, with a revised significance.

Staging, however, is more than a mode of reconstruction, because the reattachment into a new context results in a re-vision. "It gives rise to simulacra of the inaccessible, which equally cast the latter in changing patterns and as pictures fantasize hidden regions" (Iser 1992, 883). In other words, staging removes a piece from the chaotic and convoluted world so that we can understand what would otherwise not naturally be evident to the same degree, yet at the same time this piece is connected in innumerable and complex ways to the multiplicity from which it was removed. Therefore, staging completes, enacts, or simulates not just one inaccessible element, but offers a kaleidoscope of shifting meanings of that which is presented or enacted.

In the context of staging as a form of distancing, extracting from history, simulating and completing, Peter Jones (1992), a philosopher who writes about museums and what their contents mean, notes that all kinds of museums characterize, promote understanding, permit celebration and evaluation of cultures, but they do so according to a revisionist view of the original event. For Jones "museums necessarily decontextualize and then recontextualize their contents, thereby radically altering the matrices through which meanings can be projected, discerned, constructed. And necessarily the contexts in which museums exist constantly change and have their individual histories" (910). In some cases the revisioning act of a museum attempts to redress the past wrongs connected with its relics. Accordingly from the Holocaust Museum in Washington, D.C., and from the preserved fortresses built by European colonists on the shores of West Africa, we are free to see and interpret the simulated or living records of human destructive aggression.

A telling passage from Toni Morrison's novel, *Beloved*, gives us another and related perspective of what museums and colonial castles can tell us:

> I was talking about time. It is hard for me to believe in it. Some things go. Pass on. Some things just stay. I used to think it was my rememory. You know. Some things you forget. Other things you never do. But it's not. Places are still there. If a house burns down, it's gone, but the place—the picture of it—stays, and not just in my rememory, but out there, in the world. What I remember is a picture floating around out there outside my head. I mean, even if I don't think it, even if I die, the picture of what I did, or knew, or saw, is still out there. Right in the place it happened. (35–36)

The inherent immutability of a history ensures that documentation of destructive aggression remains. Even deliberate attempts to drill holes in time fail to create utter voids. What is absent is hauntingly present—somewhere. Corpses, skeletons, dismembered bodies, pictures of humans put in chains by humans, spaces purposely built to sequester and dehumanize, remain to reveal base human motivations to us.

The discovery and unpacking of the base motivations of humans points the way toward the third way station in our heuristic strategy. Museums and castles, when they preserve history, provide us with accounts of extinction of humans, stories of submission to and protest against the injunction to die, to not be, or to surrender to racism. The third rubric then is to discern the motivations behind the assumed mandate by one group to hasten the demise of another by destructive force, by gun powder, by stealth, by ruse, by co-opting collaborators within the ranks of the transgressed people themselves, and so on, and so forth.

How then may this assumed mandate to precipitously hasten the demise of a transgressed people be transformed? The question here is related to the issue of appropriation of hatred from the transgressors by the transgressed and a subsequent attempt to transform the received. Internal defensive operations such as identification with the aggressor, and turning the passive experience of having been hurt into the active experience of hurting others are one mode of transforming the received. Unfortunately, in the realm of overturning the effects of racism there is often the risk that the victim may be blamed for not being equipped to effect the transformation.

We suggest, therefore, that we adopt a mode of description that requires that we recognize the injury caused by racism as well as the subsequent attempt to heal the mental and/or physical injuries that are the result of racism. In other words, the history of outrageous injury must be mentioned in the same breath as the victim's need to attempt to transform the injury. We must do both, because the human capacity to repress the injustices of history is much too great to endorse the use of concepts that emphasize only one side of a natural bifurcation. It is for this reason that in the fourth way station of our heuristic strategy to overturn racism and its damaging effects we have proposed the concept of urgent/voluntary errands. In appropriating this metaphor from the poet W. H. Auden we see that what is "urgent" is the oppressor's demand that the victim surrender or submit to some poison without being permitted to acknowledge that it is poison. What is "voluntary" is the determination by the victim as to how the historical grievance must be transformed. The idea of an "errand" is a necessary one to draw our attention to what conscious or unconscious destructive project or mission the transgressor wills in order to precipitously hasten the demise of the innocent other. Knowing what is "urgent," knowing what is "voluntary," knowing what motivation subserves the transgressor's errand altogether constitute knowing at a deeper level one strategy that is capable of transforming humans.

Because humans are free to voluntarily determine what form transformations of racism must take, we have hope and the responsibility to create those heuristic strategies, that can combat racism. However, we may combat racism at many different levels: (1) at the level of the individual who must find ways to recognize a poisonous infusion and at the same time the appropriate means to tame the effects of that poison; (2) at the level of the family where successful strategies of recognition of hatred and its mutation can be determined and developmentally shared in child-rearing patterns; (3) at the level of the ethnic group where new forms of vaccination against the poison of racial hatred can be determined to render its members immune to repeated injury when they determine that they are not only victims but also active transformers of their own history; (4) at the level of the country where legal and sociopolitical institutions can protect groups that are transgressed; and (5) at the level of international coalitions and alliances where appropriate policies and international mandates can act in both proactive and preventive ways or in retrospective ways to combat racism. With respect to intervention, we are thus considering a series of interventions in the form of concentric circles with the individual at the center and the international community at the outermost circle.

There are some implications for such a composite heuristic strategy. We shall mention only two that relate to the place in the community of transgressed and where the infused racial hatred is stored. The first has to do with what in the United States is called black-on-black crime where the originally transgressed group has lost sight of who the enemy is. Rather, the appropriated racial hatred becomes staged in the drama of criminal activity within the community of an originally transgressed people, and consequently growth or transformation is impeded.

Just as the injected racial hatred can be stored in the transgressed community in the form of black-on-black crime and paradigms thereof, there is a second scenario that is worth a comment. The injected racial hatred can also be sequestered in splinter groups, sometimes of a rigid, fundamentally religious kind (as in the Nation of Islam or the Jewish Defense League). Recall that immediately after the Murrah Federal Building bombing in Oklahoma City on April 19, 1995, the group automatically suspected was "Islamic fundamentalists," a group stereotyped as beyond the pale of humanity. If we could treat such splinter groups not only as sites of new violence but also as the sites where the originally injected racial hatred has been stored, we may begin to see that racial harmony is not fostered when such groups are excluded in the process of conflict resolution. Rather, if we were to include them we might begin to appreciate that self and other, enemy and ally, the normal and the abnormal are yoked. In this sense, the so-called extremist groups are but a claustrum or location of a split-off site of violence that simmers in politically more centrist groups, and which must be treated as an integral part of the whole for progress to occur.

This kind of thinking that allows the split-off subgroup to be seen as a storehouse of the original racial injury permits us not only to see the split-off and the mainstream-other as equally belonging to a system of thought where one branch holds a fork, but also, it is a kind of thinking that permits a discovery of a wider horizon of a society's concealed and overt symbolic values. To know any society's concealed and unconcealed value systems we must first have the courage to face and come to grips with all of its transgressions.

In summary, we shall repeat the components of the heuristic strategy in our epistemic conversation.

1. All forms of cunning naïveté that conceal racial hatred must be unpacked and subverted.

2. We must discover all the ways in which repressed racial hatred is staged.

3. The motivation behind the transgressor's project must be discovered in its range from extinction of others to derivative forms of extinction where living occurs in the form of a psychic death, or soul murder has taken the place of an otherwise potentially fruitful life.

4. The project, mission, or errand of the transgressor must be overturned in a bifurcated way: first, by recognizing the nature of the urgently injected racial hatred and second, by voluntarily finding constructive ways to transform the received racial injury. Therein lies hope and responsibility.

If our analysis of the African American and Jewish American situation is even approximately accurate, then it can also serve as a means toward understanding and assisting in the reconciliation of such historic adversaries as Turks and Greeks, Estonians and Russians, Palestinians and Israelis, Irish Protestants and Catholics, Tamils and Sikhs, and Americans (of the United States of America) and Soviets (which the West mistakenly blurred into a single ethnonational term, "Russians") and now Russians (as in the common and provocative slurs such as "Russian mafia" and "Russian fascists"). In each case, the adversaries come quickly to brand themselves positively and their enemy or enemies negatively along the pseudobiological lines characterized by Erik Erikson (1966) as "pseudo-species": that is, each "we," as "THE human beings," special, unique, superior, and each "them" as an inferior, if not infrahuman, "race" (606).

In each instance, we must have the courage (from the French "coeur," for heart) to persevere in finding (and always rediscovering) the branch that holds the fork of our common human interests, and, in turn, our very common tree. Then and only then can we strategically develop specific methods of intervention to deal with local or circumscribed regional conflicts. Even then conflicts may remain, but thankfully they may not be malignant.

REFERENCES

Apprey, M., and H. F. Stein. 1993. *Intersubjectivity, Projective Identification and Otherness*. Pittsburgh: Duquesne University Press.

Blanchot, M. 1987. "Michel Foucault as I Imagine Him." In *Foucault/Blanchot*, by Michel Foucault and Maurice Blanchot. New York: Zone Books.

Colvard, K. 1996. "What We Already Know About Terrorism: Violent Challenges to the State and State Responses." *The HFG Review* 1, no. 1 (Fall):3–8. A publication of the Harry Frank Guggenheim Foundation, New York City.

Erikson, E. H. 1966. "Ontogeny of Ritualization." In *Psychoanalysis: A General Psychology, Essays in Honor of Heinz Hartmann*, edited by R. M. Loewenstein, L. M. Newman, M. Schur, and A. J. Solnit, 601–21. New York: International Universities Press.

Freud, Sigmund. 1930. *The Standard Edition of the Complete Psychological Works of Sigmund Freud. Volume 21: Civilization and Its Discontents*, 59–145. Translated by James Strachey. London: Hogarth Press.

Hartman, G. 1994. "Public Memory and its Discontents." *Raritan Review* (summer 1994):24–40.

Hartmann, H. 1958. *Ego Psychology and the Problem of Adaptation*. New York: International Universities Press.

———. 1964. *Essays on Ego Psychology*. New York: International Universities Press.

Herron, C. 1991. *Forever Johnnie*. New York: Random House.

Husserl, E. 1977. *Cartesian Meditations*. Translated by D. Cairns. The Hague: Martinus Nijhoff.

Iser, W. 1992. "Staging an Anthropological Category." *New Literary History* 23: 877–88.

Jones, P. 1992. "Museums and the Meaning of Their Contents." *New Literary History* 23:911–21.

Mauss, M. 1967. *The Gift*. New York: Norton.

Miller, J. H. 1992. *Ariadne's Thread: Story Lines*. New Haven: Yale University Press.

Mitscherlich, A., and M. Mitscherlich. 1975. *The Inability to Mourn*. New York: Grove Press.

Morrison, T. 1987. *Beloved*. New York: Plume/Penguin Books.

Stein H. F., and M. Apprey. 1985. *Context and Dynamics in Clinical Knowledge*. Charlottesville: University Press of Virginia.

———. 1987. *From Metaphor to Meaning*. Charlottesville: University Press of Virginia.

———. 1990. *Clinical Stories and Their Translations*. Charlottesville: University Press of Virginia.

Volkan, V. 1992. "Ethnonationalistic Rituals: An Introduction." *Mind and Human Interaction* 4:3–19.

Zulaika, J., and W. A. Douglass. 1996. "Talk to a McVeigh?" *The HFG Review* 1, no. 1 (Fall):9–11.

7

"Unlearning Racism" at Women's Music Festivals

CYNTHIA BURACK AND BONNIE J. MORRIS

Psychoanalytic theory has great potential as an interpretive tool in studies of racism and of the construction of racial identities. By reading pattern and meaning in eruption and conflict, psychoanalytic theories can help to provide a language to explain many things about self, group, and culture that seem most inexplicable. These assumptions guide the following chapter, a study of one particular cultural setting in which race and racial meaning create conflict and possibilities for dialogue and "working through" between groups.

Most analyses of racism and antisemitism begin either with a particular racial incident or with a consistent social set of beliefs, prejudices, and structural inequities. Instead, we have chosen to examine a particular social context, women's music festivals, in which conflicts between black and Jewish participants (among others) erupt. Incidents and episodes of racialized conflict at women's music festivals are both like and unlike racialized conflict in other sectors and locales of American society. Hence, examining racism and racial misunderstanding as it occurs in these festivals suggests the tenacity of racism at the same time that it demonstrates possibilities for emotional learning and "minimizing malice."[1]

Women's music festivals are large-scale events. There are over twenty such regional gatherings now held annually in the period between April and November, ranging from a local audience of several hundred to the eight thousand international campers (and hundreds of workers) at the popular Michigan Womyn's Music Festival each August. Serving a primarily lesbian, politically active crowd, the women's music festival subculture remains unknown to most Americans, yet for twenty-five years participants have subjected themselves to adverse conditions, including sometimes hostile weather and primitive campground settings, for a week or weekend of concerts, workshops, and personal transformation. A central festival ethic is honoring diversity and actively "unlearning" racism, through meetings and discussions on the nature of identity, visibility, and stereotyping. To this end, both black and Jewish women have been involved as speakers, performing artists, and workshop facilitators since the onset of festival culture in the mid-1970s.

In spite of the relative cultural invisibility of women's music festivals in American society, it is this politically progressive, largely lesbian-feminist context that offers regular and ongoing events for coalition work and dialogue between diverse groups of women. To find provocative workshops on racism and white privilege, one need only attend a feminist conference or a few of the women's music festivals held across the United States each summer. Yet women's music festivals are not only home to an explicitly antiracist political discourse; festivals are also troubled by racial conflict and rupture. Festivals are sites of racialized struggles for territory and visibility. Indeed, women's music festivals can be understood to offer conflict to their participants as part of the experience of festival culture.

RACE, RACISM, ANTISEMITISM

Because festivals are overwhelmingly lesbian in attendance, arriving on women-only land where the lesbian identity is normative can be a radicalizing moment for straight festival-goers—a contrast to daily life in homophobic society. But festivals are also overwhelmingly white. Although white festival-goers may correctly perceive festivals as radical events for *them*, marveling at woman-only, lesbian-tolerant space and accompanying freedoms, women of color often experience a familiar minority status and its accompanying stereotypes. The latter are revealed through a variety of painful incidents. Yet efforts to create safe gathering spaces within festivals for women of color are misunderstood, even resented, by white women festival-goers. White women who assume the privilege of inclusion may perceive, for example, that a workshop by and for women of color constitutes reverse discrimination.

Festivals can be nurturing, affirming, and creative ingatherings for participants; at the same time, they can also be alienating to many. One example of this ambivalent reception of festival culture is women of color searching for faces like their own. Women of color are well represented among festival performers, and most of these are African American. Yet although performers like The Washington Sisters, Melanie DeMore, Linda Tillery, Karen Williams, Bernice Johnson Reagon, and Toshi Reagon are visible members of festival culture, women of color remain a numerical minority.

It is also true that for black lesbian festival-goers and artists with limited resources, the difficulties associated with festival attendance multiply. Black lesbian comic Karen Williams humorously alludes to the fact that what seem like benign camping discomforts to some take on a political meaning for low-income women (often, although not exclusively, women of color) who are appalled by the outhouses that come with the ticket price. "Where I come from, we don't call it camping, we call it homeless," is a standard line in Williams' stage routine. Racism in the United States has an economic base; hence, while many affluent feminists enjoy camping out/doing without—albeit with rainproof camping gear, down sleeping bags, and other costly camping amenities—as a contrast to regular life, women whose families have been forced into substandard housing for generations see festivals' leaky cabins and Porta-Janes as an insult to their dignity.

As she talks about tofu, Karen Williams' comedy routine also reflects the tension between those who grew up viewing meat as a luxury and those who put down meat eaters as politically incorrect. Some white women who come to festivals as vegetarian activists lecture those festival-goers who complain about meatless meals—not recognizing cultural differences in diet and the symbolism of meat as reward, as plentitude. When white festival-goers and organizers wonder about the relative absence of women of color they don't always stop to examine the politics of diet and shelter or what sorts of diet and shelter appeal to women of different minority groups.

Where do Jewish women fit into this dynamic? It is safe to assert that the percentage of Jews among "white" women in festival culture is far higher than the 1 percent of Jewish women in the general American public. Jewish lesbian artists are among the most influential performers in what has been called "women's music," although, again, overtly feminist musicians have enjoyed very little mainstream attention. Within the subculture of women's music festivals since the mid-1970s, however, the list of Jewish artists is long: Alix Dobkin, Maxine Feldman, Sue Fink, Ronnie Gilbert, Laura Berkson, Robin Tyler, Sonya Rutstein, Judith Sloan, and Amy and Elizabeth Ziff from the trio BETTY, are but a few examples. There is no dearth of Jewish lesbian performers. But in contrast to women artists of color, whose racial difference is visible, Jewish artists often may choose not to comment on their ethnic identity from the stage, allowing themselves to be presented simply as white.

Both on and off the festival stage it can be hard to *find* the substantial percentage of Jews attending, as many Jews "pass" as WASP, retain white privilege, and refrain from addressing their own ethnic identity. Most festivals do not have a planned meeting area for Jewish women, and while festivals are as tacitly opposed to antisemitism as to racism, forums for addressing how Jews experience racism are not as common as workshops on black/white antagonisms. In workshops on racism the assumption that Jewish women have the same background of white privilege as Gentile women—or experience white privilege in the same way—often creates tension.

To any large gathering where white Gentiles predominate, both black and Jewish women bring with them a vulnerability to others'—including each other's—definitions and stereotyping. Even at a feminist festival event, lesbian identity can be insufficient to transcend ethnic tension: examples of racist and Jew-baiting comments or jokes told by lesbians at festivals disillusion those lured by the promise of cross-cultural sisterhood.

TERRRITORY AND VISIBILITY

Since the early years of festival culture, many women of color have found that festivals merely reproduce their daily experience of contending with a white majority and white privileged leadership. To counteract this imbalance, several festivals offer a specific and private meeting place where women of color can gather during the festival week and spend time together in a setting of their own majority. The Michigan festival and the New England Women's Music Retreat were original sites of separate space for women of color at festivals. The best-known Women of Colors tent is the one at Michigan, which was founded in 1983 as a clearinghouse and sanctuary for women of color and a base for discussion groups and workshops (de la Tierra 1994).

In some instances, a festival's Women of Colors tent or meeting rooms may also offer workshops to the general public at specific times, with the understanding that some workshops will be for women of color only. One example of an activity that is sometimes exclusively practiced within the group of women of color and sometimes shared with those outside the group is drumming. Indigenous drumming has always been an important part of women's music festivals; its political significance has not always been acknowledged, however. In the past decade, festival-goers have had to negotiate the racial meanings raised by drumming: What does it mean when white women play sacred aboriginal instruments onstage when few aboriginal women have the money to travel to festival events themselves? What does it mean when traditional African drumming circles are interrupted by white women who assume the gathering is a jam session for all passersby? In recent years some of these issues have been addressed through a program of cultural education and community sharing of the drumming tradition. Here the leadership of drum artist Ubaka Hill, who initiated drumming workshops, rehearsals, and performances for diverse groups of women, was a central factor.

For Jewish women, issues of territory and visibility are often even more complicated than they are for women of color. This is because many festivals do not offer Jewish women's meeting space, although this has been changing. Before its demise, the East Coast Lesbians' Festival included a Jewish lesbians tent and situated it near the Women of Colors tent for easy access and cooperation in workshops on racism. The Michigan festival offers a Jewish Women's tent, a space shared with deaf women's programming activities. At least one festival, the Gulf Coast Women's Festival at Camp Sister Spirit in Ovett, Mississippi, offers a feminist Passover Seder every year. Yet it is often the case that Jewish women's workshops substitute for actual tents, making Jewish women's gatherings "landless." Where there is no official meeting space, Jewish women at festivals sometimes find each other by holding impromptu workshops or by putting out the word that Friday night candle-lighting will be held at such-and-such a tree or table. In festival culture, many Jews simply retreat to an invisibility their high festival numbers belie (Morris 1993).

Holding services at festivals is a dramatic statement in a lesbian community pledged to acknowledging diversity but uncomfortable with religious patriarchy. When Jewish women meet for religious worship at festivals, there is always the risk associated with Jewish symbols and celebrations because of their connection with the state of Israel and Israeli nationalism. Even to speak Hebrew may be construed as racist, for it is now a national language, and not only a language of kinship and prayer. This reality has keenly frustrated Jewish women who see every other women's heritage upheld in the name of diversity. In festival space, Afrocentrism may be expressed in ways that Jewish pride cannot. After all, both the (patriarchal) religious and (Zionist) political forms of expression of Jewish pride have assumed an offensive meaning in lesbian-feminist community.

On the other hand, black and Jewish festival-goers share important characteristics. For one, blacks and Jews share an understanding of existence in a world of diaspora, of historic statelessness in a world controlled by nationalist interests. Second, African American and Jewish women share the experience of having their "tribal gatherings" taken as a threat to others' sensibilities and interests. In lesbian communities this threat has often translated to a resentment that racial, ethnic, and other groups fracture the apparent and idealized promise of women's and lesbian community.

"UNLEARNING RACISM"

Some women approach music festivals with a disinterest in examining the history of oppressions between women and with a preference for having a good time. Others invest themselves seriously in the opportunity for racial learning. Certainly, there is no *requirement* that festival-goers take part in the ubiquitous antiracism workshops, so frequently such options attract those women already committed to challenging their own assumptions and actions. Women's music festivals are one of the few sites in U.S. society where there is explicit and institutionalized dialogue about racial identity, racism, and antisemitism. This dialogue is conducted through a number of mostly informal means. However, the most formal venue is that of "unlearning racism" workshops.

Through these antiracism workshops, white participants are invited to calculate how their own attitudes have developed. They are asked to identify daily interracial contacts they may have and study the power dynamics of these relationships. They are asked to consider the privileges that white women take for granted in daily life. Sometimes a written text, such as Peggy McIntosh's essay on the litany of white privileges or the handbook *Cultural Etiquette*, produced by Blanche Jackson and Amoja Three Rivers of the Michigan festival's Women of Colors tent, may be used (McIntosh 1997; Jackson and Three Rivers 1990). If the participants in the workshop are all lesbian-identified, they may be invited to discuss interracial dating and romance experiences, their sense of social discrimination as lesbians and resulting insights into generalizations about other minorities. Language patterns, history, economic issues, visibility, mixed-race identity, and myths are addressed. Facilitators for these groups of white women are often women of color with years of expertise in workshop settings.

Central to the "unlearning racism" workshop model is the premise that racism is learned and can be unlearned; hence the importance of recalling one's earliest childhood incidents where notions of difference were conveyed by family members, peers, teachers, and the media. The model is readily adopted by a lesbian audience because most lesbians are receptive to the notion that stereotyping marginalized groups is a strategy used by more powerful groups. This they know from their own experiences of suffering lesbian stereotypes (that adult homosexuals prey upon children sexually or that they aggressively recruit heterosexuals, for example). When the emphasis remains on unlearning negatives, Jewish women have an excellent opportunity to promote the unlearning of Jewish stereotypes (e.g., that all Jews are wealthy, clever with money, and produce Hollywood films). White women are encouraged to group together in workshops, to process shared experiences with white racism, and to spare women of color the group process of bumblingly expressed white guilt. Under such circumstances, Jewish women find themselves in the difficult position of examining their own racism while being discouraged from pointing out myths that affect them as objects of antisemitism.

The failure to distinguish among "white" festival-goers in unlearning racism workshops clearly affects the process of the workshops. Jewish festival activists may readily symbolize the white oppressor to some women of color, while sharing *with* them a vulnerability to neo-Nazi rhetoric that other whites seldom experience. In the American political climate, Jewish "whiteness" remains negotiable, both contested by white supremacists and demonized by some Afrocentrists: groups that agree upon nothing but hatred for Jews. Adding to these tensions are the historic ties to Christianity in the African American community and the distress many Jews feel toward Christian fundamentalists' goals of a "Christian America." While lesbians of all colors are vulnerable to fundamentalist rhetoric, and the African American community is healthily skeptical of white-dominated Christian political groups, the ancient standoff between Christians and Jews cannot be discounted.

The ranking of oppressions, and the insistence that if one has experienced harassment oneself one cannot be oppressive in turn, is a steadfast problem for festival antiracism facilitators constructing black-Jewish dialogue. Likewise, feminism has often been vexed by claims of group-based oppression and harm in which, implicitly or explicitly, historical injustices are ranked and suffering is compared. To these claims, attentive listening and collaborative theorizing are possible responses. Although explicit opportunities for interaction and coalition-work exist in festival culture, few venues are specifically dedicated to dialogue between women of color and Jewish women.

"THE PROBLEM OF THE WILL"[2]

Women's music festivals are envisioned by many as models of cooperative community. It is striking, therefore, that racism and racial misunderstanding continue to occur in a context that is virtually defined by its political resistance—to sexism and homophobia, as well as to racism and antisemitism.

By applying psychoanalytic thought to the problem of racism at women's music festivals, we will respond to those particular aspects of festival culture that seem to us most salient to the issue of festival relations between black and Jewish women. These are: first, group definition which is accomplished (or fails to be accomplished) through spacial/territorial demarcations (tents and activities), and second, the existence and institutionalization of "unlearning racism" workshops. These are issues that have been of increasing interest to psychoanalytic theorists who address cultural, social, and political issues in a world of conflict between groups.[3]

The ways in which groups define themselves, and are defined, through possession of space and territory have been explored mostly by theorists interested in ethnic and nationalist politics. However, many of their ideas are provocative for the study of the smaller-scale politics of festival life. Particularly provocative is the concept of "psychogeographic space" employed by such theorists as Vamik Volkan and Howard Stein. These theorists suggest that the physical space claimed and inhabited by ethnic groups establish not only physical boundaries between groups but also psychological boundaries. These psychological boundaries then become invested with emotion as groups strive to protect themselves from narcissistic injuries and to maintain the goodness of the group against outsiders. For Volkan, borders that demarcate physical space become group "second skins," especially when groups step up their attempts to protect themselves from perceived threats to group cohesion, whether internal or external (Volkan 1988, 125–29; Stein 1990, 72–74).

Psychoanalytic theory also has implications for antiracist pedagogy. Virtually all psychoanalytic thinkers who address themselves to the social problem of racial conflict concede that there are dimensions of racial conflict that must be addressed through conscious and cognitive strategies. These strategies are evident in the "unlearning racism" workshops developed for women's music festivals. To the extent that unlearning racism workshops attempt to get white participants to identify the privileges associated in the United States with white skin and European heritage, they are useful and necessary. Indeed, perhaps it is well to say, not that racism can be solved by conscious processes alone, but that racism cannot be solved without conscious and willful participation of those who, consciously or not, are in complicity with it.

Yet, psychoanalytic interpretation of antiracist pedagogy would diverge from the assumption of festival antiracism to the extent that there exists a hope among many feminists that universal participation and conscious "work" on racism and antisemitism can solve the problems. Here, psychoanalysis responds that the problem of racism is actually a set of problems, some of which lie "deeper" in the psyche than conscious "work" or commitment can reach.

This characterization is consistent with the work of Michael Rustin (1991), whose attempt to theorize his ideal of "the good society" includes understanding the unconscious components of racism. Rustin suggests that race is an "empty signifier." By this he means that differences and characteristics usually attributed to "race" are traceable to sources such as culture, nationality, and experience of oppression. This understanding is consistent with other critical readings of the biologistic category of "race." Yet the "emptiness" of the racial category is psychologically meaningful; the very emptiness makes the racial category and group a ready container for feelings and amplifies the unconscious meaning associated with race. Intense, primitive, and undesirable feelings "akin to psychotic states of mind" find a target in the idea of the racial other.

Rustin explicitly addresses the knotty problems associated with antiracist pedagogy and identifies three issues that are relevant to an analysis of "unlearning racism" workshops. First, he argues that antiracist pedagogies that define racism mainly as an "ideological formation" can have the paradoxical effect of rehashing and reinscribing discredited racist theories in an attempt to reinforce the correctness of an antiracist ideology. Second, Rustin suggests that forms of antiracist pedagogy that rely upon guilt-inducing strategies, although they may enjoy some superficial and short-term success, are ineffective. "From a psychoanalytic point of view, persecution seems ill-advised as a technique for dealing with states of mind that are at root paranoid and persecutory" (Rustin 1991, 74). Finally, Rustin concludes that the psychic roots of racism must be interpreted and responded to in all groups for there to be effective antiracism. "It is hard to see how people of different 'races' can learn together about themselves if the fundamental assumption is that members of one group are guilty and members of the other are innocent" (Rustin 1991, 75).

The last two of these suggestions are most salient to the "unlearning racism" practice developed in women's music festivals. Injunctions for white women to examine their own behavior and privilege are a central aspect of learning about the construction of "white" identity in the United States and a crucial component of learning how not to engage in oppressive practices. These injunctions can also constitute public shaming, a practice that is not unknown in feminist and other political contexts. Rustin's final suggestion—that all groups must examine racism in themselves—might appear to deny the reality of social inequality and unequal legacies of harm. Nonetheless, it can be read as an invitation for groups to respond to oppression and at the same time to acknowledge in themselves and in their group the human potential for harm-doing.

OFFERING CONFLICT

We argue that women's music festivals offer conflict as part of the learning experience associated with this cultural, but also political, event. This claim has many implications. Some are obvious and provide part of the justification of structured workshops in unlearning racism. Others may not be so obvious. It may be the case that festivals, explicitly antiracist though they may be, actually *stimulate* defenses and anxieties associated with race and racial identity in many participants. This is so for four reasons. First, in festival culture, with its explicit attention to antiracism, it is more difficult than it is in U.S. society at large for white women to naturalize whiteness. Thus, white identity becomes the object of critical examination, and the "normal" unconscious operations associated with constructing the racial "other" are preempted or subjected to scrutiny.

Second, Jewish women's rituals may also stimulate defenses and primitive anxieties of both women of color and white Gentile women by problematizing the binary framework of self/other that is stabilized by the black/white difference that defines "race" in the United States. Here, Paul Berman's (1994) discussion of blacks and Jews as not "other" to one another but as "almost the same" is apropos, except that the same dynamic applies to Jews and Gentiles who share European descent. Berman's notion of "almost the same" bears, as he notes, a family resemblance to Freud's notion of the narcissism of minor differences. Both concepts would predict that projects of group differentiation in situations of some kind of "similarity," whether physiological, historical, or social/structural, become invested with heightened emotion and energy. It is, after all, a more strenuous project to differentiate ourselves from those who appear most like us, our "sisters," as it were.[4]

A third way in which festival culture might stimulate racial defenses and anxieties is related to the second. If group definitions are problematized by the presence of Jewish women, what of the presence of Jewish women who are also women of color (or light-skinned women who identify as women of color)? In fact, many Jewish women are descended from the Jewish communities of Morocco, Iran, Iraq, Yemen, Egypt, Spain, Turkey, and Ethiopia. Their presence, and self-definition as women of color, forestalls and complicates the binary of self/other for both Jewish women of European descent and women of color.

Finally, defenses and anxieties may be stimulated by the very strategies that are originally implemented to deal with palpable forms of inequality and privilege; the provision of psychogeographic space and the institutionalization of "unlearning racism" workshops may accomplish both desirable and undesirable, expected and unexpected, effects. "Unlearning racism" workshops may cause unintended effects as participants defend themselves from feelings of shame and guilt. As territory is established to create safe spaces for group members, the intended consequence can exist simultaneously with unintended, and unconscious, consequences that include paranoia and anxieties about group boundaries and purity. One reading of Bernice Johnson Reagon's famous essay "Coalition Politics: Turning the Century" (1983) is that Reagon is confronting just such unintended consequences of group boundary-making (albeit not from an explicitly psychological perspective). In this passage she writes explicitly about women's music festivals: "We've pretty much come to the end of a time when you can have a space that is "yours only"—just for the people you want to be there. . . . To a large extent it's because we have just finished with that kind of isolating. There is no hiding place. There is nowhere you can go and only be with people who are like you. It's over. Give it up" (Reagon 1983, 357).

It is not possible to specify how "working through" of feelings of fear, contempt, anxiety, and envy might be accomplished by groups in such a political context. Even so, psychoanalytic literature on group relations suggests three relevant issues. The first of these is reparative leadership that would hold and interpret aspects of the group's feelings while restraining tendencies toward separation from and denigration toward other groups. Here, Ubaka Hill's efforts to strengthen and maintain African drumming traditions among African American women, while teaching and sharing that tradition with others, is an example.

A second suggestion of a psychoanalytic group theory is the maintenance of nonjudgmental (and relatively nondidactic) dialogues within all groups about the feelings that are stirred by differences between groups. Such dialogues will not *solve* the problems of racism and antisemitism, particularly within a short span of time. What they may accomplish, instead, is the stimulation of productive conflict—conflict that is not merely suppressed until participants are safely away from the watchful eyes of other festivalgoers.

As psychoanalytically inclined writers would predict, racial conflict remains a problem even when the elimination of prejudice is part of the agenda of the gathering—indeed, even when most, if not all, participants are already committed to a politics of antiracism. It is in these circumstances that it becomes obvious, as Mark Bracher suggests, that "intolerance is caused by more than faulty knowledge and/or values" (Bracher 1996, 9). This is not to suggest that the labor of identifying faulty knowledge and values is unimportant to antiracist projects; certainly the lesbian feminist commitments to identifying privilege and unlearning racism are necessary ingredients of such a project. It is simply that more is required than this.

Psychoanalysis is a set of tools that is well suited to inquiring into our own subjectivities—cherished beliefs and unexamined assumptions alike. Thus, it is unfortunate that psychoanalysis has so often been hostile to lesbian identity, because activist lesbians, in turn, have often rejected psychoanalytic knowledge and refused to participate in its construction (Burack 1995). The consequence can be a commitment to political solutions to community problems that ignore the psychodynamic foundations and implications of those problems. Fortunately, the solution to *this* problem is closer at hand than the solution to the racial conflicts that vex us all. Psychoanalytically inclined theorists and practitioners must work to include lesbians and lesbian concerns in their moral community.

NOTES

1. The phrase is taken from Marge Piercy's poem "To Have Without Holding." Although Piercy's reference is to an intimate relationship, the ideal holds for relations between groups as well. See *The Moon is Always Female* (1980).

2. The phrase is borrowed from Stephen A. Mitchell's discussion of the psychoanalytic conversation regarding the dialectic of responsible agency and psychic determinism in the self. This notion seems particularly suited to a discussion of lingering racism in an antiracist setting. See Mitchell 1988.

3. Much, although certainly not all, of this work has been done from an object-relations perspective, and this is the perspective with which we are primarily concerned here.

4. Berman credits one of Freud's early translators, a man named only as Jankelevitch, as the originator of this idea. Berman frames the concept in terms of a falsely gender-neutral "brotherhood."

REFERENCES

Berman, Paul. 1994. "Introduction: The Other and the Almost the Same." In *Blacks and Jews: Alliances and Arguments*, edited by Paul Berman. New York: Delacorte Press.

Bracher, Mark. 1996. "Editor's Introduction." *Journal for the Psychoanalysis of Culture and Society* 1, no. 1:1–13.

Burack, Cynthia. 1995. "Mind-Mending and Theory Building: Lesbian Feminism and the Psychology Question." *Feminism and Psychology* 5, no. 4:495–510.

de la Tierra, Tatiana. 1994. "In Living Color." *Deveuve*: 46–49.

Jackson, Blanche, and Amoja Three Rivers. 1990. *Cultural Etiquette: A Guide for the Well-Intentioned*. Auto, W.Va.: Market Wimmin.

McIntosh, Peggy. 1997. "White Privilege: Unpacking the Invisible Knapsack." In *Experiencing Race, Class, and Gender in the United States*, edited by Virginia Cyrus, 2nd ed. Mountain View, Calif.: Mayfield Publishing Co.

Mitchell, Stephen A. 1988. *Relational Concepts in Psychoanalysis: An Integration*. Cambridge, Mass.: Harvard University Press.

Morris, Bonnie J. 1993. "Celebrating Jewish Identity at Festivals." *Hot Wire* 9, no. 1:38–40.

Piercy, Marge. 1980. *The Moon is Always Female*. New York: Alfred A. Knopf.

Reagon, Bernice Johnson. 1983. "Coalition Politics: Turning the Century." In *Home Girls: A Black Feminist Anthology*, edited by Barbara Smith. New York: Kitchen Table: Women of Color Press.

Rustin, Michael. 1991. *The Good Society and the Inner World: Psychoanalysis, Politics and Culture*. New York: Verso.

Stein, Howard F. 1990. "The Indispensable Enemy and American-Soviet Relations." In *The Psychodynamics of International Relationships. Volume I: Concepts and Theories*, edited by Vamik D. Volkan, Demetrios A. Julius, and Joseph V. Montville. Lexington, Mass.: Lexington Books.

Volkan, Vamik D. 1988. *The Need to Have Enemies and Allies: From Clinical Practice to International Relationships*. Northvale, N.J.: Jason Aronson.

8

Speaking the Unspeakable

AISHA ABBASI

INTRODUCTION

To write a chapter on the conflicts between blacks and Jews in America is a challenging task in itself given the complexities involved in such a discussion. It becomes even more challenging when the writer is neither black nor Jewish, as in my case, and has lived in this country for barely a decade after having spent most of my life in a country where I had no direct contact with either Jews or American blacks (I am originally from Pakistan). From a sociocultural perspective this could be a ridiculous situation, the only saving grace being perhaps the hope that I would be an "objective" discussant of the issue. From a psychoanalytic perspective, though, being invited to write this chapter—an opportunity of which I am very appreciative—does not seem very strange. In fact, I believe that this takes us to the very heart of the problem we are trying to address.

The idea that racial conflicts can be understood primarily or totally by reviewing the history and sociocultural context of the two groups involved seems to me to be an erroneous one. If this were true, the reams of writings on the subject by thinkers, intellectuals, historians, and so forth, from *both* sides, with their proposed explanations of how and why these conflicts arose, would suffice. The book for which we are currently writing would

Note: While all of the ideas expressed in this chapter ultimately reflect my own point of view, my warmest thanks go to Dr. Marvin Margolis, Dr. Mayer Subrin, Dr. Kimberlyn Leary, Dr. A. Michele Morgan, and Dr. Stephanie Stevenson, for their contributions in helping me write this chapter.

not even need to be written. Clearly then, there is a recognition that an understanding of social events and historical realities is not enough to create an understanding between Jews and blacks. We can forever talk about the sources of common and shared experiences between the two—that is, the experience of slavery of the Jewish people in Egypt and blacks being taken into slavery from Africa, persecution of Jews in different parts of the world, including discrimination against them in America, and the discrimination historically and currently against many blacks. We can also look at the factors that have created sociocultural rifts between the two groups; for example, the idea of Jews being "Christ killers," and blacks, as Christians, often being taught this early in their religious lives. In his book *What Went Wrong?* Murray Friedman (1995) refers to the autobiography of Richard Wright, who wrote "All of us Black people hated Jews, not because they exploited us but because we had been taught at home and in Sunday School that Jews were 'Christ killers' " (Friedman 1995, 28). Another contributing factor creating a rift between the two groups is the notion of Jews being privileged because of their white skin and thereby not suffering as a minority in the same way that blacks suffered. Many Jewish people resent being considered privileged when they have endured oppression and persecution, calling into question the economic situation of struggling blacks ("We were there, too. We made it; why can't they?"). Yet these questions when answered by data relying on historical events ultimately result in a sense of being deadlocked and a feeling of "Now where do we go with this?" It is here that I believe psychoanalytic thinking can be most helpful and why I feel that there may be some sense in my attempting to write this chapter. My focus will be to try to provide answers to questions about the black-Jewish conflict, not so much by formulating *explanations* but rather by trying to raise certain *questions* in the light of analytic thinking and social reality.

As we move from the realm of known and shared facts that are helpful to know, yet after a while repetitive and restrictive, psychoanalytic theory and understanding can help us look at what may be unknown and unshared among Jews and blacks with regard to the conflicts between them. It is these unknown and unshared aspects of the problem that I refer to as the "unspeakable," because these pertain to feelings that are viewed as dangerous, "politically incorrect," and inappropriate for civilized discussion. These aspects of the black-Jewish conflicts have to do, I believe, with powerful forces and beliefs, some conscious but many unconscious, in the minds of members of the two groups. It would not be enough here to attempt to understand these prejudices and their consequences as projections of unacceptable parts of one's self onto members of the "other group," with resulting denigration of that group. Such a formulation would be reductionistic since we are aware that *real* things have happened, and are *still* happening, between the two groups.

DEFINING THE CONFLICTS

One of the recurring thoughts in the literature and in talking to both blacks and Jews is that historically there are many similarities between the two groups. The similarities cited usually refer to the experience of slavery in the histories of both Jews and blacks as well as the experiences of discrimination and persecution. Descriptions in the literature of details of the slave trade resonate with the same pain and agony that is present in descriptions of massacres of Jews in Europe. The common history of slavery, the experience of being separated from the majority, of being discriminated against socially and legally, and of being the victims of violence by the majority, are common elements in the histories of both groups. It is believed by many people that these common experiences led to a sense of alliance and similarity between Jews and blacks; however, we know that, even in the midst of these similarities and the sense of alliance, a profound rift existed between blacks and Jews, and additional rifts were added during the course of history. The profound rift to which I refer relates to the religious difference between the two groups. Many blacks raised as Christians grew up with the belief that Jews were the killers of Jesus Christ. An offshoot of this belief seems also to have been the idea that Jews killed Christian children and used their blood to make matzoh for Passover. In his chapter The "New Anti-Semitism: A Geshrei," Richard Goldstein (see Berman 1994, 207) notes: "You can give guided tours of matzoh factories until kingdom come, but this idea persists in the subconscious."

The additional rifts that gradually developed include the following four topics of conflict.

1. The difference in opinion between the two groups on the subject of the state of Israel. Many Jewish people talk about feeling betrayed, disappointed, and angry at blacks for their support of Palestinians, while many black people feel that Israel is an example of American imperialism and white supremacy over oppressed people, referring here to Palestinians. Cornel West in his discussion with Michael Lerner (Lerner and West 1996) talks about the general perception among the black community of feeling a sense of empathy with the Palestinians, viewing them as oppressed and "darker skinned" (Lerner and West 1996, 60) and feeling that if Jews really understood oppression and discrimination, why would they support the formation of a state where a white Jewish society is trying to achieve supremacy. In response, Lerner points out that "60% of the population in Israel are people of color" (59) and notes that Jews feel disappointed by the failure of the black leadership and black progressives to educate American blacks about Israel.

2. A belief among some blacks that Jews who in modern-day America profess to be their allies were descendants of Jews who, in fact, had been slave owners during the years of the slave trade. From the literature it

appears that the slave trade was dominated by Arab merchants, Portuguese, and people from the Netherlands, France, and England. Murray Friedman writes that there were Jewish slave-trading families in Amsterdam and Bordeaux, and later individuals in Newport, Rhode Island, but that the participation of the Jews in the slave trade was "considerably less . . . than Protestants, Catholics, or even Muslims" (Friedman 1995, 20). There were a small number of Marranos (secret Jews) and Sephardic Jews who were more actively involved in using slave labor, but they made up a small minority of slave owners. In his chapter "The Battle for Enlightenment at City College," Jim Sleeper (Berman 1994, 249) writes about "international slavery . . . invented largely by Arab Muslims; instituted in the west by European Christians; catered to by Africans who sold blacks from other tribes." I think it is important to raise a question about why the idea of Jews being actively involved in slave buying and trading has been of so much interest to blacks, and why the fact that blacks were sold into slavery by other blacks, though accepted by many African Americans currently, becomes a muted truth in relation to the emphasis placed on the role of Jews in slavery. This highlighting of one problem at the cost of another indicates a need to deny the painful reality that certain problems within the black community are connected, not only to what others are doing to blacks, but to what blacks may be doing to each other within their own communities. I believe there is an important historical continuity in this phenomenon that is part of the "unspeakable" issues between and within the two groups of people. To turn the lights on the issue of a small percentage of Jews being slave owners, and to create a relative darkness around the issue of blacks selling other blacks into slavery, appears to reflect a need to see problems as coming only from others rather than as coming partly from others and partly from within one's own group and self.

3. The civil rights movement. The sixties were a time when Jews and blacks came together in the civil rights movement. Many Jews went South and actively participated with blacks. Even though many members of the black community appreciated Jewish support at this time, there were also mixed feelings about this. Jewish intervention was viewed by several blacks as being paternalistic, and perhaps even selfish, leading ultimately to Jews being asked to separate themselves from blacks in this movement. One sees evidence in reports of this period of a rapidly widening chasm between the two groups, with Jews feeling outraged that they lost lives during the struggle and then were told to "return to the whites," and blacks feeling that, in the words of Cornel West, "Freedom summers are one thing, but to be down there every day year after year is another" (Lerner and West, 1996, 88). However, many Jewish people feel that a major problem in the black-Jewish relationship started when the civil rights movement, with its emphasis on equal rights for all, turned into a racial movement with its focus

on equal rights for blacks. Many of them feel strongly that this emphasis detracted from the idea of all minorities having equal rights and, instead, focused on the needs and rights of blacks, with a neglect of other minorities, or other minorities being seen as "the enemy" in the struggle for equal rights.

4. The sense that although Jews certainly lost one-third of their nation in the Holocaust, they have managed to move upward in American society during the course of the past several decades. Within the black community there are different thoughts about why Jews have been able to be more upwardly mobile compared to blacks. Some of these include an emphasis on the idea that Jews were not ripped of their family connections and sense of history in the same way that over two hundred years of slavery took away a sense of tradition and history from the African blacks who were brought to America. There is a sense that the family unit and community organization that stayed intact for Jews, as well as access to education, afforded them privileges that blacks did not have. There is also an emphasis on the difference between being a person with dark skin and being a person with skin that is not dark. Whatever oppression and persecution Jews have faced, blacks point out, when a Jew walks into a store not everyone will know that this is a Jew against whom they should discriminate, whereas when a black person walks into a store it is a sign of a visible difference, often a suspected difference, because of the negative valence associated in the minds of many people with black skin and its connections to inferiority, the forces of evil, and danger. Jewish people, on the other hand, resent this assumption, pointing out that they are different from "the whites" even though their skin color may be similar at times. Michael Lerner points out that many Jews were able to move on in American society by camouflaging, or hiding, their Jewishness, and states that the "psychic trauma" (Lerner and West 1996, 68) that Jews experience is no different than the oppression currently experienced by blacks. Many blacks, on the other hand, feel that the oppression that Jews talk about was an experience of European Jews and is not a current day-to-day experience of American Jews. This debate—about whose oppression is greater, who has suffered more, and who is *still* suffering—places an emphasis in each group on the need to be recognized as the one that is most unfairly treated and, therefore, more deserving of understanding.

UNDERSTANDING THE CONFLICTS

I will first attempt to summarize some aspects of the existing psychoanalytic thinking about prejudice and my own thoughts about these ideas. In much of the literature that deals with the black-Jewish conflict there is frequent reference to Freud's idea of "the narcissism of minor differences" (Freud 1930, 114), indicating that perhaps Jews and blacks have exaggerated minor differences among themselves and ignored tremendous similarities for the sake of maintaining separate identities. I do not find myself in agreement with this idea because I feel that we are not talking about "minor differences" here. For many different reasons, it has been helpful for Jews and blacks to feel similar rather than different (i.e., two combined minorities against an oppressive majority). However, it does not seem to me that the similarities between Jews and blacks (already discussed earlier) are anywhere as close as similarities between the communities Freud was describing—for example, southern and northern Germans, the English and the Scots, Portuguese and Spaniards. The differences between Jews and blacks seem much more striking than do the differences between these groups of people. For example, the skin color difference is important, and to minimize this difference is not helpful. It is well known that in many different parts of the world the idea of black skin being inferior has been present for hundreds of years. Related as this may be to projection of one's own hostile, aggressive, unacceptable feelings onto dark-skinned people, the fact is that this problem does exist. In Pakistan, for instance, in certain northern areas where Greek armies came through in the days of Alexander the Great and there was intermingling of Greek troops with local women, many local people are now blonde and blue-eyed and are considered to be far more attractive than are other men and women who have the more usual light-brown or "wheat-colored" complexion of Pakistanis. In a country where blacks are nowhere as numerous as they are in America, this is still an important and significant problem. The skin color difference between Jews and blacks, therefore, is an important difference in that the first thing one often notices about others are their facial features and their skin color. In this way, I believe, blacks may at times be an easier target for discrimination and prejudice because of the historically and psychologically negative meanings attached to blackness. There can hardly be a more striking example of the negative power of blackness than the current plight of the black Ethiopian Jews in Israel (*New York Times*, September 9, 1996, A17). These are Jews who were brought back to Israel in 1991 and were extended full citizenship. However, their condition in Israel is already complicated by the development of ghettoes, welfare dependence, and poor education. Even as a Jew, being black has become a problem for these people in a country that ostensibly welcomed them home.

The second important difference between the two groups seems to me to reside in the fact that blacks were brought to America as slaves. They did not come here to flee persecution in other parts of the world (as many Jewish people did), nor did they come here seeking education or success or a better quality of life (as many Asians do). The experience of being brought into a place against one's will is quite different from the experience of having to come perforce to a place because it may be the only such place available. At a superficial glance the difference may not seem striking, but this difference needs to be taken into consideration in order to understand the experience of blacks. So I am not in favor of the application of Freud's idea of minor differences to the conflicts between Jews and blacks. I do find Freud's ideas about group psychology (Freud 1921) to be helpful in trying to understand these conflicts in that he saw group psychology as being "concerned with the individual man as a member of a race, of a nation, of a caste, of a profession, of an institution, or as a component part of a crowd of people who have been organized into a group at some particular time for some definite purpose" (Freud 1921, 70). Keeping this in mind, we can try to begin to understand the nature of prejudice as it relates to the black-Jewish conflict, first at an individual level and then apply it to groups to see if it can enhance our understanding of intergroup conflicts.

In a paper on prejudice Brian Bird (1957) states that

> prejudice . . . is a hastily and carelessly formed opinion about a person, group, idea, or thing; a preconceived idea not dependent for its formation on fact or familiarity. But there is more to it than that. Not only is prejudice a careless judgment, it is a judgment based upon emotions and fantasies, and thus, as well as being inaccurate, is specifically false. Furthermore, prejudice, unless otherwise defined, is always unfavorable, always against, always negative. (Bird 1957, 490)

Why is such a mechanism necessary? In working with patients in psychoanalysis many analysts have written about their understanding of prejudice as it came up in relation to the patient. Repeatedly, it has been seen that a basic aspect of prejudice has to do with projection—by which we mean putting one's own unacceptable feelings, envy, hatred, aggression, sexuality onto another person, thereby disavowing these feelings in one's self and protecting one's self from any inner anxiety related to having such feelings. These feelings then are seen as coming from another person. Goldberg, Myers, and Zeifman (1974) and Fischer (1971) all noted their patients' use of projection to deal with unacceptable impulses in themselves. Dorothy Evans Holmes (1992) notes similar conflicts in the patient she discusses in her article. For example, the Jewish analyst was at times seen as greedy. The black analyst was at times seen as uninhibited and dangerous. In the course of careful clinical work these feelings about the analyst were understood to be related to the patients' attempts to deal with these feelings in themselves and with the anxieties that such feelings aroused.

I have had similar experiences in my own clinical work where at times patients have talked about me as a "money-hungry Jew" and at other times as a "denigrated black woman." These perceptions, when analyzed, usually refer to unacceptable aspects of themselves, which these patients have viewed as "greedy" or "low-down and deprived." At other times they have had to do with identifications with their parents' prejudices or with aspects of their parents' functioning, which have not been consciously thought about by the patients until such perceptions about me came up in their analysis.

Bird (1957) appears to expand on the idea of projection by using another term, which he calls incorprojection, referring to a combination of projection and incorporation. He uses it to describe a phenomenon wherein he felt that in prejudice a person or group feels envious of another "more favored person or group" (502); however, there is fear of expressing this envy toward the envied group because of the risk of retribution. To avoid being criticized by this favored group the envious person or group incorporates the anticipated critical attitude of the envied group. At the same time, the original negative feelings are projected onto another race (a *third* race) from whom the anticipation of retribution or the consequence of loss of the relationship are less. Bird writes, "The venting of hostility against one group or individual is created as a defense against envy and hostility felt toward another individual or group" (493). This strikes me as a particularly useful idea in trying to understand the black-Jewish conflict. From time to time some authors writing on the subject have talked about the puzzling problem of why blacks and Jews are so caught up in putting each other down, whereas the larger white majority is seemingly ignored in this conflict. Is it possible then, in view of Bird's ideas, that one aspect of the hostility that blacks and Jews exhibit toward each other has to do with feelings of anger toward the larger white population and a sense of danger in expressing negative feelings toward this majority, thereby redirecting these feelings toward another minority group? This mechanism may also be at work in examples that we see of blacks burning down businesses/stores of Pakistanis, Indians, and Koreans, in certain communities—that is, could it be that some black people at times vent their hostility against Jews or whites by directing it against Asians, who are also a minority and are seen as advancing rapidly and unfairly in a country where blacks have struggled for decades to achieve recognition and success?

Analytic authors have also talked about these prejudices as being similar to competition between siblings—one hears echoes of this in the discussions between blacks and Jews about *who* has been most persecuted, *who* has been most unfairly treated and *who*, therefore, deserves more. These prejudices have also been seen as being related to feelings of anger about the oedipal phase father—that is, the persecuted group or person begins to represent, for the other person or group, the oedipal-phase father (I would say the parent) whom the oedipal child may want to destroy and castrate (Gordon 1965). How these ideas can help us in understanding intergroup conflicts is the question that we then need to address.

Since I do feel that group psychology ultimately has to do with a collection of individuals, I feel that we can expand our understanding of prejudice as seen in individuals to prejudice in groups. In doing this, however, we need to take into consideration that when individuals turn into groups they may, in order to function as a group, behave within the group "as though they were uniform, tolerate the peculiarities of its other members, equate themselves with them, and have no feeling of aversion toward them" (Freud 1921, 102). Freud was referring here to the idea that very often the kind of differentiation that individuals need to make among themselves to maintain a sense of separate identity may be given up in the formation of a group in order to maintain the identity of the group as a whole. In talking about groups that have a leader and do not have the characteristics of an individual, Freud said: "A primary group of this kind is a number of individuals who have put one and the same object in the place of their ego ideal and have, consequently, identified themselves with one another in their ego" (116). It would seem then that the very same conflicts that are understood in the individual treatment of patients are helpful to us in understanding what creates prejudice within groups. Projection/incorporjection (related to one's own unacceptable sexual, aggressive, greedy, or envious feelings) involving entire groups can certainly occur. Seeing entire groups as siblings to compete with—for attention, for money, for respect, for status, or seeing entire groups as an ambivalently loved parent—can be part of the prejudice also.

In addition to these phenomena, I feel that a consideration of the problem of trauma and external reality is very important here. The question in my mind is this. Whatever the individual intrapsychic conflicts may be that generate prejudice, what are other reasons that blacks may choose Jews and Jews may choose blacks as people onto whom to project these conflicts—that is, why do Jews sometimes see blacks as people who are content with their lot and who complain unnecessarily but who do not *really* make any efforts to move ahead? And why do some blacks see Jews as people who look out only for themselves and are selfish and miserly? I wonder if this has to do with the *narcissistic* injuries to individual and group selves that occur in the lives of people who have *genuinely* experienced discrimination. For instance, many discussants of the black-Jewish conflict write about the idea that because both Jews and blacks are minorities, when blacks see Jews doing well one of their feelings may be "even though you are somewhat like me, by doing better you humiliate me because you are thereby able to do more than I feel I can do." Could it be that prejudice in this case becomes a protective and defensive process that protects the person from further narcissistic traumas? Traub-Werner writes in "Towards a Theory of Prejudice," "What is experienced as anal, unacceptable, and derogated or castrated, is projected onto the object of prejudice, leaving little room for ambivalence or tolerance. Both the unacceptable id wishes and the original narcissistic injury are projected onto the object of prejudice, which is subsequently experienced as sadistic and imperfect" (Traub-Werner 1984, 408). Would it be useful to expand our concepts of trauma and its effects on the functioning of the ego to allow us to look at and study the ongoing repetitive trauma that occurs in the form of discrimination in certain societies, including American society? In thinking of trauma here I am reminded of Anna Freud's *Comments on Psychic Trauma*. In defining the concept of trauma she questioned, "Do I mean that the event was upsetting; that it was significant for altering the course of further development; that it was pathogenic? Or do I really mean traumatic in the strict sense of the word, i.e. shattering, devastating, causing internal disruption by putting ego function and ego mediation out of action?" (A. Freud 1964, 1967, 237). I believe that repeated attacks on the self-esteem of individuals and devaluation of the groups to which they belong, if continued over long periods of time, can be traumatic and, therefore, disrupt ego function. This disruption may be short-lived or prolonged, depending on circumstances. I think of black friends who have talked about being pulled over unnecessarily by police and interrogated because they were driving in a suburb where there were very few blacks. I think of stories of black women who a few decades ago were subjected to the "brown paper test." If they were darker than a brown paper bag they did not get the job. I think of Jewish friends who recently walked up to talk to the white men working on the driveway outside our house to find out if they could hire these men to work on their house. The construction workers, who did not know that these people were Jewish, used—in the words of my friends— "a dirty word about Jews." I think of a Jewish patient who told me that when she was picking up clothes at a cleaner and another Jewish customer walked out, the lady behind the counter smiled with complicity at my patient and said derisively "These stingy Jews." These are exceedingly muted examples of the kind of day-to-day discrimination that I believe both Jews and blacks experience in this country. Much more painful interactions take place all the time. Such repetitive disparagement of individuals and groups cannot but effect one's mental functioning, and I am referring here specifically to the functioning of the ego that needs to carry out processes of synthesis, integration, and accurate perception, in order to function well. Is it possible that prejudice becomes an easier mechanism for dealing with painful affect within groups because the ego functioning of individuals within these groups is momentarily strained and affected, thereby rendering more effective ego functioning difficult?

Could this, then, lead to a quicker and more than usual emergence of paranoid feelings, helplessness, envy, and extreme rage whenever there is a real event (for example, the black co-worker of a Jewish patient is promoted while she is not), which is ambiguous, may have many meanings in reality, but is reminiscent of earlier group traumas—and often individual rejections and abandonments as well? Could these feelings and temporary inability to modulate them, with consequent fear of feeling out of control, be then dealt with by processes of projection and incorprojection? And could it be that when there is a real event in the lives of Jews and blacks (for example, the difference in opinion between the two communities with regard to the O. J. Simpson trial, the different responses of the two groups to Farrakhan's comments during the Million Man March) that the real event serves as a stimulus whereby group rage can be rationally mobilized and expressed? Zilboorg (1947) asks:

> What better, psychologically more economical, more efficient way out of this difficulty than to find other people, other groups, and by way of projection consider them a compact herd, and by way of the same projection endow them in toto with all those repressed drives which threaten us inwardly with social ostracism and amputation from the herd? . . . What other method would permit us so efficiently to mobilize a great deal of what we hold back, return it from the repressed, and thus find a legitimate outlet or vehicle for our hate, murderous aspirations, and destructive inquisitiveness? . . . What a relief . . . it is to "discover" in time that the Jew, the Negro, the Communist, want to kill us and take our bank accounts away, and perhaps even our wives and daughters. . . . To rise and take measures . . . and kill, socially and individually, the Jew, the Negro, the Communist, the Catholic, in accordance with the best tradition. . . . We can then kill without feeling that we violate God's commandment; we can satisfy our needs and yet not only be freed from a sense of guilt, but feel noble. (321–22)

What I am stating here is that the conflict between blacks and Jews needs to be understood both in terms of its historical perspective, which I have discussed above, and also in terms of how this real history may have allowed, and continues to allow, the emergence of prejudicial feelings that arise within the minds of individuals of these two groups, using as a rational vehicle of expression the history of pain and discrimination between the two groups. My intent here is to neither minimize nor unduly emphasize the importance of either inner reality or external reality; however, I do feel that it would be most helpful in terms of understanding the painful conflicts between the two groups to keep both internal and external realities very clearly in our minds.

ALLEVIATING THE CONFLICT

I deliberately do not use words in the above heading to suggest that the conflicts can be totally eradicated. Prejudice is so rampant, and related to such powerful inner and outer forces, that its complete obliteration may not be at all possible. In addition prejudice, with all of its painful and problematic aspects, may at times serve an important tool in the functioning of a society. I am referring here to an idea presented by Bird (1957) that in prejudice, aggression is dealt with by being directed onto substitute objects and restricted to words and feelings. If indeed this does occur, then prejudice with all of its problems may be "not without a positive measure of value for the individual and, in a broad way, for society as a whole" (512). However, we do have to remember that at times words, and certainly conversion of feelings into action, may be extremely problematic for the functioning of a group and for intergroup functioning.

What can be done about these conflicts? Many attempts have been made in various ways to decrease intergroup prejudices. These attempts have met with varying degrees of success. From a psychoanalytic perspective it is important to connect our interventions to our beliefs about the possible causes of prejudice. Keeping this in mind then, from the point of view of ego functioning, I believe it would be important to educate both groups in a genuine, meaningful, and complete way about the problems that each of them has suffered and endured. In both groups there are often profound and important areas of ignorance about the history of the group to which the person belongs and about the history of the "other" group. I have found that many prejudicial feelings and beliefs are retained, despite realistic evidence to the contrary. A first helpful step then would be for both groups to begin learning more about the historical perspectives of both sides of the problem. Such an effort could be organized at different levels of our society—for example, starting at the elementary school level and going on to the middle school, high school, and college levels. It could also be done by organizing groups within workplaces and organizations. This intervention might allow certain preconceived notions about each other to be challenged in light of historical facts. However, this is obviously not a new idea, and if prejudice could be resolved simply by knowing more about each other's historical realities we would have little cause for concern. The more problematic part of the issue has to do with feelings that often have very little connection with rational thought and logic.

We then have to think about how to begin to address feelings that may have as their stimulus certain factors in reality, but that have become invested with so many other psychological meanings that they have taken on a life of their own beyond reason. (I have mentioned examples of this earlier in the chapter.) As a beginning intervention, a general elucidation of the possible psychological dynamics that can cause prejudice would be helpful. In talking recently to a group of teachers who asked for an in-service about how to handle students in culturally diverse classrooms, I was only slightly surprised to find that they were all interested in learning about such dynamic underpinnings of prejudice and that they felt it would be helpful to talk to their students about it. We should, therefore, not underestimate the capacity of the general population to utilize such psychological knowledge. Having presented such information in a general way, one could then begin to focus in a more narrow and direct way on particular feelings that black and Jewish individuals within groups have experienced and are experiencing. This intervention as part of working with black and Jewish groups on a large scale would require, I believe, the presence of psychologically sophisticated facilitators. I do not think that it would be possible to talk meaningfully about certain feelings without the help of facilitators who not only understand social reality but also inner psychological conflicts (with their roots in individual and family dynamics) that get connected to social external events and, consequently, acquire a life of their own. These powerful feelings include feelings of narcissistic injury as a result of discrimination, envy of the other, rage for what one does not have, and for what the other has accomplished.

Some of the important aspects of such discussions could be to try to focus on the sense of being "unheard." I believe that this is often more a problem for blacks than it is for Jews. Many black people feel that the Holocaust, with all of its grim meaning, is something that is currently in the awareness of most people, and that Jews have been empathized with as a result of such awareness. Blacks talk about the ongoing trauma that they experience daily in subtle and not so subtle ways as they are discriminated against, especially by virtue of their skin color. They feel that their pain is minimized and often unacknowledged. It is assumed that the days of slavery are over and that what is happening with them at this point is a problem that is not of serious magnitude. Blacks talk about how this pain, which is often not acknowledged by the majority of society, creates in them a sense of terrible rage and a feeling of helplessness, in addition to making it difficult for them to empathize with the problems of Jews and other minorities. However, it also needs to be emphasized that such rage and envy can often smoulder endlessly and can be used protectively and defensively for various purposes. Just as there is a need to victimize and put down groups of people so, too, there may be a need in certain groups to remain victimized and put down. I believe there is some evidence for this in the competition between the two groups for the role of the one that has undergone the most suffering and victimization. It seems to me that at times this is analogous to the rivalrous feelings between family members, in addition to the external factors that have obviously contributed to the problem. One must pay attention to the fact that rage and envy, if they can be dealt with directly and appropriately, can often then help to mobilize healthy ambition and accomplishment. This also needs to be emphasized in discussions within such groups.

Third, the very powerful stereotypes that each group holds in its mind about the other—that is, stereotypes of laziness, greed, and manipulation—need to be talked about as projections of one's own unacceptable feelings onto the other group. This might allow individuals to see how they may have used historical reality and created, or re-created, painful historical reality because of their own inner conflicts.

I believe that the above intervention in terms of frank discussion of the psychological underpinnings of prejudice would be the most difficult of the tasks, yet it needs to be done in some way to allow those who are prejudiced and those who are discriminated against to fully appreciate and understand the pain that each of them has gone through, and to recognize what they may have done to each other, in order to begin to pave the way for a different kind of acceptance of each other. I am aware as I am writing this that I am talking about something that may be potentially very disturbing. Yet I believe that *it is precisely these issues—that is, the derogation, hate, envy, resentment, and stereotypes, which each group holds in its mind about the other but dares not talk about openly, except when "provoked"—which might remain totally closed off despite all kinds of education and intellectual understanding of psychological dynamics.* They would then continue to perpetuate a tradition of hatred. It is one thing for people to be shocked at Farrakhan's antisemitic remarks, or to be affected by the recent Texaco fiasco where racial slurs about Jews and blacks were exposed, but it is quite another to realize that these feelings not only reside in the minds of Farrakhan and certain Texaco officials but that quietly, like underground water eroding the earth, they are present as powerful stereotypes in the minds of Jews, blacks and, indeed, all of us. These unspeakable feelings have to be spoken about in some way, with the aid of facilitators who can intervene in and modulate the discussions, thereby perhaps opening the way for a process of mourning of that which was not, and hope for that which can be. In the words of the Bengali poet Rabindranath Tagore, this might lead to the creation of a space:

> Where the mind is without fear
> and the head is held high,
> Where knowledge is free;
> Where the world has not been broken
> up into fragments by narrow domestic
> walls;
> Where words come out from the
> depth of truth;
> Where tireless striving
> stretches its arms toward
> perfection;
> Where the clear stream of reason
> has not lost its way into the
> dreary desert sand of dead habit.

REFERENCES

Berman, Paul. 1994. *Blacks and Jews: Alliances and Arguments.* New York: Delacorte Press.

Bird, Brian. 1957. "A Consideration of the Etiology of Prejudice." *Journal of the American Psychoanalytic Association* 5:490–513.

Fischer, Newell. 1971. "An Interracial Analysis: Transference and Countertransference Significance." *Journal of the American Psychoanalytic Association* 19:736–45.

Freud, Anna. 1964, 1967. *The Writings of Anna Freud. Volume 5: Comments on Psychic Trauma*, 221–24. New York: International Universities Press.

Freud, Sigmund. 1921. *The Standard Edition of the Complete Psychological Works of Sigmund Freud. Volume 18: Group Psychology and the Analysis of the Ego*. 67–143. Translated by James Strachey. London: Hogarth Press.

———. 1930. *The Standard Edition of the Complete Psychological Works of Sigmund Freud. Volume 21: Civilization and Its Discontents*, 59–145. Translated by James Strachey. London: Hogarth Press.

Friedman, Murray. 1995. *What Went Wrong? The Creation and Collapse of the Black-Jewish Alliance*. New York: Free Press.

Goldberg, Eugene L., Wayne A. Myers, and Israel Zeifman. 1974. "Some Observations on Three Interracial Analyses." *International Journal of Psychoanalysis* 55:495–500.

Gordon, Kenneth H. 1965. "Religious Prejudice in an Eight-Year-Old Boy." *Psychoanalytic Quarterly* 34:102–8.

Holmes, Dorothy Evans. 1992. "Race and Transference in Psychoanalysis and Psychotherapy." *International Journal of Psycho-Analysis* 73:1–11.

Lerner, Michael, and Cornel West. 1996. *Jews and Blacks: A Dialogue on Race, Religion, and Culture in America*. New York: Penguin Books.

Safire, William. 1996. "Helping the Black Jews." *New York Times*, September 9, A11.

Tagore, Rabindranth. 1961. *A Tagore Reader*, edited by Amiya Chakravarty. New York: Macmillan.

Traub-Werner, D. 1984. "Towards a Theory of Prejudice." *International Review of Psychoanalysis* 11:407–12.

Zilboorg, Gregory. 1947. "Psychopathology of Social Prejudice." *Psychoanalytic Quarterly* 16:303–24.

9

Sharing the Mark of Cain: The Jewish and African American Communities in America

A. MICHELE MORGAN

My initial exhilaration at being offered an opportunity to think and write psychoanalytically about the relationship between the American Jewish and African American communities quickly faded into confusion; there seemed to be so much to say about each community individually, yet talking about their relationship to each other was fraught with difficulty. The more I read and thought, the more I encountered ambivalence and contradiction.

I started with my own thoughts and feelings, as any writer does. As an African American in a field that has few blacks but many Jews, I welcomed the chance to look at this issue more deeply. Talking with others was helpful, but also increased my confusion. In conversations, in the literature, there was so much variation within each community—how could they possibly be looked at in relationship to each other when there was so little internal cohesion? Within each community existed a spectrum of socio-economic circumstance, educational levels, and political ideologies that grouping them at all seemed questionable. Still, I thought, there were clearly enough common underpinnings to be considered distinct communities, so the task must be ultimately achievable.

This, then, defined an initial problem: The black-Jewish *alliance* (or lack thereof), spoken of so freely in much of the literature, was a misnomer; it would be more precise to talk about the black-Jewish *alliances*. This distinction between singular and plural is far from being a nuance as multiple alliances, serving multiple historical, sociological, and psychological purposes, have been forged and broken over the years; this process continues.

Another difficulty was attempting to focus on the psychoanalytic, as opposed to historical and/or sociological phenomena. So inextricably are these perspectives intertwined that they defy separation; the historical and sociological remain an integral part of that understanding in the same way that both the historical background and the current thoughts and affect state are necessary to gain an adequate psychoanalytic assessment of an individual. In the United States the Jewish and African American communities have had unique experiences that have shaped their response to themselves and to each other. This is an irreducible reality.

I make a point of saying the *American* Jewish and the African *American* populations because the drama is played out against the backdrop of the American culture, a culture deeply in conflict with itself. This is a society that was founded on the principle of equality and freedom from persecution. There has been a vast difference between the ideals as they were conceptualized and the reality of how they have been put into practice. Both Jews and African Americans aspire to those ideals to some extent as well, bringing both groups into conflict with themselves and with each other.

Speaking about the conflict between these communities runs the risk of leaving the impression that conflict is the central nature of the interaction, which I believe to be untrue. In day-to-day life, the average African American or Jewish person is not principally involved in thoughts or actions related to the other community. It is important to state clearly that I strongly believe that the Jewish community, as a whole, is less racist than the non-Jewish white community and that the African American community, as a whole, is less antisemitic than the nonblack gentile community, although the research in this area has been inconclusive (Friedman 1995, 347). To a large extent, this is a war being waged between African American and Jewish scholars, whose accusations and treatises back and forth have become a subject of study in and of themselves. Nevertheless, events such as the Crown Heights riot in 1991 and the reaction to the Million Man March in 1995 indicated that *something* is going on between these two communities, and it is into that something that I will delve.

I find it impossible to talk about the problems between American Jews and African Americans separately from how those problems developed. As stated previously, the nature of the problems between these communities in the United States is deeply rooted in the American *stated* ideology of equality and assimilation, to which both communities aspire, at least in part. In this chapter, I will discuss how the quest for this equality and assimilation has drawn American Jews and African Americans into a particular relationship of cooperation and conflict. Simply put, I see the major problems between the two communities being permutations of three basic themes: reciprocally unrealistic expectations of each other, making use of the other community as Other to diminish the Other in themselves and insensitivity to the experience of the other group. These problems are interrelated, but I will discuss each of them in detail.

UNREALISTIC EXPECTATIONS

With the American culture so firmly founded on the idea of assimilation, both Jews and African Americans are seeking acceptance even while holding the conviction that they will never be accepted. Thwarted in that search by the rejection of the majority culture, African Americans and Jews have recognized each other as fellow victims of marginalization and have sought to make use of that particular alliance. This recognition and subsequent alliance, however, also led to anxiety provoking interdependence and reciprocally unrealistic expectations of the other community. These expectations took different forms for different parts of the two communities, but, simplistically and broadly stated, for some Jews, the expectations came to be that the African American community would freely accept the assistance given and, in accepting that assistance, provide an uncritical source of positive affirmation. For some in the African American community, the expectations were that Jews would absorb much of the antiwhite resentment that might be shunted their way and, most important, serve as a source of affirmation that the African American community did indeed have something to offer American society.

Both the Jewish and African American communities were using the other to alleviate internal anxieties about self-worth and marginalization and were therefore set up to "fail" each other, especially when these anxieties led them into conflict. In order to understand the nature of the "failures," it is necessary to look at some of the shared history of the two groups from the different perspectives of the Jewish and African American communities.

Although their experiences in this country have been significantly different, there have been enough similarities to forge a bond, however ambivalent. This bond has been most dramatically manifested in the cooperation between the Jewish and African American communities in the civil rights movement. It is a matter of history that Jews, along with African Americans, were actively engaged in multiple facets of the civil rights struggle, including political actions, demonstrations, and the founding of the National Association for the Advancement of Colored People (NAACP). Both Jews and African Americans sacrificed lives to advance the struggle (Friedman 1995, 177–93; Lerner and West 1995, 80–90; Walzer 1997, 401–3).

As mentioned earlier, however, this bond was not without ambivalence, which was demonstrated in the lynching of Leo Frank, a Jew, in 1913 (Friedman 1995, 63–66; Salzman and West 1997, 108). Jews, already struggling with establishing their position in American society, had a member of their community *lynched*, a barbarism used extensively against the African American community in the South. This linking with the fate of the African American community was complicated by the fact that Frank was initially tried and convicted of rape and murder on the word of a black man, something that was unheard of in the South at that time. Thus the

Jewish community had reason to fear that the violence turned against the black community could be turned against itself in a full-scale attack and felt aligned with blacks, but they also had reason to be uneasy about such an alliance. This marriage of common cause with distrust has been part of the relationship between Jews and blacks throughout American history. Much as siblings serve as sources of support as well as intense competition, Jews and African Americans have cooperated and competed with each other, their ambivalence intensified by the presence of the distant and dis-approving "parents" of mainstream society.

In the face of tremendous antisemitism in the American culture, the Jew-ish community has long looked to the African American community as a source of acceptance and confirmation of the Jewish role in the American social fabric. Jews in America, despite the diversity of the community, are generally connected by a tradition that is bound to the Torah but tran-scends the religious aspects of that tradition; that is to say, that many Jews that no longer consider themselves religious maintain a strong attachment to the philosophical mandate of transforming society toward greater fair-ness and equality (Lerner and West 1995, 81–86). Although this is part of the American ideology spoken so eloquently but practiced so poorly, the Jewish community has a better record of matching the word to the deed. The plight of African Americans in this country offered an opportunity for Jews to participate actively in this transformation, thus confirming and legitimizing their worth as a people and the right, perhaps the necessity, to exist with difference (Jewishness). The dedication devoted to this cause has been documented; that the numbers of nonblack workers in the civil rights movement were disproportionately Jewish is a matter of public record (Friedman 1995, 177–93; Lerner and West 1995, 85–86). Although the "use" to which the African American community could be put in this man-ner has been attacked by some African American scholars and historians as being self-serving, this attack has not been psychoanalytically informed. There is no act of altruism, no matter how selfless in appearance, that is without components of self-gratification, nor does that gratification nec-essarily diminish the act.

What, then, of the accusation of harm done to the African American community? What harm could be done by actively intervening on behalf of a less empowered minority? The difference in perspective must be closely attended to: African Americans did not solely want to be helped, they wanted to be empowered, to confirm that they had something of value to offer society. The cooperation between the two communities, whatever it may have been, was never cooperation between equals; the difference in access to mainstream society made this inevitable. The Jewish community has appeared to be solely in the position of benefactor, relegating the Af-rican American community to a "hat in hand" position in much of their interactions. Tremendously resentful that the assumption of such a position was necessary, some in the African American community experienced the assistance of the Jewish community as *further* humiliation. Alignment with the Jews, such as the founding of the NAACP in 1909, generated in some African Americans ambivalence much the way ambivalence had been felt by the Jews. Because blacks were initially not in a position of leadership (Friedman 1995, 45), even in this fundamental effort to restore a full sense of humanity, they were again reminded of the indignity of being less than autonomous. One way of defending against the rage and shame brought on by their position was to project onto the most accessible group: the Jews. In this way of defensive thinking, the Jews were not altruistic; indeed, the Jewish community was deliberately trying to debase and humiliate the African American community by behaving in a way that highlighted its helplessness and marginalization, the intent to actually further exploit the African American community.

In this way, the Jewish and African American communities "failed" each other by not living up to their respective expectations, however unrealistic. Part of the difficulty was that the unconscious needs of the communities were in direct conflict with each other. African Americans, making use of Jews as the white Americans that were the least rejecting, needed to emphasize their "contribution" to the Jews, while Jews needed to emphasize themselves as benefactors. Again, history and perspective are helpful in clarifying the conflict.

Jews have been locked out of mainstream America to some extent, in both de facto and psychological ways, despite white skin privilege. Because of this, the *mutual* nature of the interaction with the African American community has gone much deeper than has been acknowledged by many Jews. Many Jewish businesses remained in the communities that changed from Jewish to black; these businesses, still locked out of many nonblack communities because of discrimination, were able to contribute to the expanding economic base of the Jewish community by doing business with African Americans. This phenomenon was aided by the fact that the number of African Americans was much greater than the number of Jews. In addition to this tangible financial benefit was the psychological gratification attained from being of service to a community with fewer resources, but to fully acknowledge this benefit was to acknowledge the unmet needs of the Jewish community itself. Struggling to maintain self-esteem, as does any minority group that exists within a hostile majority, the Jews were put in a position to acknowledge that not only did they have unmet needs, but part of those needs were being met by a group even *more* devalued than themselves. For a number of Jews, this narcissistic injury was prevented by denial of mutual benefit, viewing African Americans as recipients only.

The African American community, in contrast, without the benefit of white skin privilege in a country where this is of the utmost importance, has not been able to be as directly helpful to the Jewish community. Defensiveness over this fact alone has been a source of anxiety and discomfort in the African American community; it has been experienced as a narcissistic injury to acknowledge being the recipient of benefits that cannot be reciprocated. Full acknowledgment of this state of affairs can invite further shame, a potentially intolerable position for a group already making Herculean efforts to ward off the shame and despair heaped upon it by social conditions. It became even more important for some African Americans that the mutually beneficial nature of the relationship with the Jewish community be made explicit, to validate a sense of purpose that was at times held on to tenuously; failure to do so was interpreted by some African Americans as active hostility on the part of the Jews.

This relative standoff between the two communities led the more vocal element in each community to make more strident and unrealistic demands; for Jews, this element demanded that African Americans respond to Jews only with gratitude, while the African American element demanded that Jews willingly (and uncomplainingly) absorb whatever frustrations and antiwhite sentiments African Americans might send their way.

For this faction of Jews, anything that emanated from the African American community that wasn't gratitude felt like a dangerous attack because it threatened Jewish self-esteem. The pivotal role in the collective American Jewish psyche that is given to African American gratitude is demonstrated by the increasing alarm at the perceived increase in black antisemitism. Currently at the center of this controversy is Louis Farrakhan, leader of the Nation of Islam and the highest profile African American making antisemitic pronouncements. There is little argument in any quarters that Farrakhan has made antisemitic statements, and the dismay of the Jewish population is understandable. Yet Farrakhan, at times, has been compared to Hitler, and the gross overstatement of this cannot be overlooked. A man who has *talked* about Jews in a negative, even vile, manner has been compared to a man who oversaw the systematic *murder* of millions of Jews, despite the fact that the Anti-Defamation League agrees that there have never been any incidents of Farrakhan or any of his followers committing a hate crime against Jews (Beiser 1997, 27). In reality, most Jews are cognitively aware of the fact that very few of the obstacles they have faced in the United States have come from the black community. The partly unconscious reliance on African American good will and gratitude, however, used to reassure themselves of their value as a people in the face of mainstream messages to the contrary, has caused any antisemitism in the black community to loom large in the Jewish consciousness. If black people, who have been so devalued themselves and have benefitted so much from Jewish intervention, can turn against them, what might come next? In a community that has suffered to the extent that the Jews have, this is a question of some gravity. This part of the Jewish community, therefore, has the unrealistic expectation that the African American community will serve as a source of gratification by focusing only on the role of Jews as benefactors and repudiating any antisemitism in their ranks even more assiduously than those communities that can do (and have done) the Jews real harm.

Much in the same way, some African Americans would have Jews carry the burden for all of white America. By their greater physical presence in the everyday lives of many African Americans, as opposed to the non-Jewish white population, Jews have been the target for more general anti-white frustrations in the black community. By the same token, that presence also gave many African Americans the ability to believe that other white people would ultimately cease the constant, intense attack on black self-esteem by assuming at least a *less* hostile posture. Jews, for many African Americans, came to stand for any willingness that might exist in the white community to grant dignity and autonomy for African Americans. Thus, many African Americans came to have an unrealistic expectation that Jews would behave in an idealized way toward the black community, fulfilling a deep need in that community to be treated with respect in order to consolidate self-respect. The betrayal experienced by failure of the Jewish community to live up to this ideal (as such failure would be inevitable) may account for the emergence of some of the more fantastic accusations leveled against Jews, including the view that Jews were significantly involved in the slave trade (Davis 1997, 65; Friedman 1995, 224; Gates 1994, 219). This historical inaccuracy, among others, has struck a chord among a faction of the African American population, perhaps those who are anxious to punish the Jews for being other than ideal white deliverers.

MAKING USE OF THE OTHER

The use of the Other as a tool of denial and projection is universally employed to alleviate anxieties over unacceptable impulses or traits in the self. The African American and Jewish communities are no exception to this. Their use of Otherness, however, is complicated by the fact that each group has been explicitly identified as Other within the American culture, and the indoctrination into this Otherness is so thoroughly integrated into the culture as to be inescapable; the result is internalization of the concept of their own Otherness, to varying degrees. Jews and African Americans, therefore, must deal with an experience of relating to *themselves* as Other, at least in part, often manifesting in the self-hatred that has been described in oppressed groups. Identification with the majority culture is sought as a way of diminishing their own sense of Otherness, but this identification has an inherent paradox: In a devalued group, the stronger the tendency toward identification with mainstream culture, the more intense the experience of self-hatred.

Jews and African Americans have made use of each other as a way of aligning themselves with mainstream American culture that somewhat deflects the self-hatred aspect by identifying with the hatred of another group. This means aligning themselves with mainstream America along different lines: whiteness for Jews and non-Jewish identity for African Americans. These alignments are particularly useful because they involve identifications with central aspects of the American culture that have been clearly but covertly identified as the norm. This identification takes the form of acknowledging the Jewish or African American group as Other, and relating in ways that reverberate with that of mainstream America. Thus, both Jews and African Americans can identify with mainstream American culture in ways they do not have to be conscious of most of the time, ways that diminish their own sense of Otherness but do not intensify self-hatred. Jews and African Americans, because they are less empowered than the non-Jewish, nonblack majority culture, also present to each other somewhat more vulnerable targets for the venting of frustrations, much the way siblings present a less threatening target than parents.

It must be noted that this identification with mainstream American culture is incomplete for both Jews and African Americans. The struggle with potential self-hatred, as well as the actual experience of being an identified Other, prevents complete assimilation of antisemitic or antiblack views. Identification is further hindered by an experience of shared victim status between the two groups, contributing to the cooperation evidenced by history, however complicated that cooperation may be.

An imbalance that exists in the use of Otherness between the Jewish and African American communities has to do with identifiability, a point discussed in more detail later. Average African Americans, even virulently antisemitic ones, are generally unable to distinguish a Jew from any other non-Jewish white; the distinction of "Jewish," therefore, for most African Americans, is a theoretical one. They cannot, in most day-to-day dealings they have with Jews, respond in a particular way that is different than the response to whiteness in general, even if they were so inclined. The reverse is not true, as almost all African Americans can be readily identified and therefore responded to in a particular way by Jews; this differential may contribute to the different ways antisemitism and racism manifest themselves in the African American and Jewish communities, respectively. Jews, who are so inclined, are able to respond to African Americans with action, however subtle that action might be, whether it is on the small scale of personal interaction or the greater scale of community response. Although less significant now than in the past, the most well-known (and viscerally responded to) action on the part of the Jewish community has been nonviolent: the persistent physical movement away from the African American community, as in the changing of neighborhoods, even while supporting the black community politically and in social causes. African Americans, usually unable to identify individual Jews, have responded with an antisemitism that is more verbal and symbolic, such as the attack by the Nation of Islam. The verbal attack stands in for more substantive action, prevented by the unidentifiability of Jews. In this light, it is not surprising that attacks of *action* as opposed to *words* have occurred in situations where Jews were identifiable, either through foreknowledge of Jewishness (as in the attack on Jewish business during riots) and/or physical distinctiveness, like the Crown Heights riot in 1991 (Kaufman 1997, 119–20).

INSENSITIVITY TO THE EXPERIENCE OF THE OTHER GROUP

A major source of contention between the Jewish and African American communities involves their respective insensitivities to the experiences of the other. The perception by each community of insensitivity on the part of the other community is highlighted, of course, by the previously mentioned expectation of both groups that similar experiences of oppression would render the other incapable of the projections that generally complicate the lives of minorities. This similarity in experience, living through dehumanization at the hands of others, has been instrumental in forging the bond that *does* exist; however, a bond forged in part due to shared trauma is riddled with ambivalence, as the very existence of such a bond serves as a painful reminder of second-class citizenship and Other status. Debates have raged on both the personal and the academic level over who has been the "most traumatized," Jews or African Americans, with each group feeling the other is so mired in its own pain that it cannot focus on anything or anyone else.

Part of this difficulty relates to the different relationships Jews and African Americans have to history. Jews, voluntary immigrants to the United States, came to escape persecution and make new lives for themselves. Bearing the unspeakable pain of those left behind, they have clung to their history and traditions, frequently identifying themselves as the one people that can trace their history farther than any other people on Earth. This history is significant not only for experiences with intense antisemitism, but for actual violence, including, but not limited to, the Holocaust. Many Jews therefore live with the anxiety that antisemitic sentiment may be the precursor to action, a state of mind perhaps only truly comprehensible to those having lived through actual atrocities. The fact that there are still living survivors of the Holocaust intensifies the sense that these events are not solely in the past. The Jewish culture has assumed a central role in the lives of many Jews, attested to by the number of Jews who still identify themselves as Jewish even in the absence of religious beliefs. When they speak of their history, it includes, but transcends, the Jewish experience on American soil; it includes centuries of persecution but also embraces centuries of accomplishment and steadfastness of identity.

In this context, there are some Jews who, when they look at African Americans, see a people that have suffered terribly for almost four hundred years, an undeniable tragedy, but one that pales in comparison to their knowledge of their own history of suffering. For those, the comparison of the experiences is unwarranted, even offensive.

The general American Jewish population cannot fully understand, as no one with white skin privilege in America truly can, the issue of involuntarily wearing one's mark of Cain at all times. At no point, whether the situation was merely annoying or actually life-threatening, can an African American choose to not identify him or herself as part of a particularized group. The simplicity of this belies the deep psychological impact this has on African Americans, as the perception of difference becomes intricately linked with an experience of identifiable physical difference.

For African Americans, history plays a different role. Africans did not seek a better life in the United States. Their affective experience of their history is based on a sense of having materialized out of nowhere to be captured, endure the Middle Passage, and be enslaved in America. This false but nevertheless persistent historical sense has its roots in the systematic efforts undertaken to rend the enslaved Africans from their culture and past. Those European Americans involved in the African enslavement accurately perceived that the most effective way to undermine a cohesive identity was to force a break with the past. The breaking up of family groups, separation of those with shared language, and absolute forbiddance of the practice of their own culture caused the Africans to rend with their past in a way never experienced by American Jews. The result has been a sense that African Americans sprang up on American soil, despite cognitive awareness that this is not true, and a deep abiding sense of homelessness that almost four hundred years have not been able to erase. This has been contributed to by the ongoing marginalization in America of anything in history or culture that was non-Western in origin. Although there have been fledgling attempts in the past two decades to reconnect with the lost African history (even the recent designation African American demonstrates this), these efforts are relatively new. This has the result of African Americans having a perspective particularly focused on an *American* experience, thus addressing the Jews with the perspective of almost four hundred years as opposed to thousands. African Americans cannot identify the suffering of the Jews *since their immigration to the United States* as equally painful as their own. It has been difficult to appreciate the history of the suffering of the Jews because of the affective breach that occurred in being rent from any past predating the last four hundred years; to acknowledge the previous history of the Jews is to acknowledge the perceived abyss of African history. Jews and African Americans are speaking to each other around the barrier of a history that must be clung to for shared meaning on the one hand, and a history that must be denied because it is unknown on the other. Norman Podhoretz spoke of this disparate experience with history between Jews and African Americans, stating: "I think I know why the Jews once wished to survive (though I am less certain as to why we still do): they not only believed that God had given them no choice, but they were tied to a memory of past glory and a dream of imminent redemption. What does the American Negro have that might correspond to this? *His past is a stigma"* (Podhoretz 1994; 91; emphasis is added). Podhoretz also makes the mistake of confusing the breach in the history of African Americans with the true lack of any significant history. He, too, speaks as though African Americans sprang forth on American soil, unconsciously identifying with the marginalization of anything non-Western.

Another area of insensitivity toward Jews centers around physical visibility, particularly skin color. As previously mentioned, Jews have some insensitivity regarding the impact of this difference on nonwhite Americans. African Americans have come to relate the experience of discrimination, with its resultant humiliation, shame, and struggles with self-image, with skin color. The experience of Otherness is intimately associated with easily identifiable differences, along with whatever nonvisible components that might be involved. It is difficult for many (and impossible for some) African Americans, therefore, to appreciate discrimination that is based less on physical difference but on heritage or cultural difference in the *absence* of physical identifiability. That Jews enjoy white skin privilege renders many blacks less sympathetic to whatever persecution Jews experience. This is exacerbated by the relative affluence of the Jewish community as compared to the African Americans community; if discrimination is perceived in terms of relative poverty and physical identifiability, Jews are seen as less affected and subsequently less traumatized.

The rising popularity of a figure such as Farrakhan is understandably alarming to Jews, perhaps giving rise to the erroneous (I believe) belief that African Americans are more antisemitic than other non-Jews. Although some studies have supported the view of greater African American antisemitism, the data has been contradictory (Friedman 1995, 347). What many in the Jewish community fail to realize is that most African Americans respond to the positive message of self-sufficiency and community uplift and are able to dismiss, perhaps too easily, the antisemitism of his message. Because of the strength of his pro–African American message, it should be noted that Farrakhan has also been allowed to be more critical of the African American community than almost anyone else.

Thus, I have postulated that marginalization in American society has fostered cooperation as well as competition between Jews and African Americans, leading to unrealistic expectations, making use of the Other, and insensitivity to the experiences of the other community. These are clearly interrelated phenomena; for example, the perception of the other community as Other enhances the degree of insensitivity and vice versa. Jews are able to use African Americans as a source of psychological gratification as well as a source of reassurance that Jews are not the most marginalized group in America. African Americans have used the perceived whiteness of American Jews as a means of alleviating anxiety about total marginalization (when focusing on the "alliance") but also a more readily accessible target for resentment (when focusing on relative distance and higher social status). Each community has used the other in an attempt to master its own internal anxieties about its place in society, leading to a relationship that is volatile at worst, tenuous at best.

"SOLVING" THE PROBLEMS

The delineation of problems, no matter how confusing or difficult, is never as problematic as the generation of solutions. This, already being the more difficult task, is complicated by the fact that analysts don't *solve* problems per se—they work toward enlightenment and clarity with the hope that this will enable people to solve their own problems. Having said this, any changes that occur between American Jews and African Americans will have to include realistic goals; the elimination of discrimination or the human need of the Other will not be brought about by Jews or African Americans. Differences, at times tensions, will continue to exist between two groups that are likely to continue to be devalued in the larger culture for some time to come. As in individual psychoanalysis, the most important changes will be less dependent on changed external circumstances as they will be on *internal* shifts within each community.

For the Jewish community, this will include a reckoning with the anxiety of unmet needs and partial marginalization in a country whose stated doctrine is so close to their own cultural doctrine. By reckoning I do not imply acceptance, as I believe it imperative that neither group ever accept the devalued status it has been assigned, but that this anxiety is more constructively dealt with on a conscious basis. Although many Jews have a conscious anxiety about their status in American society, I believe much of the intensity remains unconscious. As long as this anxiety is allowed to remain unconscious, there will be a corresponding (and equally unconscious) need for an Other that is even more devalued; it will remain important to relate to this Other in a devalued way as well, if that Other is to serve the purpose of warding off anxiety about Jews themselves. There is no other group in the United States better situated to serve as that Other than African Americans, and tensions between the two communities will escalate.

What does this mean on a practical level? Frankly, Jews must acknowledge the existence of white skin privilege and the difference that makes in American society. This does not imply that Jews are completely unaware of the advantages conferred by being considered white in America; if that were the case, they would not have made the efforts they have over the years. This also does not imply that Jews should be required to make any sort of formal acknowledgment to African Americans, as the focus here is on *internal* shifts, but rather be prepared to examine how deeply racist feelings may go in their own community and how that racism might show itself. There is no elimination of racist feelings any more than there can be elimination of the human need of the Other, but increased awareness can modify action, and this is the only reasonable goal.

African Americans, on the other hand, have felt such a need to protect themselves that the process of self-criticism has been impaired. It is difficult for them to criticize a message such as Farrakhan's because it is so positive in many respects, yet the antisemitic element needs to be identified and protested; silence, not to mention defense, in the face of such statements has been interpreted as consent. To reject antisemitism, for some, will mean giving up the sadistic pleasure of being able to project onto another group when one's own group is so devalued. The necessity of this is not to appease the Jewish community, but to preserve integrity in the struggle to improve group self-esteem.

Again, in practical terms, African Americans must be willing to speak up, whether as individuals or in groups, when antisemitic comments are made and examine themselves for antisemitism. The ideas that blacks cannot be prejudiced because of their own experience or that prejudice that cannot be acted on doesn't count must be rejected. As with Jews, this confrontation with inner struggles is not for public consumption, it is an internal process with the expectation of internal results.

I stress the necessity of an internal process in each community preceding any interactive process between the two communities because I believe the internal anxiety can only be dealt with in a private process. How can communities of this size have "internal processes"?—by closing off the dialogue to anyone else. One of the reasons Farrakhan has been able to criticize the African American community, sometimes sharply, is because he has closed the dialogue to whites. He is willing to interact with whites but makes it clear that his comments are for the African American community, and has thus been able to have criticism taken in and considered by a community that is often intensely sensitive to criticism; he has successfully established a forum in which African Americans can speak frankly among themselves. This type of "within community dialogue" is possible in both the Jewish and the African American communities, as both communities have modes of communication that are utilized primarily by the community itself. Both communities are also insular enough such that at least some time is usually spent in the absence of members of other communities. This period of "closing off" may be necessary to establish the safety to explore sensitive issues in much the same way that the analytic situation of privacy slowly establishes the safety to explore internal conflict on an individual basis. Just as it is not necessary that a patient withdraw from his or her everyday life to undergo analysis, it would not be necessary that the Jewish and African American communities withdraw from or change their way of interacting with the other community while this process took place.

Many of those looking at the conflicts between Jews and African Americans have suggested increased dialogue between the two groups as a way of establishing less conflicted relations. I feel this would be helpful only after an internal process had taken place or at least had been started; to do otherwise would risk increasing anxieties, therefore increasing the need for the defenses that are already hampering less conflicted interaction. I have similar feelings about solutions that call for education—this could be helpful, but the difficulty between Jews and African Americans is not principally one of lack of information. Information cannot be taken in until both the Jewish and African American communities feel more secure in their abilities to contain their own anxieties and rage about their status of Other in America without having to recruit the other community so intensely.

This "solution," in the end, is inadequate and incomplete. It is inadequate because there is no absolute self-awareness, as an individual or as a group, and incomplete because some of the projections of both Jews and African Americans do in fact exist. History has demonstrated that in this conflict, as in others, external threats to both groups will enhance cooperation and external threats to one (or certainly threats that exist between the two groups) will intensify tension, but the alliances will continue to be forged and broken. Perhaps the internal process described will facilitate overall collaboration.

REFERENCES

Altman, Neil. 1995. *The Analyst in the Inner City: Race, Class, and Culture Through a Psychoanalytic Lens.* Hillsdale, N.J.: Analytic Press.

Beiser, Vince. 1997. "Farrakhan Talks to the Jews." *The Jerusalem Report* 8 (June): 26–32.

Berman, Paul, ed. 1994. *Blacks and Jews: Alliances and Arguments.* New York: Delacorte Press.

Burack, Cynthia. 1997. "The Sexuality Revolt in Black and White." *Journal for the Psychoanalysis of Culture and Society* 2 (spring): 65–74.

Davis, David B. 1997. "Jews in the Slave Trade." In *Struggles in the Promised Land: Toward a History of Black-Jewish Relations in the United States,* edited by Jack Salzman and Cornel West. Oxford: Oxford University Press.

Friedman, Murray. 1995. *What Went Wrong? The Creation and Collapse of the Black-Jewish Alliance.* New York: Free Press.

Gates, Henry Louis, Jr. 1994. "The Uses of Anti-Semitism, with Memoirs of an Anti-Anti-Semite." In *Black and Jews: Alliances and Arguments,* edited by Paul Berman. New York: Delacorte Press.

Harris, Herbert W., Howard C. Blue, and Ezra E. H. Griffith. 1995. *Racial and Ethnic Identity: Psychological Development and Creative Expression*. New York: Routledge.

Kaufman, Jonathan. 1997. "Blacks and Jews: The Struggle in the Cities." In *Struggles in the Promised Land: Toward a History of Black-Jewish Relations in the United States*, edited by Jack Salzman and Cornel West. Oxford: Oxford University Press.

Lerner, Michael, and Cornel West. 1996. *Jews and Blacks: A Dialogue on Race, Religion, and Culture in America*. New York: Penguin Books.

Mama, Amina. 1995. *Beyond the Masks: Race, Gender, and Subjectivity*. London: Routledge.

Podhoretz, Norman. 1963, 1994. "My Negro Problem—and Ours, with Postscript." In *Blacks and Jews: Alliances and Arguments*, edited by Paul Berman. New York: Delacorte Press.

Salzman, Jack, and Cornel West, eds. 1997. *Struggles in the Promised Land: Toward a History of Black-Jewish Relations in the United States*. Oxford: Oxford University Press.

Walzer, Michael. 1997. "Blacks and Jews: A Personal Reflection." In *Struggles in the Promised Land: Toward a History of Black-Jewish Relations in the United States*, edited by Jack Salzman and Cornel West. Oxford: Oxford University Press, 1997.

Young-Bruehl, Elisabeth. 1996. *The Anatomy of Prejudices*. Cambridge, Mass.: Harvard University Press.

10

The Conflict Between Blacks and Jews: A Lacanian Analysis

MARK BRACHER

Psychoanalysis offers three basic resources for solving social problems, and each can be of use in dealing with the black-Jewish conflict. First, psychoanalysis offers a model of subjectivity that allows us to hypothesize what sorts of basic forces are producing a particular behavior. Second, psychoanalysis offers a particular technique for identifying the specific psychological forces that are producing any given behavior, including the behaviors involved in the conflict between blacks and Jews. This technique involves analyzing the discourse of the people whose behavior is in question in such a way as to discern the desires, fantasies, enjoyments, anxieties, conflicts, and defenses that are motivating these people. Third, psychoanalysis provides two fundamental strategies for intervening effectively and ethically (i.e., in a manner that is neither authoritarian nor seductive) in these psychological roots of the social problem. The first strategy (the properly psychoanalytic one) involves helping the people concerned to gain greater awareness and ownership of the intrapsychic forces that are motivating their destructive behavior. The second involves providing alternative, less destructive objects or pathways to gratification for these psychological forces.

MICHAEL LERNER'S PSYCHODYNAMIC ASSESSMENT

How these resources of psychoanalysis can be used to help resolve the black-Jewish conflict can be explained most economically via a critique of what is arguably the most insightful account to date of the causes and possible cures of that conflict: Michael Lerner and Cornel West's co-authored book *Jews and Blacks: A Dialogue on Race, Religion, and Culture in America*. In this book, Lerner contends that the root causes of present racial tensions are similar to those that gave rise to the horrors of the Holocaust, and he argues that to resolve the present conflicts we need to take a crucial action that those opposed to the Nazis failed to take—namely, recognizing the psychological needs that are motivating the aggressors: "Instead of demonizing the fascists (yes, they were demons, but saying so didn't win any support among those who didn't already share that perception), they [the opponents of the fascists] should have been asking, 'What psychological, emotional, and spiritual needs are these people speaking to that gets such a powerful response, and how do we speak to those same needs without reverting to anti-Semitism or xenophobic nationalism?' " (238). Meeting these psychological needs, Lerner maintains, "is precisely the only strategy that will ever significantly help African-Americans in this country. . . . The only way to ever have stopped the rise of fascism would have been for Jews and the Left to have recognized that pain, addressed it, and offered alternative solutions to it besides those offered by the fascists" (240).

Lerner's questions are perhaps *the* most important questions to ask regarding the conflict between blacks and Jews. But Lerner's answers to these questions, while insightful and useful, reveal themselves to be incomplete when viewed from a psychoanalytic perspective. Lerner's answer to the first question—"What psychological, emotional, and spiritual needs are these people speaking to?"—is what he calls "meaning needs": "The alienation and the decline in solidarity and trust that undermines long-term relationships and families and friendships is based on the frustration of the psychological, emotional, and spiritual component of our being that I call our 'meaning needs.' This deprivation of meaning is also *real* oppression, and leads people to despair, to violence, and to living lives of pain every bit as experientially real as pain generated by poverty" (231). "The deprivation of these [meaning] needs," Lerner contends, "can often lead people to shoot each other on the street, just as much as the deprivation of economic needs can lead to family violence, alcoholism, and drug abuse" (241).

Lerner's answer to the second question—"How do we speak to those same needs without reverting to an anti-Semitism or xenophobic nationalism?"—is "a Politics of Meaning that challenges the ethos of selfishness and the economic institutions that generate that ethos, a politics that is as much concerned about alleviating the pain of whites as it is to alleviate the pain of Blacks, and that recognizes that in a fundamental way both pains are rooted in the system of organized selfishness" (240). "A Politics of Meaning," he explains, "involves exposing the ways that the dominant cynicism and materialism all contribute to people believing that the only rational thing they can do is to continually narrow their arena of caring and to shut their eyes and ears to the pain of others" (257). Thus, he argues, "the Politics of Meaning, with its call to change the dominant discourse from selfishness to caring, is a way of addressing the dynamics that undergird American racism" (178).

Lerner's view of the psychodynamics of the conflict sees it as basically a conflict between the narcissistic ego and its reality principle, on the one hand, and the ego ideal and its values of altruism and caring on the other:

> In my own work as a psychotherapist, I've found that most people, while caught in the dynamics of selfishness, would actually appreciate and yearn for a different kind of society—one based on caring. There are millions of Americans who show this in small ways—they volunteer in public and private agencies, they pitch in when their communities offer them opportunities to do so, and they happily engage in generous acts toward friends and family. But they also have come to believe that it would be crazily self-defeating for them to act on this caring ethos in the larger society, in their economic or political life. They've been taught that the world is governed by materialism and narrow self-interest, and that they would be irrationally self-destructive if they were to act on a different set of assumptions. So what you see happening in this society is that people are pulled between a part of them [their ego ideal] that really wants to act according to their own highest moral vision and another voice inside [their ego and its reality principle] that tells them that they would be stupid to do that. (256)

In Lerner's view, then, it is largely the quest to actualize one's highest ideals that leads people to embrace racism and antisemitism:

> Most people, while responding to the reality of a society in which everyone else can be expected to act on narrow self-interest, and in which they must themselves act that way for self-protection, nevertheless hate this way of being and desperately seek an alternative. They seek communities of meaning and purpose which transcend the selfishness of the competitive market society. Sometimes they find those kinds of communities in religious or nationalist forms that are benign, but all too often they find those communities inextricably linked to racist anti-Semitic, homophobic, or xenophobic programs. Our task as liberals and progressives is to develop a Politics of Meaning that can address these same needs for a community that is committed to caring for each other, but which does not link that caring to a denigration or assault on "the evil Other" (be they African-Americans, Jews, gays and lesbians, or anyone else). (256)

In sum, Lerner argues (and West seems largely to agree) that the root causes of the conflict between blacks and Jews are a general lack of meaning in our society today and a dominant discourse and ethos of selfishness, and he maintains that what is needed to resolve the black-Jewish conflict, as well as other instances of social conflict and injustice, are a new discourse and ethos of meaning and caring. "The major problem facing the Black community," Lerner says, "like the major problem facing the rest of the population, is the dominant ethos of selfishness and reckless disregard for others, an ethos that then allows so many Americans to turn their backs on the poor, a majority of whom are white, but also turn their backs on the concentrated suffering of the Black community" (250).

Lerner's analysis is of considerable value, first, because it recognizes that reducing the black-Jewish conflict requires identifying and addressing its psychodynamic roots, and second, because it identifies narcissistic wounds (or "meaning needs") as a major cause of the aggressivity that fuels the conflict. However, Lerner's analysis overlooks a number of crucial factors that psychoanalysis can identify, and as a result, his proposed solution is destined to be less successful than it could be if it took these factors into account.

The "meaning needs" that Lerner identifies are certainly important components in the black-Jewish conflict. But Lerner's account needs to be supplemented in two important ways. First, the nature of the "meaning needs" requires greater clarification and precision. What are these "meaning needs," exactly? Where do they come from? How can they be filled? Can they be changed? If so, how? Second, there are other needs besides "meaning needs" that play a crucial role in the conflict between blacks and Jews, and these additional needs must be explored as well. In what follows, I want to explain both the meaning needs and the additional psychological needs and show how the black-Jewish conflict is largely a function of how these various needs of each group are either filled or frustrated by the other group. To explain these needs and the intergroup dynamics that they involve, I will make use of Lacan's theory of discourse, which identifies four fundamental needs that are the basic components simultaneously of individual personalities and of groups and societies. That is, the same needs that define individual identity and determine individual behaviors also function to define group identity and determine intergroup relations.

BASIC PSYCHOLOGICAL NEEDS ACCORDING TO LACAN

S_1 (Ego Ideal): Identity, Ideals, Values[1]

The first need that Lacan identifies is what we might call the need for identity, the need to be someone, to be recognized as a certain person or type of person, and to be able to recognize oneself as a particular person or type of person. This need is filled by various identity-bearing signifiers, which are a subclass of what Lacan calls "master signifiers." A master signifier is a term whose meaning and value go without saying. They are the "god-terms," the words that are used to define, evaluate, and situate other terms, without appearing to need any justification or evaluation themselves. We all need to feel that we embody some such terms if we are to feel that we have any worth. Common identity-bearing master signifiers of this sort include signifiers of one's gender, ethnic, religious, professional, and national identities, which form the core of one's ego ideal. This aspect of our identity-construction begins when we begin to learn language. In learning language, we come to recognize ourselves as either male or female and as being of a certain race, ethnic group, class, religion, and nationality, as well as being "good" or "bad," "smart" or "dumb," "strong" or "weak," "big" or "small," and so on.

These signifiers of our identity are very precious to us, for they are quite literally essential elements of our being. Our embodiment of signifiers valorized within a code can provide us with a profound sense of well-being and enjoyment, and, conversely, our failure to embody such a signifier, or our embodiment of signifiers denigrated within a given code, can cause us severe anxiety or depression or evoke powerful feelings of aggression in us. Thus a fundamental and continuous aim, present to some degree, although not necessarily consciously, in virtually every utterance and action, is to consolidate and enhance our ego and its sense of identity by allowing the ego to recognize itself as embodying the signifiers constituting its ego ideal. We can see the significance of this identification with signifiers by observing the extent to which people will go to defend both the integrity of their identity-bearing master signifiers, as well as their own claim to these signifiers: Most people become upset when someone denigrates one of their master signifiers—as, for example, in the statement, "Men are pigs!" or when someone threatens to deprive them of one of their master signifiers, as with a statement like, "You're not a real man!" or "You're not a true American!"

S_2 (Ego): System, Knowledge, Belief

The second psychological need identified by Lacan corresponds to what Lerner calls "meaning needs." This need, which is met by knowledge and beliefs of various sorts, as well as by one's membership or participation in various organizations, is a need for relationships between oneself and other people and things and among other people and other things. This need for relationship is both a cause and an effect of one's need for identity. Identity is an effect of relationships: as someone who helps others learn and is paid by the state for doing so, I am a teacher. Identity is also a cause of relationships: If I want to identify myself as a scholar and a teacher, I need to have some sort of productive relationships with ideas and with students, respectively. Meaning is a function of one's identity having consequential relationships with other persons and things. Insofar as my being has little consequence for other persons or things, or insofar as the persons or things are themselves seen as inconsequential, my life lacks meaning.

The most meaningful knowledge and beliefs concern one's own most consequential relationships to the most consequential of other beings. But even trivial knowledge, of the sort that for all intents and purposes is totally inconsequential, and of persons or things that apparently have no significant relation to us, can provide a modicum of meaning, through the abstract, purely formal order, stability, and comprehensiveness that it offers us. All of us use knowledge to some extent in the way the autistic Raymond employed his encyclopedic knowledge of baseball statistics and the television schedule in the film *The Rainman*: to provide ourselves with a sense of order, stability, and meaning in the face of an uncertain and ever changing environment. This need to possess or inhabit a system, however abstract or inconsequential it might be, can be inferred from the gratification we get from recalling, rehearsing, and expressing all sorts of inconsequential knowledge concerning sports, entertainment, art, literature, and many other topics—not to mention the lengths to which we will go to acquire, produce, preserve, protect, and/or defend our systems of religious, metaphysical, epistemological, political, social, and historical knowledge or belief. Meaning is thus a function not only of the consequences of our positions for other positions, *but also of our grasp of all these positions*: meaning increases not only to the extent that our position is one of dominance and consequence (as noted above), but also to the extent that we have a firm grasp of all the positions and their consequences for other positions. When our knowledge or our position is challenged in some way, we thus respond with anxiety and aggressivity.

The *a* (Id): An Object or Quality that Escapes or is Excluded by the System

In subjecting ourselves, in our quest for identity and meaning, to certain signifiers or positions and to the systems or organizations of which they are a part, we inevitably sacrifice certain aspects of our being. The most obvious sacrifice comes in the realm of gender identity, where the polymorphous perverse infant, in order to become either a "boy" or a "girl," must repress certain physical desires and pleasures, as well as certain types of behavior and relationships to others. Boys, for example, are traditionally pressured to give up passive desires and behaviors, while girls are made to give up more active, aggressive impulses and actions. At the same time, the infant grows further and further from that primordial and ineffable bliss that it experienced in the dyadic relationship of its polymorphously perverse body to the mother's body. The oceanic feeling of satiation at the mother's breast, of the soothing provided by the mother's gaze, by the tone of her voice, and by the phonemes she uttered, and of the uncoerced and unfettered release of urine and feces and enjoyment of genital sensations—these experiences are reduced to vague memories that form the ambivalent prototypes for what the subject of identity and meaning has lost and/or transcended. The objects of such experiences—which Lacan calls the object *a* and identifies as the breast, the phallus, the urine, the feces, the gaze, the voice, and the phoneme—function variously as the objects (either alluring or repulsive) that on the one hand threaten one's identity and meaning and on the other hand promise to restore that (mythical) primordial lost jouissance and fullness of being. In its positive aspect, an object *a* is any priceless commodity or special substance that promises to provide ultimate bliss or wholeness of being. Any object or substance that we yearn for or lust after—including a certain person, food, drink, drug, product, material, or quality—is an instance of the positive object *a*. Any object or substance that repulses us, horrifies us, or makes us anxious—that is, anything that threatens our bodily, intellectual, or moral homeostasis, including a particular person, food, drink, drug, material, or quality—is an instance of the negative object *a*.

A positive object *a* functions much like a fetish object: It allows us to disavow the structural deficiency of the Great Other—that is, the incapacity of the System (God, Society, Nature, Language) to provide us with absolute meaning and fulfillment—by promising that the object itself will provide this fulfillment for us. Fantasized, idealized sexual partners such as celebrities function as this sort of object *a* for many people, who are convinced that if they could only possess the idealized person, their bliss would be absolute and their lives complete. Advertisers often try to position their products as positive objects *a*. Examples include the car that promises to transform one's life, the perfume that will make one irresistible, and the makeup or clothing that will transfigure one's body. Groups and entire societies can have positive objects *a*, such as a particular piece of land the possession of which, it seems, would fulfill the nation's destiny.

A negative object *a* functions much like a phobic object, or scapegoat: It too allows us to deny the structural deficiency of the Other, and hence our own inescapable vulnerability or lack, by attributing this lack to a particular agent (either human or nonhuman), the avoidance or destruction of which promises to free us from the lack that plagues us. The quintessential example is the way in which Jews functioned for the Nazis and continue to function for many militias and other antisemitic groups in our country: as the purported cause or secret agent responsible for whatever real or imagined economic or political woes plague the antisemite. As Elisabeth Young-Bruehl has shown, the antisemite often describes the Jew in terms of filth and excrement—that is, as the negative object *a*.

Being the object a

In addition to the active need to *possess* (or control and destroy) the object *a*, we also have a powerful (if unconscious) need to *be* the object *a* that the Great Other, or the System, is lacking or has rejected. Whenever one performs an action, assumes a function, or occupies a position that is to a significant degree outside a system or Symbolic order, resisting assimilation by the system, one is functioning as an object *a* in relation to the system. The object *a* can function in relation to the system either as something positive—that is, as a special something that complements, supplements, and completes the system—or as something negative, something that frustrates, challenges, or thwarts the system. Either way, the person or group embodying the object *a* experiences a heightened sense of being. Since we have all suffered loss of being as a result of being socialized by the various systems to which we are subject, we find a dual gratification in positions outside the system: (1) as an object that frustrates the system, we (a) gain a sort of revenge on our aggressor (the system) and (b) have a basis of existence or being that is not subject to or dependent on the system, and (2) as an object that the system needs or lacks, we gain recognition by the system and a certain value within the system precisely by being outside the system (the most obvious instance being the criminal who becomes one of the "ten most wanted" individuals in society).

We can occupy the position of the positive object *a* by virtue of products that we produce, services that we provide, or other functions that we have in relation to the System or Symbolic Other. For example, insofar as members of a group feel that the group is producing a uniquely valuable product or providing an indispensable service, they are assuming the position of object *a* in relation to society as a whole. Certain occupations—farming, medicine, law enforcement, and so on—lend themselves particularly well to assuming the position of object *a* in relation to society as a whole, since these occupations enact functions that are essential for the preservation of life.

The negative instance of the object *a* is found in various kinds of rebels, outlaws, and counterculture members. Any kind of activity that is radically disjunctive from the Symbolic order or official system can provide an individual or group with the status of a negative object *a*. Subversive or nonconformist individuals, as well as gangs and various countercultural groups, including subgroups such as Marxist teachers, legal services attorneys, and so on, can occupy the position of a negative object *a* for society as a whole insofar as they function as gadflies, obstructionists, subversives, or revolutionaries. Such a position can be quite gratifying. Within a university, one can see faculty, many of whom have unspectacular records as teachers and scholars and who have thus probably not gained significant narcissistic gratification within the official university culture, performing as various instances of the negative object *a* in relation to the official organization. I am familiar with a number of faculty, for example, who have devoted a large portion of their energies for most of their academic careers to fighting administrators at the departmental, college, and university levels. In most cases, the ostensible reason for a particular fight is little more than an excuse, and usually these individuals don't want any official powers or administrative positions themselves, since they derive their gratification not from power per se but from obstructing the system.

"Service departments"—that is, departments that are not part of the central production process, that do not contribute to the organization's public profile or identity, and that function as the poor stepchild or the beast of burden within a system—can also function as instances of the negative object a. They are the refuse that the system does not recognize as part of its official, public identity but without which the system could not function. In the university this includes departments whose main function is teaching basic level required courses (e.g., freshman English or foreign language courses) to undergraduates rather than producing significant research or preparing majors for significant professional activity. Members of such departments sometimes gain satisfaction by claiming that their work is more "real" than that of administrators or members of more prestigious departments, or by emphasizing that their function is crucial to the university or society as a whole despite the fact that it is not recognized as such.

$ (Superego): The Divided Subject, Expression of Intrapsychic Conflict and Pursuit of Integration

The fourth psychological need identified by Lacan is the need for the divided subject—split between its identity and meaning on the one hand (S_1 and S_2) and its lost jouissance and being on the other (object a)—to bridge the gap between these two sides of itself. Subjects, that is, need an opportunity, a venue, a space, or a ground upon which to confront their self-division—their alienation in S_1 and S_2 and their lack of loss of a—and to attempt to resolve this self-division. People fill this need to mourn, to complain, to rebel, to critique, to destroy, and to rebuild in the confessional, in conversations with friends, in the therapist's office, in their diaries, in some high school and college classes, and, increasingly, in identifications with suffering protagonists in TV programs and in films, as well as in books. Such expression can lead to several different forms of resolution. One resolution involves renouncing the a and mourning its loss, which entails altering S_1 (values, ideals) and S_2 (system, knowledge) so as to accommodate this renunciation. Another resolution involves embracing the a and altering S_1 and S_2 so as to accommodate the a's incorporation. A third resolution is sublimation of the a, which occurs by assimilating the a into the preestablished social ideals and values (S_1) and knowledge, systems, or practices (S_2)

THE FOUR NEEDS IN GROUP DYNAMICS

These four basic needs, according to Lacan, constitute the key elements out of which all social bonds—both alliances and oppositions, on both the individual and the collective level—are formed. Alliances—and hence groups—can be formed when any one of these needs takes the same form in several individuals. As Freud pointed out in *Group Psychology and the Analysis of the Ego*, groups can be based on shared ideals or values (S_1), shared knowledge, beliefs, or system membership (S_2), a shared object of fantasy (either the positive or the negative form of a), or a shared desire or sense of lack (\$), which Freud names hysterical identification.

Group identity and individual identity can also be constellated around an individual—a leader—who embodies or fills any one of these four needs in such a way that a significant number of people identify with the leader and take him/her as the externalized embodiment of their own need. Thus visionaries, masters, heroes, and celebrities lead by embodying attractive positions, ideals, or values (S_1) and/or enacting pursuit or possession of a special quality or state (a). Experts, bureaucrats, and administrators lead by appearing to possess knowledge, *savoir faire*, or wisdom offering solid meaning. Criminals, stars, and anyone else above and beyond the law can gain a following by appearing to offer access to transcendence of the System in the object a. And rebels, protesters, critics, reformers, and poets attract followers by expressing the self-division (\$) that others have lived but have been unable to articulate.

In addition, each of these needs can contribute to intergroup conflict and enmity in one of three basic ways. First, the quest to fill each need can lead to competition, rivalry, and even enmity with another group that threatens to deprive one of the means to satisfy a particular need. Second, an enemy can help fulfill a particular need by serving as a foil or defining antithesis for the fulfilling object. And third, an enemy can relieve one of a particular need, and of the intrapsychic conflict it entails, by functioning as a receptacle into which one can deposit that need. Each of these functions is a causal factor in the conflict between blacks and Jews.

THE DYNAMICS OF THE FOUR NEEDS IN THE BLACK-JEWISH CONFLICT

Threats to S_1 (Master Signifiers: Ideals, Values)

The conflict between blacks and Jews involves each of the four needs in one or more of these three ways. In the first place, each group in some way threatens each of the four needs of the other group. Much of the threat derives from the profound similarity of the two groups, which involves them in what Freud called the narcissism of minor differences, the fear that the other is encroaching upon and stealing part of one's identity. As Cornel West explains, "Jews and Blacks have been linked in a kind of symbiotic relation with each other. Whether they are allies or antagonists, they are locked into an inescapable embrace principally owing to their dominant status of degraded Others. . . . Both groups not only have a profound fascination with each other; . . . they also have much at stake in their own collective identities as a pariah and 'chosen' people" (Lerner and West 1996, 4). As a result of their common status as "degraded Others," there is a competition over which group is the most victimized—that is, which group really possesses the master signifier "victim"—and each sees the other as threatening to steal that identity from it. Lerner observes that "many Jews have the perception that . . . Blacks have seen Jews trying to rob from them their identity as 'the most oppressed group' " (7). Noting that "to be a Jew means to be oppressed, to be struggling, to be a certain moral conscience of the nation and so forth" (222), he states: "It looks as if people of African descent more readily meet the criteria of what it means to be Jews, suffering, chosen, getting kicked in the behind, still keeping on, you see. They figure, 'Wait a minute, we are the real Jews' " (222). Lerner responds: "This is one of the pathetic things . . . , to hear the followers of Leonard Jeffries and other Afrocentrist Blacks telling us, 'Oh you Jews aren't really Jews, you stole that identity from us Blacks.' There are so many ways that the Black people could create an identity for themselves. Why in the world should they need to take our identity and claim that it was theirs or, as some do, that our Torah is really their Torah. Yet you hear this pathetic and hostile articulation from some of them who talk about 'so-called Jews' " (7, 221–22). One of the causes of conflict between blacks and Jews is thus clearly the threat that each group poses to the other's claim to embody the S_1 "victim."

Threats to S_2 (System: Knowledge, Belief, Organization)

As Lerner's comment about the Torah indicates, S_2 is clearly involved in the conflict as well. In some cases the conflict is over who owns a particular body of knowledge or belief. In other cases the conflict over S_2 concerns whose S_2 is the truth. For example, does the truth lie in beliefs of certain blacks that Jews were major slave-traders, and that the precise numbers of Africans who perished as a result of slavery is much greater than most historians estimate? Or does the truth lie in the contrary beliefs that Jews were not a major force behind slavery and that fewer blacks perished than are claimed by some Afrocentrists?

Each group also threatens the type of S_2 or System that the other inhabits. Jewish people have invested more energy in, and have been more successful at, assimilating into the dominant academic, social, economic, and legal systems, many of them becoming quite accomplished scholars, social scientists, bankers, entrepreneurs, and attorneys. As West points out, "Jewish power and influence—though rarely wielded in a monolithic manner—in the garment industry, show business, medical and legal professions, journalism, and the academy—has had a major impact on the shaping of American life. We are reminded of the fundamental centrality of learning in

Jewish life, when we realize that as of 1989, of fifty American Nobel Laureates in the medical sciences—such as biochemistry and physiology—seventeen were Jews" (3). The greater success of Jews in achieving a place in the System is also demonstrated, according to West, by the contrary results of the respective nationalist movements of blacks and Jews: "The emergence of Black Nationalism around the turn of the century coincided with the appearance of Zionism. Fifty years later, after the Holocaust, the nascent and embryonic expression of Jewish national self-determination that was Zionism has become a nation state. Primarily owing to historical events, Jews were able to convince others of the Zionist case. At the same time, the Black nationalist movement is experiencing more and more set-backs, even in persuading folks in the Black community" (108–9).

Recently this perceived discrepancy between the presence of blacks and Jews in the System has been intensified by the establishment of the United States Holocaust Memorial Museum, as West explains:

> Now in Washington, D.C., you've got this powerful museum sitting at the very center of the capital of the nation. And you've got the series of evils which have historically sat at the center of American civilization uncommented on. When is America going to come to terms with its own legacy of injustice and evil toward indigenous people, the slave trade, Jim Crow, the suppression of the workers' movement? What this does for me is to raise the question, why this Jewish specific situation as opposed to these other specific situations? . . . The reason why you have the Holocaust Museum is not simply because the Holocaust was one form of evil, distinctive and unique, but that American Jews have levels of unity and influence and resources such that they can pull this thing off. Whoever really has the power to create such an event, that's who gets center stage. As long as Black people don't have the power to do it, nobody's going to give a damn about slavery, nobody's going to give a damn about lynching. . . . It just becomes a question of who has the money. If you have the money to do it, you can keep your memory going; if you don't, you can't. (145–46)

Thus it is, as West explains, that "Farrakhan sees Jewish unity . . . in the last twelve years as an obstacle to Black unity" (108).

Blacks often appear to have a different kind of privilege within the System. Excluded for centuries by slavery and the Jim Crowism from any significant roles in these systems, African Americans have developed a greater presence in underground, countercultural, or subcultural systems of knowledge, belief, and social relations, including affirmative action, the welfare system, and even the prison system. These systems, insofar as they share in the resources of the social system as a whole and thus provide recognition (however negative it may be) by that System, can be seen by Jews as providing special treatment or commanding a disproportionate share of the System's resources, for blacks.

Threats to the Positive *a* (Precious Object) and the Negative *a* (Refuse, Trash)

Each group also threatens the other's claim to embody Society's positive object *a*, that special something that will complete the social order or fill its lack. For Jews, this status has traditionally been embodied in the notion that they are God's chosen people, a notion to which Lerner gives the following contemporary construal:

> The notion of Jews as a chosen people is part of a religious system that requires Jews to act with a high level of morality toward each other and other people. . . . Jewish identity as constituted by the Torah tradition consists of being a witness to God as the force in the universe that makes possible the transformation of that which is to that which ought to be. . . . Human beings are created in the image of God, and charged to be partners with God in the process of changing the world from that which is to that which ought to be. Jewish destiny is to be part of the vanguard that brings this understanding to the world, that becomes a light to the nations precisely because it proclaims this possibility, and to be involved in the healing and transformation process. (55, 8–9)

Blacks threaten this status in several ways. One way is by pointing out the extent to which Jews are part of the System and thus part of the problem rather than the solution. Another is by rejecting Jewish aid in the black quest for equality, which, as Lerner explains, has the effect of evicting Jews from the position of devotees of universalistic, moral aims. "I don't know where to go now," Lerner says to West, "because you've thrown me away from the one place that seemed to be my community: namely, one struggling for a universalistic, moral goal. That was my community and you Black people are now telling me it is yours alone because right now you are the real victims of oppression" (87). And finally, blacks threaten Jews' status as the chosen people by echoing antisemitic stereotypes and referring to Jews as "bloodsuckers," which convert positive notions of Jewish exceptionalism into negative images of Jewish excessiveness—excessive usury, importunity, and ethnocentrism—which drains or pollutes the system rather than enhancing it.

Blacks' embodiment of the positive object *a* is designated most directly in the notion that black people possess soul, a certain style, quality, or *je ne sais quoi* that permeates black music, food, clothing, sexuality, and, indeed, black *being*. This object *a* manifests itself in what West calls "a history of Black styles and mannerisms: ways of singing, praying, worshipping, and communicating" (92). West's description of his sense of black style during his youth is another instance of blackness as a positive object *a*: "To be black at that time was a question of style, of being able to revel in a cultural way of life. We knew we had our own world, with its lingo, its way of walking and talking. It was also a highly sexualized state because we also felt a certain superiority over a lot of the white boys in relation to women. We had a certain suave style, a cool style: we believed it, a lot of other people believed it, and it was one way in which our blackness was set apart from whiteness," (20).

The Jewish threat to this positive object a derives primarily from Jewish entrepreneurship, and it finds its articulation in the black characterization of Jews as "bloodsuckers." At one level, this "bloodsucking" has a clear economic referent: Jewish business people making money from black customers. But in addition to this fact, the notion of "bloodsucking" expresses the black perception that their unique cultural and spiritual quality—their essence—is being appropriated and in some cases expropriated by white businessmen, of which Jews are perceived to constitute a prominent proportion. The most obvious instance of such expropriation may be in the music industry, where, for example, black blues musicians provided much of the substance—the soul, as well as the particular lyrics and melodies— of the music that made white rock musicians (beginning with Elvis) and music company executives (beginning with Sam Phillips, Elvis's first producer) rich and famous. This same scenario has repeated itself, with some variation (i.e., more black performers are achieving wealth and fame), in the case of Rap music, where the large majority of black rap musicians remain anonymous and impoverished.

Another way in which Jews threaten the black positive a is through their complicity in stereotyping blacks as lazy, oversexed, and immoral—that is, as exceeding the social order in a negative rather than a positive way: welfare cheats, drug dealers, vandals, and rapists who drain and pollute the system rather than contributing to it, or as the polluters of Jewish neighborhoods, "the cause of Jews losing the value of their investment in housing" (162).

As discussions of S_1 (master signifiers) and S_2 (system) have revealed, blacks and Jews also constitute threats to each other's claim to be the most victimized group. While this threat bears upon the S_1 and the S_2 of each group, it operates most centrally in each group's investment in its own position as exceeding, transcending, or excluded by the System (i.e., its position as object a), and its status as a divided, suffering subject ($). Here it takes the forms of arguments about, respectively, which group has been the most denigrated in history and which group has suffered more. The black threat to Jewish embodiment of the negative object a is articulated in Lerner's statement that "many Jews have the perception . . . that in the post-Holocaust years Blacks have seen Jews trying to rob from them their identity as 'the most oppressed group' " (7). The United States Holocaust Memorial Museum is the culmination of a series of events beginning with the Nuremburg trials, the documentation of the horrific realities of the concentration camps, and the establishment of Israel that recognized the monstrous degree of abjection and abnegation to which millions of Jews were consigned. Seeing no comparable recognition of their own status as abject object, some blacks have responded by inflating the numbers of blacks who perished in the slave trade and grossly exaggerating the role of Jews as slave traders (with the implicit logic that a group of slave masters could not also be an abject group). What is at stake in such arguments is thus not only each group's knowledge or status in the System; it is also, and perhaps even more important, the status of each group as a negative object *a*, or abject object.

Threats to One's Struggle with and Attempt to Overcome Lack: $

Closely related to each group's threat to the other's status as abject object is the threat that each group poses to the other's opportunity to voice its pain, to recognize and mourn its losses and thus attempt to move beyond them. Lerner explains one dynamic operating here: "The people who are the most oppressed are hurting so much that they can't think about this other guy's pain because it looks less real and hurtful than their pain. So the people who are hurting feel the need to say, 'Only my pain is real, and your pain is less.' In a way, it becomes people's only claim to dignity—that they can claim the uniqueness of their oppression" (241). Here again, phenomena such as the Nuremburg trials, the establishment of (and the United States' continuing support of) the Jewish State, and the erection of the United States Holocaust Memorial Museum are important resources for Jewish people: these all constitute substantial resources through which Jews can have their losses recognized and engage in mourning them. Insofar as there are no parallel resources for black people, black self-division—alienation, loss, anxiety—is repressed and the opportunities to reduce it are diminished. On the other hand, some Jews feel that the recognition of black suffering provided by initiatives such as affirmative action threatens to divert attention from the antisemitism that continues to threaten Jews today.

An Enemy as an Identity-Enhancing Antithesis

Conflict between blacks and Jews is thus produced and exacerbated by threats that each poses to the other's fulfillment of the basic psychological needs. At the same time, however, the conflict is also supported by the fact that an opponent or enemy can help a group in various ways to formulate and consolidate satisfactions of each of these needs. In the first place, enmity is a valuable contributor to identity (S_1) because identity is established only by differentiating oneself from—that is, opposing oneself to—various Others. Identity, as we have seen, is a function of master signifiers (such as "man," "woman," "white," "black," "African American," "Jewish," and so on), and signifiers mean what they mean only by virtue of their difference from and opposition to other signifiers. Being one thing is thus a function of not being its opposite, and humans often go to great lengths to avoid association with signifiers that are antithetical to their identity-bearing, or master signifiers. This fact is demonstrated, for example, by the way little boys often react when a playmate calls them a girl or suggests that their situation, demeanor, or activity is that of a girl. An enemy, as an entity emphatically opposed to oneself in crucial ways, thus becomes an excellent resource for defining oneself, constituting one's identity.

Thus, for example, Jewish people can define their unity and universalism in contrast to the apparent particularism and lack of unity of blacks and their possession of a distinct religious and national basis for identity in contrast to blacks' much greater acceptance of the religion and nationality of their oppressors. On the other hand, blacks can fortify their sense of independent identity by contrasting their civil rights and black nationalist activism against their oppressors with Jews' relative passivity in the face of the Nazi threat. Each group thus serves as a foil for the other, by which the other group can accentuate and consolidate its own sense of distinct identity. This dynamic can be seen in some of the stereotypes that each group has of the other: for example, Jews who view blacks as lazy and inept, as a way of seeing themselves as industrious and effective, or blacks who view Jews as scheming and manipulative, which lets them see themselves to be more guileless, open and honest—righteous.

The same is true with S_2, each group's knowledge, belief, or membership in or control of a system. Jews can take greater pride in their success in assimilating into and appropriating the System of their oppressors by observing the considerably lesser extent to which African Americans have done the same. Black people view the same phenomenon, but reverse the valence, so that Jewish assimilation becomes a sign of Jewish weakness and passivity, which then sets off favorably the black exclusion from the System, which now becomes a measure of black independence and strength and of black construction of an alternative or countersystem within the System. This dynamic can be seen, for example in street-wise black youth who contemptuously view academically successful Jewish youth as uncool—nerds—while these same Jewish youth regard themselves as sophisticated intellectuals or budding professionals and see their African American detractors as ignorant and morally bankrupt. Each group thus possesses or inhabits an S_2 as the truth that the other group lacks, rejects, or tries to destroy.

The same dynamic between the two groups operates with the object a. What blacks experience as the special something that sets them apart from other groups—their soul, or style, or sexuality—is often perceived by Jews and others as black sexual excess, or economic lassitude, or immaturity, which drains the System that Jews inhabit. From such a perspective, the black a becomes negative, and it is instead the Jewish devotion to the System—their status as chosen people—that has inestimable value. From the perspective of some African Americans, however, this devotion to the System—which Lerner describes in terms of a wholistic concern for actualizing latent possibilities in the System (see 8–9), and which Jews often experience as their universalism and higher moral standards—is rather the basis of a usury and commercial exploitation that makes Jews into nothing more than parasites—"bloodsuckers"—on the System that blacks inhabit. In this light, blacks are the System on which Jews are the parasite. Each group's object a thus has its value enhanced by being scorned by the other group and the System this group inhabits: the object a becomes the stone that the builders of the other group's System rejected, but which now becomes the cornerstone of something much more grand than the System from which it was excluded. Its value is also enhanced insofar as the other group tries unsuccessfully to assimilate it or to steal it.

A group's embodiment of the $, the expression of and attempt to overcome its own self-division, is also fortified by an enemy group. The most common and the most destructive function of an enemy group in relation to the $ is as a scapegoat, in which the enemy group is seen to be the cause of a group's pain, suffering, alienation, frustration, or lack. Jews and blacks sometimes function this way for each other, in several respects. Most obvious is perhaps the claim of some blacks that Jews are largely responsible for the enslavement of blacks in the first place and hence for the continuing suffering that blacks must endure as a result of the enslavement of their ancestors. Jews who see black welfare recipients as depriving Jews of their Social Security benefits are another example. Such scapegoating allows one to formulate a simple solution for overcoming one's self-division—eliminating or policing the other group that is seen as responsible—and thus enables one to avoid recognizing the inherent, structural grounds of one's lack and mourning one's loss.

When we have an enemy, the fact that we are always lacking something, always desiring—a fact due in part to the jouissance that we sacrifice in order to assume an identity in the Symbolic order—is not accepted as an inevitable consequence of the structure of human subjectivity but rather is attributed to a specific event or condition that was caused by a specific agent and thus might have been avoided and could possibly be rectified. The enemy is someone who, we imagine, has either stolen our jouissance, or is threatening to steal it, or someone who, we imagine, possesses a surplus of jouissance that threatens us and/or evokes our envy. Blacks and Jews serve as such enemies for each other.

An Enemy as a Suitable Target for Externalization

As should be evident from the preceding discussion, each group's perception of antithetical defining elements in the other group is never purely objective and is in many instances colored, if not wholly constituted, by projection. Enemies help us consolidate our identity not only by embodying antithetical defining qualities but also by harboring the actual or projected qualities that we must reject in order to embody effectively our own master, identity-bearing signifiers. To maintain an identity that we have assumed, we must disown and expel behaviors, relationships, attitudes, desires, and feelings that are antithetical to this identity. Thus, for example, in order to maintain one's identity as a boy, one traditionally had to avoid playing with dolls, being passive, feeling afraid, and so on. Enemies help one to get rid of such antithetical parts of oneself by offering what Vamik Volkan calls "suitable targets for externalization"—that is, objects onto which we can project and thus effectively rid ourselves of attributes that contradict the identity we have assumed. Thus boys who need to deny their own fear will often project it onto another child, chanting "Fraidy-cat! Fraidy-cat!" at the child. In so doing, they effectively deny the existence of their own identity-threatening attribute, the object a.

In offering an easy means for disposing of one's identity-threatening attributes, enemies who have become containers of one's disowned and projected qualities provide another benefit as well: They function as a new target at which one's superego can now direct its aggressivity and sadism, which can reach the point of physical violence. Thus a boy who has projected his own fear onto a playmate may proceed to berate and persecute this child for possessing the boy's own disowned attribute. One of the most obvious large-scale social persecutions produced by this process is gay bashing. In black-Jewish relations, such aggressivity manifests itself when members of one group attack members of another group for qualities that the first group itself secretly harbors and feels guilty about, such as guilt about one's own victimization. As Lerner points out, "[Some Jews say,] 'Yes, there is social misery, and you know who is responsible? The Blacks. They have brought this on themselves because they are irresponsible. . . . ' When you read *Commentary* or *The New Republic*, you sometimes get a feeling that [these Jews] just can't hold back their delight at the prospect of throwing Black teenage mothers off of welfare or Black youth into an ever-expanding prison system" (153).

In addition to serving as a suitable target for superego aggression, an Other onto whom we have projected our own disowned attributes also functions as a means for us to continue to receive unconscious gratifications from the attributes we have disowned, by participating unconsciously in the imagined gratifications that the Other is receiving from them. A good example of this dynamic is the censor who, in externalizing his own "prurient interests" onto the supposed audience of pornography, manages through the activity of assessing films or books for pornographic content to gratify these prurient interests unconsciously while at the same time experiencing the conscious gratifications of having a clear conscience and indulging his superego aggression in condemnation of the overt consumers and producers of pornography.

We cannot fully understand the conflict between blacks and Jews unless we grasp how each uses the other as a target of externalization and how this process enhances the respective identities of each side and provides each side with surplus jouissance (particularly of aggressivity). The most significant instance of this dynamic lies, perhaps, in the relation between the Jewish S_2 (knowledge, system membership) and the black a (qualities excluded by the system). Cornel West describes such a dynamic operating between the Jewish ego and the black id:

> When you have a culture [i.e., the Jewish culture] that has put such a premium on critical intelligence—what Freud would call the ego—then you do get a preoccupation with the id: the irrational, pleasure-seeking forces of the body and sexuality. Jewish culture has revolved around education to which Blacks were denied access. There's no doubt that in American culture there has been a certain Jewish preoccupation with the id in a variety of forms, one of which is a fascination with Black culture and the Black body. A special relationship has evolved between the two groups, which functions on a deep cultural psycho-sexual level. It's not rational: it's to do with need. The Jews need to feel they have a special relationship with the people associated with id. The Black community needs to have a special relationship with the people associated with the ego. (138)

What West is describing is a division of psychological labor that blacks and Jews have worked out unconsciously in their relations with each other, whereby blacks have assumed embodiment of the a (physicality, sexuality, soul) and Jews of the S_2 (ego, System, superego). This division of labor, which has undoubtedly come about through a combination of projection, projective identification, and externalization, provides several psychological benefits for each group. First, it allows each group to eschew responsibility for a major dimension of psychological functioning. Insofar as Jews are perceived as dominating in the fields of commerce, law, and education—S_2—and blacks are perceived to excel in such activities as popular music, athletics, and sexuality—a—each group feels, first of all, that they need not take on these tasks, because someone else is already doing them quite well and, by identifying (unconsciously) with this other, they can share this success vicariously without having to pursue the activity themselves. In addition, each group feels that their own efforts in these fields will inevitably fall short of the other group's success and that therefore it is better not to exert oneself in this field. And each group rationalizes this decision through the reaction formation that the other group's enterprises really aren't that interesting, or valuable, or gratifying anyway. Yet at the same time, each group often feels envy and resentment at the other's successes in their fields, indicating that the original psychological investment still exists, and suggesting that, as Volkan points out, one continues to enjoy and unconsciously identify with those impulses and attributes that one has projected onto the enemy or rival group.

Another manifestation of this division of psychological labor concerning the S_2 (system) and the a (excluded element) is found in the respective strategies of blacks and Jews regarding the question of whether to assimilate with or to separate from the dominant culture. Historically, both Jews and blacks have functioned as the abject object upon which the System relies (in different ways). But more recently, many Jews have tended toward assimilation (Lerner and West, 8), partly because since the Holocaust, the West and the United States in particular have moved officially to integrate the formerly abject object into the system and even to valorize it: witness the trials of Nazis for crimes against humanity, and more recently, the establishment of the United States Holocaust Memorial Museum. For many blacks, however, the earlier attraction to assimilation (passing) has largely passed, and now there is greater emphasis on black identity and even separatism. But each group continues to be attracted to the rejected strategy (and the corresponding rejected aspect of themselves). And as a result of this dialectic of externalization, each group needs to emphasize that it is not the other by rejecting the other, directing its superego attacks onto the external instance in order to keep their superego from attacking the internal instance of their own rejected qualities and impulses. Moreover, through the unconscious identification with the other's assimilation or separation, each group continues to enjoy its own disowned impulses and attributes through the other. Thus Jews who are ashamed that they didn't rebel like blacks (see Lerner and West, 36) can enjoy such rebellion through their secret identifications with blacks who did rebel, and blacks who envy Jewish unity (see 108) can enjoy that unity through unconscious identifications with Jewish people. As West says, "There may be resentment [by some African Americans] of Asian upward mobility, but the greater preoccupation with Jews is generated by Black identification with them" (137).

STRATEGIES FOR REDUCING THE CONFLICT

Psychoanalysis thus reveals that the psychological needs that are being served by the conflict between blacks and Jews involve more than the "meaning needs" identified by Lerner. Or, alternatively conceptualized, the "meaning needs" served by the conflict are much more diverse and complex than Lerner's account indicates. Whichever formulation one adopts, the consequence of the psychological roots of the conflict revealed by psychoanalysis is that more is needed to resolve the conflict than simply the discourse of caring and ethos of unselfishness that Lerner offers as a solution. Lerner's proposed solution—a Politics of Meaning based on a discourse and ethos of caring—is insufficient for two major reasons. First, it is unjustifiably optimistic about the possibility of introducing new values and knowledge from the top down—that is, of the masses accepting this new values (S_1) and beliefs (S_2) from an authority. And second, it overlooks the fact that the conflict between blacks and Jews derives from more than just the presence of inadequate values (S_1) and knowledge (S_2); it also derives, as we have seen, from other psychological needs. Lerner's own comments include the observation that a big part of the problem is not just that people lack the right values, but that although they possess precisely these values, these values fail to control their thoughts, feelings, and actions. The reason these values fail to guide people's actions is because, as we have seen, people have other psychological needs which, in these cases, prove more powerful than these values. While a vigorous promotion of values such as caring and empathy by national leaders might shift the balance of power more toward these values and away from the other psychological needs, what is really needed is an opportunity for both blacks and Jews to encounter, recognize, identify, and assume ownership of their other psychological needs—that is, of their various repressed drives, desires, fantasies, enjoyments, anxieties, and defenses that we have seen to be at the root of their conflict.

What is needed to reduce the conflict between blacks and Jews is a process similar to the process of feminist consciousness raising of the 1960s and 1970s in which women in significant numbers began to recognize and reclaim psychological needs—such as the need for sexual gratification and the need to be assertive—that had been repressed. This process took many forms, but two factors were crucial, and these same two factors must be mobilized if a similar process is to occur with blacks and Jews. The most important factor was the commitment that many women made to examining their own feelings—their anxieties, desires, and enjoyments—and to acknowledging qualities and impulses that they were ashamed of or uncomfortable with. A second, ancillary factor was the public acknowledgment and ownership by feminist leaders and writers of precisely such feelings and qualities, thus reducing the degree of shame attached to these feelings and making it easier for others to accept such feelings in themselves. Prior to this process, it was very difficult for most women to acknowledge, even to themselves, powerful libidinal and aggressive impulses. As a result, many women repressed such impulses, for which they paid a significant price in symptoms such as depression and psychosomatic disorders.

Many blacks and Jews are in a position similar to that of women before the 1960s and 1970s, and one of their major symptoms is their conflict with each other. What is thus needed to dissolve this symptom is an opportunity to recognize and own the various unacceptable libidinal and aggressive impulses—such as the desire to be the object *a* (positive or negative) in relation to the System, or the desire to make the other group the object of attack by one's own vicious superego. As with feminist consciousness raising, two sorts of activity can increase the opportunity for such recognition and ownership. First, members of each group need some form of respected Other to model a less severe superego, a superego that does not condemn one for having the kinds of psychological needs that we have discussed here. Such an other can be a trusted friend, a respected leader or authority figure, or public discourse itself—which means that the more we expose, describe, and explain the kinds of psychological needs we have been discussing, the less shameful and hence difficult it will be for individuals to acknowledge that they themselves harbor such needs.

Such individual acknowledgment, however, is the sine qua non for significant psychological change here. Simply acknowledging the existence of such needs in general, without confronting them in oneself, will be relatively inconsequential. Thus in addition to altering the public discourse to enhance public awareness and acceptance of the existence of such needs, we also need to provide opportunities for people to encounter and work through such needs in themselves. For some, reading or hearing about others' acknowledgment and working through of such needs can be opportunity enough. Others need a more personal, concrete, and sustained interpersonal interaction with other people in order for such a process to occur. For them, churches, synagogues, and other organizations might play important roles in facilitating such self-examination and self-encounters.

Perhaps the most promising model for such self-encounter, however, is a respectful and honest dialogue between blacks and Jews such as that which West and Lerner have exemplified in their co-authored book. Such dialogues promise to be particularly effective if they are structured and conducted according to principles such as those formulated by the psychoanalyst and international relations expert Vamik Volkan and others for reducing international and interethnic conflicts. Herbert Kelman (1990) explains the process as follows:

> The core of the process that we try to generate in problem-solving workshops is analysis. Participants are encouraged to put aside the typical adversarial mode of interaction and, instead, to approach the conflict analytically: to probe its meanings, its causes, the factors that exacerbate it, and the constraints that operate against its resolution. Emphasis is placed on enabling the parties to understand each other's (and indeed their own) perceptions of self, the enemy, and the conflict, and to share their differing perspectives. Analysis, however, is not meant to be a cold, disengaged process. As in insight therapy, we stress the importance of expressing and dealing with emotions. ... In effect, we try to create opportunities for corrective emotional experiences, for the engagement of strong emotions simultaneously with the freedom and the requirement to analyze them. (155–56)

Facilitating the establishment of such groups, and such dialogue, is perhaps the most promising way to promote resolution of the conflict between blacks and Jews by addressing the psychological needs that are at the root of the conflict.

NOTE

1. For a fuller discussion of these four psychological functions, see Bracher 1993, 19–52.

REFERENCES

Bracher, Mark. 1993. *Lacan, Discourse, and Social Change: A Psychoanalytic Cultural Criticism*. Ithaca, N.Y.: Cornell University Press.

Freud, Sigmund. 1921, 1955. *The Standard Edition of the Complete Psychological Works of Sigmund Freud. Volume 18: Group Psychology and the Analysis of the Ego*, 67–143. Translated by James Strachey. London: Hogarth Press.

Kelman, Herbert C. 1990. "Interactive Problem Solving: The Uses and Limits of a Therapeutic Model or the Resolution of International Conflicts." In *The Psychoanalysis of International Relationships. Volume II: Unofficial Diplomacy at Work*, edited by Vamik Volkan, 145–60. Lexington, Mass.: Heath.

Lerner, Michael, and Cornel West. 1996. *Jews and Blacks: A Dialogue on Race, Religion, and Culture in America*. New York: Penguin.

Volkan, Vamik D. 1988. *The Need to Have Enemies and Allies: From Clinical Practice to International Relationships*. Northvale, N.J.: Jason Aronson.

Young-Bruehl, Elisabeth. 1996. *The Anatomy of Prejudices*. Cambridge, Mass.: Harvard University Press.

11

Black-Jewish Relations:
A Social and Mythic Alliance

LEE JENKINS

A MYTHIC BROTHERHOOD: SIMILARITY YET DIFFERENCE

Do Jews and blacks feel any special affinity that is not expected to apply between blacks and other whites and Jews and other whites? Is there a moral imperative in their recognition of a mutual interest or bond such that the undermining of such a position is a cause for alarm?

An arresting depiction, though perhaps an unintended evocation, of this idea of affinity was Art Spiegelman's rendering of a kiss between a Hasidic Jew and a Caribbean-appearing black woman on the cover of a Valentine's Day issue of *The New Yorker*. Unavoidable was the suggestion of needed reconciliation between the two in the aftermath of the racial disturbances in Crown Heights, Brooklyn.

Much has been made of the collaboration between blacks and Jews in addressing social inequity and opposing intolerance in the nation in the fight to make a reality of its democratic egalitarian promise. The similarity of historical experience of being victims of intolerance gave both groups the possibility of a mutual recognition and a common cause. It has often been pointed out that both groups experienced slavery, collective oppression, minority status in Christian societies; both were subject to stereotyping, restrictive laws, intimidation and violence; both subjected to a pariah status on the basis of personal identity, viewed by the majority as the Other, the outcast.

The response to such a plight brought about membership in liberal organizations and progressive labor movements with increased social activism and civil rights agitation, reaching a high point in the triumph of the 1960s civil rights campaigns. Though there was a basis for cooperation, there were always differences in the assessment of group self-interest and the most effective means to promote equality; and there was a degree of conflict inherent in the racial difference and the extent of mutuality experienced as a result. Jews confronted, just as blacks did, the question of the extent to which integrationist or separatist strategies might be adopted, but Jews were nevertheless whites who were afforded the prospect of eventual assimilation unavailable in the same way to blacks.

The extent to which there was collaboration between the two groups is also reflected in a linking of the two in the mind of the nation and a conflicted view that the two hold of each other as sharers in a brotherhood of victimization. Perhaps also at work here is a mythic conception in which white interest in black well-being has often been rendered: to be sympathetic to their cause is to love them, as in the epithet "nigger lover" applied to whites who were sympathetic to the black cause during the period of segregation. To love them is to be one of them is perhaps the unconscious thought. For the Jew to identify with the black is to acknowledge his own history of victimization at the same time that he might strive to resist the stigma resulting from such an identification.

There may be a mutual recognition of kinship between Jews and American blacks based on many things, with a genuine feeling on the part of Jews for the suffering experienced by blacks. Doubtless there is also a recognition that the social circumstances of the two are no longer the same, if they ever were, though the identities of the two are still linked in some way. As James Baldwin has suggested, the Jew may know just enough about the black situation to be "unwilling to imagine it again" (Baldwin 1967, 38), if imagining it means, as a result of sympathetic feelings for blacks, being identified with them as well as being made to reexperience the stigma and heartbreak that Jews too have had to endure.

The casting of the two groups as victims is a reflection of their historical plight as well as of the attitudes toward them that initiated the victimization and are still maintained in stereotyped thinking. Being black, for instance, can signify many negative things in our culture, and it can do so on a common level of acceptability in our psychic life. Jews can also be viewed in a similar unflattering way.

In this chapter I will suggest that the historical basis of the intolerance expressed toward Jews and blacks has cast the two in a mythic kinship, while at the same time the emphasis upon the similarity of historical and social experience has served as a source of ambivalence and conflict between the two groups. They are mythic doubles, each seeing both an unwanted reflection of itself in the other and a mutual recognition of similarity, yet driven by the self-evident experience of the uniqueness of a separate identity and a necessary emphasis upon such difference.

KINSHIP, SHARED SOCIAL ACTIVISM, DIVERGENT ASSIMILATION

In many ways the black is conceived of as the Other, as the negation of the idea of the self that is socially approved of and honored. Joel Kovel in *White Racism* (1984) speaks of the way in which Communists and Jews as well as blacks have been seen as the Other in the white West, though the Jew, at present, has had his position altered as a result of the integration of Israel within the ranks of the nations of the West—and now the Russians too may be candidates for exclusion from the category of the Other, with the collapse of communism, leaving the black in his status as Other as yet undisturbed.

The main stereotypes of Jews refer to ideas of group achievement and insularity, intellectuality, influence and power, rapacious and profane pursuit of self-interest, while those of blacks emphasize physicality, primitivism, inadequacy and defilement, profligacy. Both groups share a derogatory reference to stereotyped notions of physical appearance: the Jew may be swarthy; the black by definition dark-skinned, each with supposed coarse physiognomy. Such references call to mind the idea of the projection upon these two groups of disowned qualities unacceptable to the ideal white self-conception. Additionally, both Jews and blacks may be thought of as morally deficient, as "transgressors of the sacred," to use the social philosopher Cornel West's phrase (West 1993, 105). While the Jew may be thought of as choosing such a course to serve some nefarious purpose, the black is viewed as acting by default out of a corrupt nature.

The Jew is recognized as the originator of a powerful patriarchal myth inextricable from Western civilization that projects the conception of God and a relationship to God that reveals the unfolding of a divine plan for the salvation of mankind. As the social critic Ellen Willis said in "The Myth of the Powerful Jew," this means that Jews are also the upholders of the highest ethical standards and the providers of rules for ethical conduct. This makes them "revolutionary figures," "superego figures" subject to admiration, resentment, rage, and envy (Willis 1979, 195). The rules for moral conduct imposed as a binding obligation between men and God involve renunciation, the censoring of instincts, and the submitting to a hierarchal order emphasizing higher and lower desires, mind versus body, distinctions based on class, ethnicity or sex, dominance and submission, the ideal and the ignoble.

It might be imagined that the unconscious rage generated by the civilized renunciation of desires expected under such a system is expressed toward Jews in the treatment of them as scapegoats who, especially in times of social unrest, may be pointed to as the source of collective problems, just as blacks can be imagined as the unassimilable Others whose very presence is the source of the problems of the majority.

The ambivalent potential of such a perception of Jews is seen in their insider and outsider status, the envy of and readiness to expose them as well as the resulting guilt and recognition of them as historical examples of moral excellence and divine favor. The Christian adherent may struggle with the moral obligation to accept the contradiction Judaism poses to Christian orthodoxy and the need to resist submitting to the impulse to eradicate it, as one experiences the tension between preaching tolerance and trying to practice it. The Jew is therefore a powerful cultural figure, and the desire of the antisemite is to reduce him to a powerless victim, since it is Jewish *success* that supports the fears of Jewish subversion and conspiracy. Though the Jews had once been slaves, they were liberated by the Almighty Himself, and they may have the expectation—challenged by the Holocaust but not defeated by it—of thereafter being subject to a similar elevation. Judaism's success is the justification of its affront to Christianity and of the Jewish refusal to convert. The power of this opposition cannot be posed, however, if Jews are powerless, outnumbered, easily defeated.

Racism too depends upon blacks being powerless, preferably as an impotent and suffering mass, as an indication of the judgment to which they have been subjected and the burden they bear, justifying the treatment the racist would enact against them. The power of the ambivalence and the psychic resonance these two figures hold in the Western mind is revealed in the extreme and ludicrous stereotypes applied to them. The omnipotent and sacrilegious Jew, the rapacious black, the one possessing demonic horns and needing the blood of Christian children to make matzoh, the other a body without mind, an embodiment of pure instinct and appetite. If the Jews are the repository of the ambivalent attitudes toward conscience, then the blacks are the embodiments of the violation of conscience and the punishment to be visited upon the violator as a result, thought of as revealed in their differing color and appearance. A reversal of this situation would be one in which blacks in the world wielded power in the way that whites now do. *Black racism* would then doubtless view and oppress whites in a manner similar to what is the reverse today, with there being nothing special or favored about being white, a situation that for some people cannot even be imagined.

The commitment to humanism and democratic liberalism was a way to combat the prejudice directed against the two groups. American society was fundamentally liberal and in time might make Jewish acceptance a reality, especially since Jews were afforded the advantage of white skin, which would facilitate assimilation. The black problem was the ongoing one of encouraging a liberal society to act in accordance with its liberal principles that had been betrayed in their denial to the black on the basis of his color. There was a desire to fulfill the promise of free individualism and free the society of prejudice and superstition, undoing the Jewish experience of being an unloved minority. Black political agitation for change and the Jewish liberal drive to accomplish equality had much in common but were also different. The black was often dependent on government initiatives to enforce equality through the recognition of the group exclusion of blacks and a need to secure individual rights through protecting of the rights of the group.

Not until recently, with the general increase in emphasis upon ethnicity and group consciousness, have Jews been receptive to any attempt to make political issue of their Jewishness as a basis of political or civic recognition. They wanted instead to preserve the ideals of individual freedom that allow them to live and prosper as a group, freed from the prejudices and restrictions that had for so long been directed against them as a group. It is precisely Jewish autonomy and/or prosperity that for so long resisted absorption or elimination that have been the basis of antagonism toward it.

The Jews were white and at last, in America, could as whites blend in but still be Jews. The blacks as black could not blend in and remained outcasts. Their blackness would never be overlooked, so they were forced to claim it as the essential defining feature of their being, just as Jews, in a dominant white Christian society that did not adhere to liberal democratic principles of tolerance and inclusion, would forever be condemned as long as they insisted on affirming their Jewishness, the essential feature of their being, which took precedence over their being white in their eyes as well as in the eyes of the white Christian majority.

American Jews are predominantly middle class with characterizing class attitudes in spite of their outsider sympathies. American Jewry is no longer a German or Eastern European offshoot, as Julius Lester reminds us, but an independent distinctly American group (Lester 1994, 172). Jews have lost their distinctiveness also because American blacks and other minority groups are even more distinctive. The Jews have, therefore, become comfortably white, in triumph over their long history of having been viewed as aliens, non–Anglo Saxons. Jews of European descent probably certainly see themselves as white and are classified as such, though Jews as a group are a multiracial people. Jewishness as such is therefore not a racial category. Indeed, as Ellen Willis (1979, 188) argues, to be Jewish is to refuse to be identified in racial terms, to repudiate race as a classifying category, and to oppose institutions and practices that perpetuate racial hierarchies. Though this may be contradicted by right-wing conservative Jewish thinking or the hard-right sympathies of some present-day Israeli politicians, nevertheless one sees the historical point affirmed by many that Jews are a people who remain one without regard to race as the defining feature of their cohesiveness. To the white Christian West with its nation-states based on color as well as on their delineations of history and other defining features of national character, the Jewish cohesiveness is a feature of their sameness with a difference. This is the context in which the presence of white supremacy results in the expression of both racism and antisemitism, in which a recognition of the individual and his worth depends upon his membership in and allegiance to the race of white people.

As a consequence of being beneficiaries of American democratic liberalism, Jewish life has been transformed, leaving behind the deprivations and hardships of the historical past with the experience of assimilation and prosperity in the present. The similarity to the blacks may still be the recognition that no amount of success can produce a state of mind free of vulnerability unless Jewishness itself is escaped, but the story of Jewish success is a radical contrast to the continuing imperiled status of blacks.

CONFLICTING SOCIAL GOALS, BROKEN ALLIANCES, MUTUAL ANTAGONISM

The extent to which the contrasting fates of blacks and Jews, and their opposing priorities, have come to epitomize enmity and conflict is dramatized in the Crown Heights disturbance. The conflict over affirmative action and the argument over Zionism and the Palestinian question were signal events, against a backdrop of disagreement between blacks and Jews over economic and political goals. A decline in Jewish support occurred after the 1967 war followed by a resurgence in both groups, and in the country at large, of ethnic awareness and group interest as positive concerns.

Though the racism blacks faced had been ameliorated, and laws had been instituted to provide black citizenship rights, it had nevertheless not been eradicated. The political and economic disenfranchisement of blacks was felt as a worrisome, intractable problem. The measure of black success always depended on the aid of whites, often disproportionately Jews. The need to appeal to the conscience of the white majority, which characterized the civil rights movement, to fulfill its liberal principles was no longer necessary, many black leaders felt, when blacks began to feel the appeal and strength of Third Worldism, global anti-imperialism, in which people of color were a worldwide majority and the attempt to make a flawed liberalism work appeared to be a self-defeating and self-deluding task. Strength and self-respect were increasingly thought of as resulting from affirmation of the group identity.

On the home front this meant agitating for affirmative action as a concrete political initiative that would oppose group discrimination by giving qualified *individuals* the recognition they might otherwise be denied. This unfortunately came to be perceived only as giving recognition to group members, not giving qualified members of a group the recognition that might be denied because of their group membership. Thinking of this kind inevitably linked the idea of quotas to the initiative, undermining the egalitarian assault upon discrimination that had been its intent.

Even when the Jewish group consciousness also involved sentiments that turned away from an exclusive emphasis upon secular integration and more upon an awareness of group self-interest, it did so without an appeal to government to promote policies that favored group interest, whereas blacks emphasized the necessity of governmental help to enhance their advancement. So progress and egalitarian inclusiveness would have to be facilitated by government intervention. This, however, was taken as only the establishing of group quotas without regard for competence.

It was a prospect understandably resisted by Jews, remembering their own group persecution, their exclusions from universities and other areas of public life on the basis of their group membership; this development seemed a black betrayal of the egalitarian liberal alliance. In addition, as middle-class white Americans, Jews were also voicing the class interests of whites concerned about "reverse discrimination" and preserving equal opportunity as well as the advantage of their own status and position.

The concern about "reverse discrimination" and a conviction about a decline of standards was opposed by the conviction on the part of blacks that equal opportunity did not prevail and no matter how competent they were they would be subject to denial or restrictions in hiring and promotions. The refusal to acknowledge this possibility on the part of whites was seen by most blacks as typical hypocritical examples of bad faith, similar to the reluctance on the part of Christian whites to acknowledge the persistence of anitsemitism that causes Jews to be watchful and wary.

To the problem of affirmative action was added the controversy over Zionism and the Palestinian question. The liberal Jewish defense of Israel in spite of its poor, often dehumanizing treatment of the Palestinians was seen by many blacks as an abandoning of the common cause shared with Jews in the fight against injustice and oppression in favor of a hypocritical pursuit of self-interest. The Jewish stance was viewed by some as an outpost of European imperialism with the imposition of racist hegemony upon the other or nonwhite residents of the region. Liberal Jews saw Israel as the minority defending humanistic liberal freedoms against those who undermined them, but these Jews were surprised to find their position cast as a Zionist conspiracy advancing its own interest while at the same time it appeared to stand on the side of the oppressed. Perhaps to some blacks, the Jewish attitude toward the Palestinians was no different from that toward the blacks—betrayal and exploitation—in view, for instance, of the most recent rejection of affirmative action.

If Jews, in response to a history of antisemitism and uprootedness, felt entitled at any cost to a nationalism expressed in the absolute need to preserve Israel, so too did blacks see themselves entitled to the benefit of affirmative action in the face of continuing racism. Unfortunately, the two groups could never arrive at categories that would facilitate the discussion of differences and airing of critical inquiry without being mutually perceived as intolerant, racist, or antisemitic.

This sense of mutual betrayal has initiated the present state in the crisis of black-Jewish relations. As Cornel West observes, the two must become able to evaluate the moral content of the black and Jewish positions and of their consequences (West 1993). Blacks must reject antisemitism and affirm the intensity of Jewish commitment to the survival of Israel, and Jews must reconcile their fight against injustice and intolerance with a refusal to countenance Palestinian subjugation in the Mideast and a refusal to succumb to racist dealings with blacks in the United States.

RESURGENT CONSERVATISM, JEWISH RACISM, BLACK ANTISEMITISM

Meanwhile relations between the two groups have settled into a watchful wariness or impasse. Reagonism, neoconservatism, and a rightward drift have blunted Jewish sympathy and brought forward Jewish racism. Black crime, the threat to neighborhood safety, and the eroding of upward mobility have become rallying points. The antiurbanism and attacks upon those who are poor, marginal and different can be sympathized with by Jews as an expression of the measure of their own assimilation, even though many of the attitudes with which they sympathized might have been directed by the larger society against the Jews themselves. The Jews *had* overcome poverty and become assimilated, so why hadn't the blacks? The extent to which they had is the measure of their identification with the mainstream white population and less with the dispossessed. The black might ask, What if Jews had had to fight too in America for the realization of liberalism against the same kind of resistance that blacks have had? They have not had to do so, however, because racism seems a more entrenched bias to American whites than antisemitism.

The black perception of the effects of racism sometimes embitters its view of the immigrant success story. Many blacks feel that some of the immigrants, though they can be subject to intolerance, do not occupy the positions of pariahs, the quintessential Other who is the opposite of all that has come to be signified by the ideal white self. There are of course many blacks—perhaps a third of the black populace, 5 or 6 million individuals— who have experienced the success of upward mobility and prosperity; but remaining are the one-third who are working class and struggling and the other one-third who are marginal and/or members of the so-called underclass (Ploski and Williams 1989). If Jews have rejected suffering and come to embrace acceptability and bourgeois comfort, a sizeable portion of poor and marginalized blacks has rejected suffering and come to embrace nihilism or forms of desperate black self-affirmation in an attempt to stave off feelings of hopelessness or unworthiness.

Black political and economic disenfranchisement, and the legacy of racist mistreatment, are the root causes of expressions of black antisemitism. This antisemitism is in the first instance an expression of anti-Americanism and antiwhiteism. Attacking Jews gives blacks a false sense of insider status and provides the assurance at last of singling out a white target that will hear and react. The moderate, informed or morally principled black voices can be upstaged by the more extreme antisemites. A further objective of black attacks upon Jews is to make them vulnerable again, as victims, in the same way that blacks are.

This new black antisemitism is usually not expressed with any real historical knowledge of the treatment of Jews in the past and of what such utterances mean. It is often simply an expression of feelings of disappointment and betrayal, seeking a scapegoat. Since the Jew can make use of white skin privileges, many blacks feel that, to some extent, to accept such privilege is to accept the system of racial exclusivity that underlies it and the racist sentiments it can harbor or breed.

Black antisemitism is also an attempt on the part of black demagogues to exploit black denigration and substitute themselves as the leaders of the black masses in the place of any multiracial egalitarian alliance, since media attention will be given to them and their agendas. Henry Louis Gates Jr. has reported minister Louis Farrakhan as avowing that the real purpose of the present-day bible of black antisemitism, *The Secret Relationship Between the Blacks and Jews*, was to "rearrange a relationship" between blacks and Jews that "has been detrimental to us," not just to sever but to convert what had been friendship and alliance into enmity and distrust (Gates 1992, 221).

It is a self-defeating tactic to seek to promote black affirmation through a stance of antisemitism. It is also an immoral action that should be condemned unequivocally, but it is an outcome of the social context of blacks that has given rise to it. It is a tragic situation in which the blacks act out their own version of the antisemitism of the larger society without appreciating how they become agents of the intolerance that will also be expressed against themselves. It encourages Jews to think that now blacks are the only antisemites, not the conflicted surrogates for the expression of such generalized attitudes in the culture. Christian fundamentalism and the antisemitic aspects of black nationalist thinkers do not exist apart from the sanctions such views receive from the society at large.

Some black antisemitism, especially on the part of young blacks, is an expression of resentment of Jews feeling a basis of shared suffering and having formed an alliance in accordance with such feelings, while blacks, in an attempt to assert a category of racially distinct suffering, say that there can be no comparable Jewish suffering in America. The unfortunate aspect of such "authentically black" assertions is the concomitant sentiment that there can be no universally shared feelings, that only blacks can understand black suffering, as in "It's a black thing; you wouldn't understand." It's the black version of the retreat to ethnic authenticity in general, presently so tragically being played out in other areas of the world.

All of this expresses the breakdown of a sense of mutuality that was an especially strong expectation between blacks and Jews. Blacks may have been unrealistic in having wanted Jews to have avoided any bigotry expressed toward another victim. Human failings are an inextricable human reality, but the unique history of the Jews as the sufferers treasuring the human ideals that elevate human nature plays a role in the desires of blacks to have Jews, more than other whites, be able to confront their racism and change it.

There is real Jewish antiblack racism that causes some blacks to be antisemitic in response, but the expression of this response is often viewed merely as antisemitic intolerance, so that condemnation of the black experiencing such feelings produces further rage and a righteous indignation at the existence of a moral double standard. The matter is complicated. Cynthia Ozick (1983) reminds us that major black leaders and institutions have made antisemitic assertions, while expressions of antiblack racism in this country cannot be attributed, as perhaps has been the case in Israel, to institutionalized Jewish leadership, only to individual Jews and fringe organizations. Jews have been more receptive to the black cause than any other group of whites, and Jews seem responsive to the need to morally assess their behavior and thinking and to expunge or rectify attitudes of intolerance or bias.

This tendency might also result in a desire on the part of some people to put expressions of Jewish racism, when they do occur, on a different level from other expressions of racism (Hacker 1994). Are Jews not to be permitted the same range and depth of human failings as other humans? Is it appropriate to think that they, as a result of their experience, would be less prone to be racist or intolerant? Is the white readiness to expect more of Jews—just as did blacks—an expression of our need to comply with Jews' own acceptance of a group moral superiority, precisely *because* of their sense of a higher accountability to God?

It is a similar situation to the Jewish expectation for blacks to condemn hate speech on the part of other blacks because they're black, though blacks are no more at fault for the existence of antisemitism in the culture than are whites and cannot as a group alone be responsible for eliminating what is a culturally embedded phenomenon. Is the Jewish wish to have blacks, especially, abstain from its expression an example of Jews holding blacks to a similar higher standard that blacks have held Jews? It sometimes seems that the black is expected to prove his humanity by repudiating the inhumanity of another black. The black is expected to criticize the racism of another black as a black person, as if he has some inevitable link to the other on the basis of color, instead of responding simply as a morally outraged human being, not because he is a black morally outraged human being.

Blacks must oppose antisemitism because it is wrong to countenance any form of intolerance, and the moral authority of the black cause depends outright upon condemning acts or expressions of prejudice. Blacks also must oppose antisemitism because they owe not only something to Jews, as fellow humans, but also something to themselves. They cannot avoid their status as souls who have been demeaned and despised, but they must acknowledge this affront without forfeiting their humanity, and eventually even triumph over it, as so many are called upon to do daily. Jews must be accorded the respect due them as fellow human beings that blacks will not withhold because it was withheld from blacks. Blacks must not let the prospect of resentment of another victimized minority group that has escaped its brutal past prevent them from recognizing that the human bond blacks share with Jews is not abandoned because of that accomplishment. Neither should that bond be abandoned by Jews because of that accomplishment.

RELIGION, AFROCENTRISM, GROUP TRANSCENDENCE

A lot of the black religious experience in the United States has echoes of identification with Old Testament Jews, who were enslaved, who suffered, and were ultimately liberated. The identification of black religious celebrants with the Hebrews typically prescribed a stance of resistance to antisemitism, even as the social reality of their present-day, sometimes negative, contact with Jews in commerce and as agents of institutionalized authority made for attitudes of ambivalence. The suffering Hebrews of the Bible—the identified-with children of the God of old—and the relentless shopkeepers of the present could not be one and the same to many of these black celebrants. Their life-preserving religious rapture caused them to conclude that these Jews were not the same, merging disappointment of the immediate black experience with the age-old white Christian notions of Jewish conspiracy and self-serving duplicity.

The black Muslim minister Khalid Abdul Muhammad offers the latest version of this notion of double dealing. In a similar manner that white Christians express anxiety about the primacy of Judaism or Christianity with respect to ultimate salvation and favor with God, so now these black Muslims speak disparagingly of Jews, casting them as impostors, just as the Jews have been accused of having displaced others in their Christian host societies. Muhammad proclaims that the Talmudic scholars had contrived the conception of a divine curse upon blacks that has been the cause of so much anguish and the negative attitude with which they have been viewed in the white West.

This is the most poignant and direct presentation of the ambivalent merging of love and hate, the distinguishing between the one who is like oneself but is not. The black has become the Jew, in an Afrocentric re-creation of history that confers historical recognition and respect. I think what is meant by saying blacks are the true Jews is that to be Jewish has always been to be the symbol of eternal outcast, but one favored by God, the eternally different ones in the Christian West. When Jews therefore become assimilated into society, they lose as a consequence the moral authority of the protesting outsider. They cease, in effect, to be Jews, and only blacks, eternal outcasts, remain, who cannot assimilate until the basis of their difference disappears.

Furthermore, I think that blacks claiming to be the real Hebrews are claiming for themselves the honor of being the true victims of history and the moral authority of being the living representatives of principle that has been denied. They present the moral authority of victimhood, which ever asserts a stance of righteous opposition in the face of the oppressor. I think that this is the real meaning of the ongoing attempt to answer the question of who has suffered the most, black or Jew. This is the black attempt to give meaning to the black historical plight beyond that of mere victimhood, unregenerate and meaningless suffering, suffering that neither ennobles nor ends.

The black may see himself as the unique exemplar of suffering in the world, the symbol of moral challenge, and the ultimate bearer of divine judgment and vindication, since otherwise his suffering has been meaningless. The attempt to promote such a conception through the antisemitic traducing of his closest spiritual rival, the Jew, reveals the depth of a loving and hated identification. The soul-wrenching denial of the commonality of human nature that is racism remains the abiding preoccupation of the black. He may not want to forgive the Jew, despised in his own right as a victim of intolerance, for acquiescing in any way to the perpetuation of American racism or benefiting from its practice.

Blacks as purveyors of antisemitism not only betrayed the transracial liberal alliance with Jews but also frightened and dismayed them. There had been a commitment of especial urgency to the defense of the poor and deprived that had been nurtured by the Jewish experience as well as it had been an expression of Jewish values. The intensity of this response brought to the fore the conflicts of the Jewish commitment to the black cause. What did it mean to the Jew to encounter a victim even more despised than himself? Did blacks afford Jews the opportunity, as they became more prosperous, of keeping alive militant liberalism as well as they served as objects to assuage Jewish guilt. Were blacks the obverse reflections of Jews as victims, promoting an identification with their suffering but a pity for their helplessness? Did Jews need blacks in order to continue to feed their sense of moral superiority and challenge, to verify their status through history as the righteous ones unjustly suffering, by making a vicarious identification with blacks? What was the Jewish conflict of leaving behind the sense of outsidership, the possibility of the loss of moral authority that might have been posed in the form of the lessening of the principled empathy with the underdog and the defense of the weak against the strong, in light of bourgeois success and the possibilities of complacency?

In his famous essay on black-Jewish relations, "My Negro Problem—and Ours," Norman Podhoretz (1963) spoke of another aspect of the way blacks are the obverse reflections of Jews. Podhoretz indicates the anxiety attendant upon his perceptions of the black youths of his boyhood as victims made tough and intransigent by their victimization, in contrast to an image of Jewish timidity and intellectuality. Instead of these black boys being worse off than whites, to Podhoretz's youthful eyes they appeared better off than all whites. They were more ruthless, better athletes and dancers, on special terms with their bodies, emphasizing the cultivation of the physical, not the mental. They were not bound by the conventional proprieties, and they resisted socialization. In short, they were the image of the ones who could not be assimilated.

In their ruthlessness and rebellion, they made Podhoretz feel faceless. He hated them because of their power to humiliate him. They were not afraid of their enemies the way Podhoretz had been afraid of his. Podhoretz acknowledges that when the Jewish boys fought with other whites they did not do so with the same ferocity that they all felt when fighting the black boys, because the white boys, in spite of ethnic differences, saw themselves as "Americans," sharing a common street culture different from the culture at home.

The retreat into Afrocentrism and ethnic identity politics is an understandable response made by disillusioned or demoralized blacks to the seemingly intractable or ineradicable problem of racist inhospitality abetted now by the nation's political conservatism that has worsened the plight of the masses of blacks. It is a situation that has occurred in spite of legislation protecting the citizenship rights of blacks, in spite of increased upward mobility of blacks into the middle classes, and the ongoing evolution of the national will toward the realization of democratic liberalism.

Black leaders who speak for the disaffected masses can speak to their despair with powerful effect. Their power is derived from the perception that they are the only ones who take the blighted life circumstances of the masses seriously. These are leaders who understand the costs of persistent black survival, the heroic but disrespected strivings of blacks, their generational failures, bitter wounds, and resentments. How to address the stigma of shame that wages such constant warfare against self-respect? The black, in being despised, has learned to be ashamed. The Jew, though despised, had a history that could protect him against such shame.

The militant blacks' new "antiracist politics" can call into question the legitimacy of the entire liberal democratic establishment, seeing it as a pretext for preserving the influence and biases of white authority under the guise of a universalism that is only a partisan defense, not a true integration of the black into a democratic liberal body politic. The experience of blacks in all areas of public life, from the schools to the court system, can be seen as submitting to a contaminating white hegemony harmful to the well-being of blacks (Sleeper 1994). This is why, for instance, the response to the O. J. Simpson trial so easily put the majority of blacks on one side and whites on the other. This is why even the National Association for the Advancement of Colored People equivocates now on whether racial integration in schools is still a desirable objective.

One must imagine the state of mind of people continuously concerned with the differential consequences of status inequality (Jenkins 1994). The diminished social life and public image of the oppressed individual are allied to chronic and pervasive depression and the rage it masks. So much pain has been absorbed by blacks in merely surviving that the resulting state of being, extreme as it is, seems normal. So much of the psyche has been submerged it is little wonder that even successful blacks feel a sympathy for the rebellious black who speaks out (French 1993). This is why a leader such as Louis Farrakhan, who is obviously antisemitic in the statements he has made, is not readily denounced. Even his bigoted sentiments are inextricable from the perception held of him by many blacks as one who has been seared by the same mistreatment as they have and who will not be quiet about it. It is unfortunate that the craving for black self-assertion and respect so powerfully expressed in this charismatic man is tarnished and blighted by contrasting sentiments of an ignoble and inhumane kind.

CLOSING COMMENTS

No solution to the black-Jewish conflict can be offered that is different from what our approach must be in general in the effort to cope with the problem of religious, ethnic, or cultural difference. We must recognize the necessity to oppose, never to tolerate, the prejudices that can result from the need to emphasize one's own distinctiveness in a manner that excludes or disparages others. Ethnic difference, like color, gender or nationality, is inevitably expressed in the circumstance of the living of one's life. It is the signature and celebration of identity. But the more distinct identity is, and the more autonomous one is, the greater is the recognition that one is not alone.

It is only through the establishing of true selfhood that one is able to recognize the individuality of another as one like oneself capable of being loved. Identity promotes identification. This is why even enmity and bitterness, powerful though they be and rife in all corners of the world, can always be opposed or subdued in the imagination—or thought that they *ought* to be subdued—by an even greater force. That force is the notion of the sanctity of a common humanity, the conviction that one violates the ideal of humankind, human commonality, and harms oneself when harm is done to others. This is what unites the commandment *Thou shall not kill* with the precept *Inasmuch as you have done it to the least of my brothers, you have done it to me.*

The United States stands uniquely on the brink of the creation of the first genuinely multiracial heterogeneous society. Liberalism is the expression of the desire to transcend parochial differences. Liberalism seems to supplant difference in favor of a oneness of *individuals,* their bond being civic membership in a body politic with responsibilities and privileges in a community of human beings, as an ultimate basis of identity, before consideration is given to other allegiances such as race, ethnicity, class, or religion. This seems to me the ultimate triumph of humanism—human beingism—not as a social or religious doctrine, as in "secular humanism," but as a realization of the respect and the inalienable worth accorded each individual that makes our dealings with each other humane.

Our primary task in life may be no more than to know who we are as individuals and to fulfill ourselves as such. It is not easy to embrace the conflicting aspects of selfhood, the lonely birthright of our separateness, and the continuing need to strive for wholeness, which for many people cannot even be conceived apart from membership in a clan or allegiance to an ideology. But race, religion, social class, and ethnicity are not the same as individuality, the final and irreducible measure of identity, though they obviously contribute to the making of it. Knowing what kinds of behavior, good and bad, characterize us as human beings can cause us to accept ourselves and recognize our human nature in others, as an expression of the uniqueness of individuality yet a recognition of the sameness of our kind.

Individual rights guarantee the right of individual dissent without necessarily being seen as merely an exercise in the pursuit of self-interest. People can differ on issues of principle and express such differences within an atmosphere of tolerance. Likewise, individual rights undergirds the right to the existence of individual group identities as part of a whole. This can be good when the individual group identities willingly defer to the primacy of the greater good of the whole, which must take priority over individual group interests. This can be bad when the individual groups deny the primacy of the greater whole, which provides the security for the very existence of the individual groups. This can be as true for chauvinistic black Afrocentric tendencies as it is of insular Jewish groups who exist within the civic politic but are not part of it.

I think the question of the response to miscegenation, or race mixing, is an indication of the position one occupies with respect to true receptivity to democratic liberalism. Would race mixing—better put as the natural proclivity for interrelations among people when the opportunity is present, indicating the recognition of the sameness in individual difference—promote the intermingling of individuals and lessen the emphasis upon group distinctions, in line with the principles of humanistic liberalism? The children of such unions may initially be black—or brown or yellow—but eventually will make it difficult to provide a basis for determining what one's color is or what one's group identity is. They might even cause us to begin to question the narrowness of such definitions. One will at last be truly multiracial, multicultural, emphasizing the shared genetic basis of the races in the first place—but is this realization of Oneness something that is by many people truly desired?

REFERENCES

Baldwin, J. 1967, 1994. "Negroes Are Anti-Semitic Because They're Anti-white." In *Blacks and Jews: Alliances and Arguments*, edited by P. Berman, 31–41. New York: Delacorte Press.

French, A. 1993. "Black Despair: John Wilson and the Plague of African-American Depression," *The Washington Post*, June 20, C1, C4.

Gates, H. L., Jr. 1992, 1994. "The Uses of Anti-Semitism." In *Blacks and Jews: Alliances and Arguments*, edited by P. Berman, 217–23. New York: Delacorte Press.

Hacker, A. 1994. "Jewish Racism, Black Anti-Semitism." In *Blacks and Jews: Alliances and Arguments*, edited by P. Berman, 154–63. New York: Delacorte Press.

Jenkins, L. 1994. "African American Identity and Its Social Context." In *Race, Ethnicity and Self: Identity in Multicultural Perspective*, edited by E. P. Salett and D. R. Koslow, 63–88. Washington, D.C.: National MultiCultural Institute.

Kovel, J. 1984. *White Racism*. New York: Columbia University Press.

Lester, J. 1994. "The Lives People Live." In *Blacks and Jews: Alliances and Arguments*, edited by P. Berman, 164–77. New York: Delacorte Press.

Ozick, C. 1983, 1994. "Literary Blacks and Jews." In *Blacks and Jews: Alliances and Arguments*, edited by P. Berman, 42–75. New York: Delacorte Press.

Ploski, H. A., and J. Williams. 1989. *The Negro Almanac: A Reference Work on the African American*. 5th ed. New York: Gale Research.

Podhoretz, N. 1963, 1994. "My Negro Problem—and Ours." In *Blacks and Jews: Alliances and Arguments*, edited by P. Berman, 76–92. New York: Delacorte Press.

Sleeper, J. 1994. "The Battle for Enlightenment at City College." In *Blacks and Jews: Alliances and Arguments*, edited by P. Berman, 239–53. New York: Delacorte Press.

West, C. 1993. *Race Matters*. New York: Vintage.

Willis, E. 1979, 1994. "The Myth of the Powerful Jew." In *Blacks and Jews: Alliances and Arguments*, edited by P. Berman, 183–203. New York: Delacorte Press.

12

Some Practical Psychoanalytically Informed Suggestions for Communal Leaders for Improving Black-Jewish Relations

ALAN HELMREICH AND PAUL MARCUS

As we noted in our introduction, psychoanalysis has been strongest on the theoretical level as a mode of understanding the underlying, frequently unconscious, psychological conflicts, anxieties, wishes, fantasies, and defenses that are quite likely factors contributing to black-Jewish conflict in different contexts. Psychoanalysis has been more limited in its ability to generate pragmatic "solutions" to the problems that it formulates are at the root of black-Jewish conflict. While the editors are in no way claiming that a psychoanalytically informed approach to black-Jewish conflict and relations is a panacea, we do believe that along with other approaches deriving from different theoretical perspectives, it can make an important contribution to creating the conditions for making things better.

The editors are also aware that many of the chapters in this book are not easily accessible to a lay audience who are not versed in psychoanalytic theory and practice. While we have tried to avoid unnecessary jargon and obfuscation, the fact is that some of the best theoretical insights contained in the foregoing essays, may not be easily applicable to those people who are involved with ameliorating black-Jewish conflict on the "front lines." In our view, if these individuals are not able to appropriate some practical ideas on how to tackle black-Jewish conflict, then this book will surely be one of the many ineffective volumes on the subject that is relegated to the tombs of academia, destined to oblivion. Thus, in this conclusion we would like to offer a few pragmatic suggestions geared to lay people who are charged with improving black-Jewish relations and reducing black-Jewish conflict. We offer only some general suggestions that of course need to be tailored to the specific situation when it arises. These suggestions are only "food for thought" and in no way strive to be comprehensive or rigorously systematic.

One of the first observations that strikes the discerning reader of this volume is that what one takes to be the "problem" between blacks and Jews is largely a function of one's theoretical presuppositions and where one situates oneself in the discourse. So, for example, from the point of view of Mortimer Ostow, a psychoanalytic/Jewish scholar, black-Jewish conflict is largely due to black antisemitism, to nationalist leaders like Louis Farrakhan spurring pathological hatred at undeserving Jews who, ironically generally have been the white group most supportive of black freedom and empowerment. In contrast, Victor Wolfenstein, a psychoanalytic/Marxist scholar, views black-Jewish conflict more in terms of white racism and black liberation, a Jewish tendency to misunderstand and overreact to blacks as a consequence of their history of European antisemitism and a wish to maintain their present power and economic class interests.

Most other contributors have taken more intermediate views in their way of formulating the problem. They have suggested that black-Jewish conflict is best understood not only in terms of black antisemitism and white racism and Jewish power but also in terms of extremely complex, frequently co-produced psychosocial processes and social realities. For example, one of the most interesting formulations was put forth by Alford, and in a some-what similar manner by Jenkins, with his notion of a symbiotic-like "mythic kinship" between blacks and Jews. Alford has argued that blacks and Jews desperately need each other as enemies in order to define them-selves by dissimilarity. They are as groups thoroughly enmeshed and pro-foundly identified with each other. Emblematic of this is when Khalid Abdul Muhammad claims that the Jew is not truly Jewish and blacks are the authentic Jews. This suggests that the identification with the Jew/enemy is so deep and pervasive that the initial step to improve things must be to tease apart the confused thinking and unconscious identification, foster psy-chological separation, and a reclamation of the lost projections—and not reconciliation as usually understood and approached such as in conven-tional "healing" dialogues.

Some of the other psychoanalytically oriented formulations and concepts that have been applied by authors, alone and/or in combination to illu-minate black-Jewish conflict include: narcissistic injuries and narcissistic rage and the narcissism of minor differences; unresolved collective internal grief and the broken line of disrupted lineages (e.g., the Holocaust and slavery); struggles for territory and visibility, projection, projective identi-fication and externalization (e.g., stereotyping and scapegoating); truncated empathy and insensitivity; unrealistic group expectations, permutations, and combinations of "primitive" envy, jealously, and rivalry; shame and guilt; fear and hatred. As this partial list suggests, psychoanalytically oriented thinkers have provided us with a rich and interesting set of ways of conceptualizing black-Jewish conflict. So where do we go from here? What can we do to intervene in the context of this incredibly complex, ambivalent black-Jewish relationship to make things better?

IMPROVING BLACK-JEWISH RELATIONS

One possibly helpful way of looking at the problem of "solutions" to black-Jewish conflict is to conceptualize it in terms of two general approaches. The first approach looks at black-Jewish conflict as a problem of improving relations, or rather fashioning the experiences that help create the conditions of possibility for improved relations. Political coalitions and other acts of cooperation and solidarity between blacks and Jews against racism and antisemitism are examples. The second approach is geared to conflict resolution, that is, to intervene when there is trouble, or there is likely to be trouble, between the two groups. Workshops meant to reduce racism and antisemitism on college campuses is an example.

Before we present some suggestions pertaining to the first approach it is important to keep in mind a few cautionary points. First, neither the black nor Jewish communities are homogenous or monolithic; there are a wide range of views and spokespersons within each community so that it is impossible to speak about either community as if they necessarily acted in unison and held similar views. Thus any generalizations about the black and Jewish communities need to be highly qualified and contextualized.

Second, there is considerable evidence that the state of black-Jewish relations in this country is not nearly as bad as many think. Blacks and Jews on the "grass-roots" level have reached out to each other to build bridges and to promote racial harmony. As Professor Philip Freedman, the director of research at The Foundation for Ethnic Understanding, wrote in his summary of "The State of Black/Jewish Relations: 1996":

On the side of cooperation, Jews marshaled monetary, moral, and political support for Black congregations whose churches had been burned in the wave of destruction that overtook the nation. In meetings and demonstrations, Jews expressed solidarity with the Black sisters and brothers, frequently noting that their empathy flowed not only from a moral position but from their memory of the notorious Kristallnacht. In regard to communication, synagogues, Black churches, and civic organizations mounted ever increasing, programs of dialogue to examine questions of mutual concern, to confront differences that have arisen between the two societies and to prevent or contain the flash points that have, periodically, generated bitter rhetoric. These organizations have also sponsored inter visitation between Jews and African-Americans of all ages with an emphasis upon gaining insight into the culture and experience of their opposite numbers. A number of congregations have conducted joint services during important holidays; Jews and Black youths, in specially designed exercises, visit locales that are deeply significant to both communities. Clearly, substantial numbers of Jews and blacks are determined to reach out to each other in friendship and solidarity. (Freedman 1997, v)

Hugh Price, president of the National Urban League, in the same report, noted in his short statement the "arduous and effective work of people of good will, all across America, to repair the breach and rebuild trust. . . . The roster of cooperative efforts offers welcome evidence of forward progress and helpful clues to best practice" (ibid., iv).

The above summary statements raise the question of whether the perceived magnitude of black-Jewish conflict is to some extent a function of media coverage and amplification, especially of the more provocative stories concerning, for example, Louis Farrakhan, Khalid Abdul Muhammad, and Leonard Jeffries. Moreover, as A. Michele Morgan has pointed out in her chapter, the bulk of books written about black-Jewish conflict has been generated by academics and scholars, by individuals who make their living and derive considerable narcissistic gratification from writing books and touring the country talking about black-Jewish conflict (the editors of this volume perhaps can also be indicted here). Without sounding overly cynical, it is worth keeping in mind that they and the community professionals who are paid to work on improving black-Jewish relations, have a stake in keeping the so-called problem a problem, or at least magnifying it. In other words, in our view, there are many good things going on between blacks and Jews on the local level that go unreported because they are not media events, thus amplifying the perceived amount and intensity of black-Jewish conflict.

In addition, as far as we can determine, the average black and Jew in this country is probably not thinking that much about the other unless of course there is an obvious problem that emerges between them. Most of the time, most blacks and Jews are going about their everyday business trying to go about their business like everybody else, usually trying to avoid conflict in their lives wherever possible. Finally, it should be noted that the available research suggests for example, that many African Americans have positive views of Jews and see them as less prejudiced than other segments of white America. Most blacks are also aware and appreciative of the fact that Jews have historically been on their side. And black representatives in Congress have supported Israel by a margin of about 3 to 1 over the years (Helmreich 1995). Murray Friedman has noted a 1992 study done by the Anti-Defamation League that showed that "the American people overwhelmingly reject anti-Semitism and that most Blacks do, too" (Friedman 1995, 348). Moreover, there is still a sizeable group of liberal-minded, activist Democratic Jews who have not abandoned their commitment to social justice and helping the black community improve their economic and social situation in this country. These and other findings and trends remind us of the dangers of negatively generalizing about black-Jewish relations.

BUILDING BRIDGES BETWEEN THE COMMUNITIES

As suggested above, in order to improve relations between blacks and Jews it is essential that there be increased positive contact between the groups. The "contact hypothesis," as it has been called, indicates that increased positive contact between groups reduces stereotypes that flourish on lack of personal, direct information about others. In psychoanalytic theory, this is a way of saying that, in general, it is more difficult to project and externalize one's "bad" parts on to the other if the other is a known entity and viewed favorably. As we have seen, projection and externalization are key mechanisms for the development of interethnic conflict in general and black-Jewish conflict in particular. As Gordon Allport (1954) has pointed out, in order to foster the kind of contact between blacks and Jews that will help reduce projection and externalization (e.g., prejudice), frequently the basis of conflict between blacks and Jews, it is important that:

1. The groups should possess equal status in the situation. For example, blacks and Jews who come together to work together and/or learn about each other should come from a similar social class background, at least initially and as far as possible. This condition tends to level the playing field and minimize any obvious prejudicial attitudes about perceived status between groups.

2. The groups should be seeking common goals. For example, blacks and Jews joining forces against racism and bigotry or fighting crime.

3. The groups should feel the need to work together to obtain their goals. For example, it should be perceived as in the best interests of both blacks and Jews to work against racism and bigotry or to learn about each other in order to strengthen friendship and solidarity. The hallmark of cooperation is shared outcomes. Furthermore, cooperation increases favorable attitudes toward the people you are working with.

4. Authority, law, and custom should support contact between the groups. To the extent that others, such as like minded non-Jews and nonblacks, people of good will, clergy, and local government support interaction between the groups, the interaction is more likely to be positive.

These four principles described by Allport are useful guidelines for reducing prejudice between blacks and Jews. It should be emphasized that many of the successful programs described above have been developed cooperatively by blacks and Jews, and they have incorporated these very principles. The programs that are most important to develop are the one's that reach out to children for they are more receptive to new ideas and represent the future. Intergroup trips to museums, participation in parades and festivals, and watching films are some concrete examples of how to truly reach children by inculcating them against the appropriation of prejudicial attitudes via positive experiences with each other. Films are especially important because today's children tend to respond more to auditory and visual stimuli than to the printed word.

Perhaps one of the most psychologically astute and successful programs that has put into practice many of the above described psychological principles for promoting cooperation between blacks and Jews is the one developed by Steve Sherman. Sherman's Young Leaders United (YLU) started in 1990 when he organized a multiethnic basketball game. Building on the camaraderie and comfort level Sherman observed between black Americans and Jews on the basketball court, he created the YLU. Since its founding, YLU has hosted educational seminars and engages in communal work, held workshops on racism and antisemitism, conducted a hate crimes forum, hosted business-related dialogues, participated in a walkathon to benefit the United Negro College Fund, helped deliver food packages to Jewish needy and planned informal social activities. Moreover, in 1996, the Anti-Defamation League joined forces with the Chicago Urban League to provide institutional support and programming to help YLU encourage black and Jewish professionals "to resist racial division and stereotypes" (Anti-Defamation League 1997, 13). In our view, this program, and others like it, which builds on the strengths of each community and their common moral vision, are clearly on the right track toward building bridges between the black and Jewish communities.

Thus, one of the best ways to promote healing and harmony between blacks and Jews, psychoanalytically speaking, is to reduce the possibility of either group being able to dehumanize the other, that is, use the other as a suitable target of destructive projection and externalization. Encouraging direct, cooperative, and positive interaction between the two groups is the most promising way to work against those destructive tendencies that are always a danger in all intergroup relations.

REDUCING BLACK-JEWISH CONFLICT

While we have suggested that black-Jewish relations are not nearly as bad as some believe, there are real problems between the two groups that need to be addressed. It is here that a psychoanalytic perspective and the group technology that emanates from it, may be most helpful.

From a contemporary Jewish perspective and on a manifest level, the current problem with the black community largely emanates from the speeches by Louis Farrakhan and his cohort and by a number of academics. Put simply, Jews see Farrakhan and Leonard Jeffries of the City University of New York among others, as the personification of antisemitism. Jews also get angry when more "mainstream" black leaders who Jews feel they have supported in the past, don't vigorously and publicly criticize Farrakhan. From a black perspective, some black leaders view the Jewish community as overreactive about Farrakhan and feel that he does not represent the "mainstream" black community. Nor should Jews be dictating to blacks how they should react. Black leaders are also distressed by what they see as a reduction of Jewish commitment to affirmative action and other social programs and a lack of a clear response to the issue of race as a factor in drawing congressional district lines (Freedman 1997, v). There have of course been other situations of conflict in recent years (see chapter 1, "The Time Line of Black-Jewish Relations")—the ones described above are only illustrative.

However, as the chapters in this book have argued, there seems to be a lot more going on below the manifest level to account for black-Jewish conflict, a wide range of complex passions and psychological motivations. So, for example, Farrakhan's antisemitic speeches and absurd allegations that greatly exaggerate the role of Jews in the slave trade and stimulate in the identified Jew extremely intense anxieties about security and survival. The Holocaust of course serves as a psychological/historical context from which Jews interpret these speeches. For identified Jews, it is possibly conscious and unconscious annihilation anxieties that get generated by Farrakhan's antisemitic utterances and tone. For blacks, the perceived reduction of Jewish support for causes that represent to them freedom from racism, and autonomy and empowerment, may well stimulate in them intense abandonment anxiety and feelings of betrayal. Moreover, for blacks, racism, like antisemitism, is a reality that is interpreted within the historical context of slavery and institutional racism in this country. Racism thus also probably stimulates annihilation anxieties in many blacks, experienced in many cases as a kind of "soul murder."

We are not trying to reduce Jewish and black allegations against each other to the above described psychological anxieties, that kind of reductionism is not very illuminating. However, if we assume that these and other kinds of anxieties and fears are operative in the minds of blacks and Jews, anxieties that may interfere with their ability to empathically, constructively, and reasonably communicate with each other, then what is needed is a forum for addressing these issues in an honest, direct, and validating manner. In fact, such psychoanalytically informed group technologies exist for helping conflicting communities "work through" their anxieties and fears and to develop more effective ways of communicating.

Nearly every chapter in this anthology has made a similar point, namely, that blacks and Jews need to communicate more effectively with each other. However, what makes these recommendations different from the conventional call for direct face-to-face dialogue is the nature of the dialogue. That is, the kind of dialogue that is psychoanalytically and psychologically informed and guided and tends to address those wishes, anxieties, and needs that are usually not spoken about and explored in other contexts. These are the "unspeakable" themes that Aisha Abbasi has described in her chapter.

For example, Vamik Volkan (1988, 1990) and Herbert C. Kelman (1997) have developed independently a small group workshop model for helping to reduce conflicts between groups. These workshops are easily adaptable to a variety of settings such as urban sites of conflict and the college campus. Basically, Volkan and Kelman bring together influential and respected private citizens and community leaders for a number of days, to explore the conflict between them and possible solutions to their problems. These workshops are "led" by, for example, psychoanalytically trained "neutral" facilitators who are well versed in conflict theory, group process, and the specific problems facing each community as well as each community's aspirations. The facilitator's function is not to impose solutions or assume a position of arbitrator of the truth or worthiness of views put forth. Rather, the facilitator's functions are to generate a psychologically "safe" atmosphere where everything can be discussed, establish mutually acceptable norms, and make periodic interventions meant to foster free and open discussion between the parties as individuals. This is in marked contrast to how conflicting communities generally communicate where leaders usually address their constituencies or other influential third parties. Problem-solving meetings are thus intensive meetings that are completely private and confidential, there is no audience, no publicity, and no record. In fact, one of the central ground rules according to Kelman, is that statements made during a workshop cannot be quoted with attribution outside of the workshop setting (1997, 214). These and other conditions are designed to facilitate the workshop participants to engage in a type of free and candid communication that is usually not available to parties in intense conflict with each other. Thus, as the workshop proceeds, there tends to be less of the self-serving finger-pointing hyperbole and "positioning" that takes place in public contexts.

What also makes these types of meetings different from conventional types of dialogues is that the focus is less on the manifest demands that each group makes to the other group, especially the demands that are geared for public consumption. Rather, the focus is more on the "deeper" desires, security and identity needs, and existential anxieties that each group has as well as generating psychologically acceptable solutions. The assumption is that only after the psychological obstacles are addressed between the conflicting groups can reasonable, fair, and durable solutions be generated. Kelman aptly describes some of the salient features of these workshops in the international conflict context, but much of what he says has applicability to the black-Jewish conflict in America:

Once both sets of concerns are on the table and have been understood and acknowledged, the parties are encouraged to engage in a process of joint problem solving. They are asked to work together in developing new ideas for resolving the conflict in ways that would satisfy the fundamental needs and allay the existential anxieties of both parties. They are then asked to explore political and psychological constraints that stand in the way of such integrative win-win solutions and that in fact, have prevented the parties from moving to (or staying at) the negotiating table. Again, they are asked to engage in a process of joint problem solving, designed to generate ideas for "getting from here to there." A central feature of this process is the identification of steps of mutual reassurance—in the form of acknowledgments, symbolic gestures, or confidence-building measures—that would help reduce the parties' fears of engaging in negotiations in which the outcome is uncertain and risky. Problem solving workshops also contribute to mutual reassurance by helping the parties develop—again, thorough collaborative effort—a nonthreatening, deescalatory language and shared visions of a desirable future. (Kelman 1997, 214)

These and other similar types of workshops are designed to bring about changes in the workshop participants themselves, especially in the negative way that they see the group they are in conflict with. Workshops are also geared to improved psychological understanding of the others' perspective and their own priorities, increased insight into the psychodynamics of the conflicts (e.g., the "need for an enemy" and the variety of projections and externalization's that are operative), and new reality-based ideas for resolving the conflict and overcoming the psychological barriers to creating a solution to the problems they are facing.

Most important, perhaps, these changes on the individual level are a way of promoting change on the policy level of the conflicting parties. In other words, says Kelman, the aim of the workshops is to maximize the likelihood that the new insights, ideas, and proposals developed in the course of the workshops are slowly fed back into the political debate and the decision-making process within each community. It is the task of the facilitator to help create the conditions for the workshop participants to maximize the transfer of these insights and new ideas into the policy process that gradually lead to change on the "grass-roots" level (ibid.). Eventually, at the right time, reparative public symbolic gestures from respected leaders from each community can be done to signal both cooperation and solidarity between the conflicting parties as well as signaling the fact that it is "safe," without debilitating shame and guilt, to speak about one's more deeply felt anxieties, fears, and wishes. The latter is especially important as Mark Bracher has indicated in his chapter, for without a respected model of a less severe superego that encourages acknowledging the kinds of psychological vulnerabilities and wishes that we have been describing, it is unlikely that members of conflicting groups will face and begin to "work through" these feelings in themselves. Without altering public awareness and acceptance of the existence of such feelings and needs, altering public discourse will be difficult and change on the "grass-roots" level slow in coming.

Obviously, one of the important considerations in terms of the likely success of these workshops is the make-up of the groups, that is, who is invited to participate. Participants need to be able to use the workshop experience, they need to have the interest and intellectual and emotional capacity to engage in the kind of group process described above. Moreover, they need to be respected in their communities and be viewed as representative of the conflicting parties.

In the black-Jewish context, this raises the thorny issue of whether Louis Farrakhan and other black nationalist leaders and "extremist" members of the Jewish community like the Jewish Defense League should be invited into the workshops. In our view, they should be, providing they agree to "play by the rules" and behave in a manner that is compatible with the parameters of the workshops as defined by the facilitator and other participants. We believe that in the case of Reverend Farrakhan it is essential that the members of his organization participate because he clearly represents an important and sizeable subgroup of the black community and psychoanalytically speaking, he embodies their intense anger and feelings of outrage associated with white racism, as well as black pride and empowerment. Both of these elements are key underlying issues in the black-Jewish mix. Moreover, as far as we can tell, the Jews' difficulties with the black community largely emanates from what Jews view as black antisemitism and Farrakhan and his cohorts clearly have kept the pot boiling when it comes to antisemitic utterances. This issue therefore needs to be dealt with head-on, if possible, in a workshop context although not necessarily in the first workshop. Preliminary work with more "mainstream" and moderate community leaders would probably be the best starting point.

A word should also be said about another major site of black antisemitism, the college campus. As Michael Walzer has pointed out, "anti-Semitic demagoguery, when the demagogues are Black, resonates powerfully in the Black community today," especially on the college campus (Walzer 1997, 405). He notes that the ideologically driven (segregationalist and Afrocentric), politically ambitious, vaguely leftist in tone version of antisemitism seen on college campuses is most troubling because it appeals beyond the ghetto, among the Afrocentric intelligentsia and in parts of the new middle class (ibid., 406). Murray Friedman too, cites a study that suggested that "Black elites, including better educated Blacks, are more inclined than other Americans to endorse negative comments about Jews," pointing to why antisemitic diatribes on campus by Farrakhan and others may be having some impact (Friedman 1995, 347). As Walzer further notes, in the speeches of Khalid Abdul Muhammad, for example, at Kean College in 1993, but in many more less–well-publicized college forums, the Jew is characterized in classical antisemitic terms: as an international figure, veiled and threatening who supposedly ran the slave trade, who controls the banks, and the mass media. The Jews are the oppressors of blacks, Third World peoples, the Palestinian Arabs, and anyone who fits the bizarre mythic fantasy of these demagogues. The fantasy itself is detailed "in pseudo-scholarly books and articles. It is the work of people who study in libraries, collect weird footnotes, imagine themselves radical intellectuals" (ibid., 406).

We believe that the sort of people described above should also be invited into group workshops at the appropriate time and setting. They too should not be excluded, not because their views are in any way condoned by Jews and most "mainstream" blacks, but rather because psychoanalytically speaking, they represent important communal black affects (especially narcissistic injury and rage), fantasies, and wishes that need to be addressed in terms of improving the overall black-Jewish relationship. Moreover, the "message" of these campus demagogues probably resonates to some extent in other more "moderate" blacks who privately identify with aspects of their expressed anger, outrage, and power strivings. (The same dynamic is also operative for some Jews who privately identify with aspects of Jewish demagogues like the late Rabbi Meir Kahane.) Black campus demagogues also have a sizeable following that may one day become more than rhetorically menacing to Jews, and this is another reason why they need to be included in the workshops.

While we feel that these campus demagogues and similar personalities need to be included in the workshops, we are well aware that they will probably not take up the offer, and if they do, they will be difficult to manage in the workshop context. We say this for two reasons. First, most of the campus spokespersons mainly thrive in the public context where they can "play to the crowd." They require many contextual props to bolster their message and frequently rely on intimidation derived from group dynamics to assert their views and shield themselves from criticism and accountability. And this is one of the reasons that black demagogues will quite likely not want to take part in workshops. They don't want to make themselves available to reasoned critique by others or self-critique, for to do so would mean confronting aspects of reality they don't want to face, as well as their own personal narcissistic deficits. Workshops, as we have described them, require people who are committed to honest self-exploration, who are open to criticisms, and who are willing to examine the assumptions underlying their own taken-for granted views. Campus demagogues are not inclined to want to do this, and when they can't hide behind the various props associated with large public group gatherings, their presentation, as they must somewhere sense, is hardly impressive. So chances are, the above described antisemites on campus and elsewhere will have to be fought using conventional tactics, politically and educationally, and through ostracism by Jews and like-minded blacks (Walzer 1997, 406).

We also believe that before workshops get started *between* blacks and Jews, it is necessary for each group to meet themselves as a group in workshops designed to address the issues relevant to black-Jewish relations and conflict. That is, as A. Michele Morgan pointed out in her chapter, Jews and blacks as communities need to look *within* to establish for themselves what they actually want from the other side and what is realistically possible. It would be helpful for each group to address these questions within the context of their anxieties pertaining to their security as a minority in this country, anxieties that are frequently overlooked especially within the Jewish community. Moreover, each group needs to face up to the underside of their community, for example, the generally unacknowledged white privilege in the case of Jews and antiblack attitudes and antisemitism and antiwhite attitudes among blacks. In addition, blacks and Jews have to decide how they are going to handle the more "extremist" elements in their communities when they participate in black-Jewish workshops. Blacks have to decide how they want to do deal with Farrakhan and campus demagogues just as Jews will have to decide how to handle some of the Jewish bigots that exist on the fringes of the Jewish community. Ideally, both communities have to work out their intracommunal differences, at least to some degree, as it pertains to Jews and blacks, before intergroup dialogue is likely to be maximally effective. In other words, when it comes to interethnic conflict, some things are best dealt with "in house" in private before trying to work it out with the other party in the conflict.[1]

Along these lines, C. Fred Alford's advice, to "give it a rest" may also be wise psychoanalytically inspired counsel. As he and others in this anthology have noted, Jews and blacks are in a certain sense like a pathologically enmeshed "dysfunctional" couple. They can't "live with each other and they can't live without each other." It may perhaps be best at this time in their roller-coaster history if they separate for a while and strengthen and "actualize" themselves as individual communities. That is, blacks and Jews probably should concern themselves with other things pertinent to enhancing their own communities as well as sorting out internal communal problems that each has not adequately dealt with. For Jews this includes, for example, the problems of assimilation, intermarriage, creating affordable Jewish day school education, helping the Jewish poor as well as combating antisemitism, and maintaining the security of the state of Israel. For blacks, economic and political empowerment, increasing job training and opportunities, cultural independence in the form of the development of an extensive network of hospitals, day care centers, welfare agencies, and mutual aid societies comparable to what the Jewish and Catholic communities have, the "melt down" of the urban black family, black-on-black crime, affirmative action, and fighting institutional and other forms of racism, are pressing issues and problems that need to be more effectively dealt with. Moreover, psychoanalytically speaking, both groups would probably do well to focus more on building coalitions with other groups, be they Asians, Hispanics, or newly arrived white immigrant groups. These groups do not have the same cultural baggage and psychologically conflicted history regarding blacks and Jews and may be more receptive to overtures of working together. Such coalitions may help relieve some of the pressure that has come to be a part of black-Jewish relations as well as reduce black-Jewish enmeshment. Perhaps then, by each community "giving it a rest" and concentrating on developing greater and more adequate separation and individuation (in the psychoanalytic sense)—with a little luck—blacks and Jews may generate a new-found appreciation of each other.

It is tempting to end this book on an optimistic note, suggesting that blacks and Jews are well on the road to "healing" their relationship, working out their problems with each other, and that psychoanalysis can somehow almost magically make things better. While we are cautiously optimistic about the future of black-Jewish relations, we think it is better to conclude our anthology with some difficult to digest "tragic" psychoanalytic realism as it relates to the larger question of improving black-Jewish relations in the political context. That is, as Freud's tragic, ironical, and stoical views suggest, and Max Weber wrote, conflicts of values are the driving forces of history and politics (Gray 1997, 8). In this view, the purpose of politics is not to create ideal harmony among social goods (and between communities). It is to maintain a shaky coexistence between irreconcilable ideals and interests. Skillful and wise leadership can intervene in and mediate conflicts of values especially between communities, but these conflicts can never be finally and fully resolved. As Gray further notes, "The vocation of politics is tragic, because no such balance is ever achieved without irreparable loss" (ibid). Political life, he continues, including interethnic relations, in a certain sense will always remain a realm of "warring gods." In other words, unresolvable conflicts, ambiguous settlements of political issues, and ambivalent relations between ethnic groups are not indicative of a phase of historical development that may soon be overcome but are perpetual aspects of the human condition. Blacks and Jews who are working so hard to make things better would do well to keep this tragic view in mind when the going gets tough and the frustration feels unbearable. Resignation without despair, the Freudians wisely call it.

NOTE

1. The kinds of groups we have been describing can be organized and "led" through a number of institutions. For example, Herbert C. Kelman, Department of Psychology, William James Hall, Harvard University, Cambridge, MA 02138; Va-

mik D. Volkan, The Center for the Study of Mind and Human Interaction, University of Virginia, Blue Ridge Hospital, Drawer A, Charlottesville, VA 22901; Paul Marcus, The National Psychological Association for Psychoanalysis (The Center for the Psychoanalytic Study of Social Trauma), 150 West 13 Street, New York, NY 10011, in affiliation with William B. Helmreich, co-director of the City College Conflict Resolution Center.

REFERENCES

Allport, Gordon. 1954. *The Nature of Prejudice*. Reading, Mass.: Addison-Wesley.
Anti-Defamation League. 1997. *On the Frontline* (The National Newsletter of the ADL). September/October, 1–14.
Freedman, Philip. 1997. "The State of Black/Jewish Relations: 1996." In *Report on Black/Jewish Relations in the United States. Cooperation, Conflict, Human Interest*. Foundation for Ethnic Understanding, January 20, 1997.
Friedman, Murray. 1995. *What Went Wrong? The Creation and Collapse of the Black-Jewish Alliance*. New York: Free Press.
Gray, John. 1997. "The Tragic View." (A review of *Max Weber* by John Patrick Diggins). *Times Literary Supplement*, September 26, 8.
Helmreich, William B. 1995. "Black-Jewish Relations: What Is the Problem and What Can We do About It?" Paper presented at the conference "Racial and Ethnic Conflict in America: Black/Jewish Tension in New York," sponsored by The National Psychological Association for Psychoanalysis, May 7.
Kelman, Herbert C. 1997. "Group Processes in the Resolution of International Conflicts." *American Psychologist*, March: 212–20.
Luel, Steven. 1994. "Bettelheim on Education." In *Bruno Bettelheim's Contribution to Psychoanalysis*. A Special Issue of *The Psychoanalytic Review* 81, no. 3 (fall):565–80.
Volkan, Vamik. 1988. *The Need to Have Enemies and Allies: From Clinical Practice to International Relationships*. Northvale, N.J.: Jason Aronson.
———. (1990). *The Psychoanalysis of International Relationships: Volume II: Unofficial Diplomacy at Work*. Lexington, Mass.: Heath.
Walzer, Michael. 1997. "Blacks and Jew." In *Struggles in the Promised Land: Toward a History of Black-Jewish Relations in the United States*, edited by Jack Salzman and Cornel West, 401–10. New York: Oxford University Press.
West, Cornel. 1997. "Walking the Tightrope: Some Personal Reflections on Blacks and Jews." In *Struggles in the Promised Land: Toward a History of Black-Jewish Relations in the United States*, edited by Jack Salzman and Cornel West, 411–16. New York: Oxford University Press.

Index

About the Editors and Contributors

AISHA ABBASI, M.D., a psychoanalyst and member of the Michigan Psychoanalytic Institute, grew up in Pakistan and now is in private practice and teaches psychiatric residents at Michigan State University. She is a published poet in her native language, Urdu, and a frequent participant at Urdu poetry readings in America.

C. FRED ALFORD, Ph.D., is professor of government at the University of Maryland, College Park. He is the author of dozens of articles and eight books applying psychoanalysis to social theory, including *Melanie Klein and Critical Social Theory*, *Group Psychology and Political Theory*, and *What Evil Means to Us*. He is a member of the A. K. Rice Institute and a frequent consultant to what are often called Tavistock groups.

MAURICE APPREY, Ph.D., is professor of psychiatry and associate dean for minority affairs, University of Virginia School of Medicine. He is trained in child psychoanalysis at the Anna Freud Center and is the English translator of Georges Politzer's *Critique des Fondements de la Psychologie*. He is also the co-author of *Intersubjectivity, Projective-identification and Otherness* and co-editor of *Ethnicity, Medicine and Psychoanalysis*.

MARK BRACHER, Ph.D., is professor of English and director of the Center for Literature and Psychoanalysis at Kent State University. He is a graduate of the Cleveland Psychoanalytic Institute, author of *Lacan, Discourse, and Social Change: A Psychoanalytic Cultural Criticism,* and co-editor of *Lacanian Theory of Discourse* and *Lacan and the Subject of Language.*

CYNTHIA BURACK, Ph.D., is assistant professor in the department of Political Science and the Center of Women's Studies and Gender Research at the University of Florida and the author of *The Problem of the Passions: Feminism, Psychoanalysis, and Social Theory.*

ALAN HELMREICH has a degree in philosophy and political science from Columbia University. He is currently a journalist in New York who has reported on the black and Jewish communities with special attention to the aftermath of the Crown Heights riots.

LEE JENKINS, Ph.D., a psychoanalyst and member of the National Psychological Association for Psychoanalysis, is professor of English, John Jay College of Criminal Justice and author of *Faulkner and Black/White Relations: A Psychoanalytic Approach.*

PAUL MARCUS, Ph.D., is a member of the National Psychological Association for Psychoanalysis and founder of its Center for the Psychoanalytic Study of Social Trauma. He is co-editor of a number of books including *Healing Their Wounds: Psychotherapy with Holocaust Survivors and Their Families* and *Psychoanalytic Versions of the Human Condition: Philosophies of Life and Their Impact on Practice.* He is also the author of *Autonomy in the Extreme Situation: Bruno Bettelheim, the Nazi Concentration Camps and the Mass Society.*

A. MICHELE MORGAN, M.D., graduated from the University of Texas Medical School and trained in psychiatry at Sinai Hospital in Detroit. She teaches psychiatric residents and maintains a private practice while she completes her psychoanalytic training. Her main interest is in the psychoanalytic understanding of racial and ethnic identity.

BONNIE J. MORRIS, Ph.D., is professor of women's studies at George Washington University. She spends her winters writing and her summers working at women's music festivals throughout the United States. She also tours with her one-woman play "Revenge of the Women's Studies Professor." Her work has appeared in over twenty different anthologies, and she has authored two books on the recent history of American Jewish women.

MORTIMER OSTOW, M.D., is chairman, Sandrow visiting professor emeritus of pastoral psychiatry, Jewish Theological Seminary of America; president, Psychoanalytic Research and Development Fund; and a member of the New York Psychoanalytic Institute. He is the author of a number of books including *Ultimate Intimacy: The Psychodynamics of Jewish Mysticism* and *Myths and Madness: The Psychodynamics of Antisemitism.*

HOWARD F. STEIN, Ph.D., a psychoanalytic anthropologist is professor of family and preventive medicine at the University of Oklahoma Health Sciences Center. He has co-authored four books with Maurice Apprey including *From Metaphor to Meaning* and *Clinical Stories and Their Translations.*

E. VICTOR WOLFENSTEIN, Ph.D., is professor of political science at UCLA and a member of the senior faculty at the Southern California Psychoanalytic Institute. He is the author of *The Victims of Democracy, Malcolm X and the Black Revolution,* and *Psychoanalytic-Marxism.*

ISBN 0-275-95666-0

90000>

EAN

9 780275 956660

HARDCOVER BAR CODE